THE HOWLEYITES

TORONTO'S CHANGING CITY, A STADIUM RISING, AND THE CHAMPIONS OF 1926

D.M. FOX

**August
Publications**

The Howleyites: Toronto's Changing City, A Stadium Rising, and The Champions of 1926

August Publications
215 10th Av. S., Unit 621
Minneapolis, MN 55415
augustpublications.com

ISBN 978-1-938532-96-2 (Print)
ISBN 978-1-938532-97-9 (eBook)

Cover design: Natalie Nowytski

PRAISE FOR THE HOWLEYITES

"We all know about Toronto's passion for baseball and the Blue Jays, but **The Howleyites: Toronto's Changing City, A Stadium Rising, and The Champions of 1926** takes us back in time, through the deep history baseball has here. D.M. Fox does an outstanding job illustrating how both the love of baseball and the city itself grew alongside one another 100 years ago. We learn how teams were put together, how stadiums were built, and ultimately how a championship was won. It's a great trip back in time to when baseball was just putting its roots down in Toronto, and it's a great read for the current baseball fan."

—**DAN SHULMAN**, VOICE OF THE TORONTO BLUE JAYS, SPORTSNET

"D.M. Fox has done a masterful job of re-creating the Toronto of the mid-1920s, a city bursting with civic pride that was reflected in its new lakefront state-of-the-art ballpark, and the championship team that played in it."

—**JAMIE CAMPBELL**, HOST OF BLUE JAYS CENTRAL, SPORTSNET

"A captivating look at a transformative time in Toronto sports history. Doug doesn't just chronicle a championship season, he expertly captures a city on the rise and its enduring love of baseball. By bringing the 1926 season back to life, he has created a must-read for baseball fans and history buffs alike."

—**GREGOR CHISHOLM**, TORONTO STAR BLUE JAYS REPORTER

"Doug's passion for the game of baseball is never more palpable than when he's telling the stories that paved the way for the game we know today. **The Howleyites** offers a fun, entertaining look back on a part of Toronto's past—the baseball, and the city—that even a hardcore fan may not be familiar with. As the Blue Jays celebrate their 50th season, this is an excellent way to appreciate a rich baseball history that paved the way for baseball in Toronto in 2026."

—**BLAKE MURPHY**, HOST OF JAYS TALK PLUS ON SPORTSNET THE FAN 590 TORONTO

"The day before Maple Leafs Stadium opened in 1926, the *Globe* urged Toronto baseball fans to 'Get right in behind Dan Howley and the Leafs, and we'll show the world what kind of ball town Toronto is.' This book taught me so much about what kind of ball town Toronto was, but also made me better appreciate the kind of ball town it's become a full century later. **The Howleyites** captures the rich baseball history of Toronto that long predates the Blue Jays and the growth of the city right alongside it. This is a must-read for baseball fans."

—**KEEGAN MATHESON**, BLUE JAYS REPORTER FOR MLB.COM AND AUTHOR OF **THE FRANCHISE: A CURATED HISTORY OF THE TORONTO BLUE JAYS**

CONTENTS

FOREWORD: WILLIAM HUMBER

At the risk of using a little-known word—not only to baseball fans, but most people—I'll venture down a thorny path. The word *palimpsest* describes the erasure of one type of past, allowing for another layer to be imposed upon it. It could be a manuscript from which text has been scraped or washed off in preparation for reuse by another document. It has been used to describe a landscape in which an old world of the countryside has been built over by a new urban built one. Every so often, however, the old one can't help leaking through reminding us of what was there.

Sports history is like that. Before the Toronto Blue Jays and their days of triumph, there were spectators in a baseball past who shared in these moments. They were in places long since abandoned, erased, and often built over. And there were players and owners whose leadership resides only in aging online newspaper files.

Such is the story of Dan Howley and the 1926 Toronto Maple Leafs in their brand-new playground, Maple Leaf Stadium, at the bottom of Bathurst Street, culminating in their penultimate triumph in that season's minor-league Little, or Junior, World Series. I have a panoramic photo of that team that includes the irrepressible owner Lol Solman, one of the true entrepreneurial and sporting geniuses in the city's sports history, but now long forgotten. Despite only a brief appearance in the Leaf uniform, Lionel Conacher is there. He was one of the athletic giants of Canadian sports. Possibly the greatest pitcher in Toronto baseball history—step aside Dave Stieb, Roy Halliday, and Kevin Gausman—was future Hall of Famer and New York Giant Carl Hubbell proudly staring out at the camera. And of course there is their manager Dan Howley and his aide-de-camps, including the too-often-overlooked Toronto boy Bill O'Hara.

It was an era when the team went on the road on Sunday because of the Lord's Day Act's prohibition on games on that day. It was an era when another kind of Prohibition was capitalized to remind everyone of the difficulty in finding a drink. It was an era when the minor leagues might be below the majors but were by no means subservient as they eventually became. Most of all, it was a different world recovering from the slaughter of the Great War and not aware it would lose its nomenclature to an even more violent World War Two. It was an era when every economic sign pointed to never-ending prosperity, little imagining the Depression ahead. It was an era when women had finally broken out of their long second-class status to enter the workplace, demand and then get the vote, and finally challenge men for sporting audiences from hockey to softball, and basketball to track and field.

Baseball and sports had entered their own golden age, topped by the ebullient stardom of Babe Ruth, a man eventually claiming he deserved more money than a President of the United States because he'd had a better year. Howie Morenz and Canada's female athlete of the half century, Bobbie Rosenfeld, electrified hockey arenas. Jack Dempsey fought Gene Tunney for heavyweight glory, and Big Bill Tilden made people care about tennis.

Of all the treasures of the age, the new Maple Leaf Stadium seemed to be Toronto's ticket to the big leagues, but scaling back its construction from 35,000 to 20,000 seats would have long-term implications. I was fortunate enough to go to that stadium many times in its last glory years of the 1950s. I saw the Havana Sugar Kings and Montreal Royals. I saw Rocky Nelson hit home runs in 1958 before joining the Pittsburgh Pirates for their improbable World Series win in 1960. I remember the combined odor of 25-cent hot dogs (which my dad thought too expensive to splurge on), stale popcorn, and cigar smoke from the right-field grandstand. I recently discovered that the first Toronto baseball team known as the Young Canadians was a roster of tobacconists sponsored by Wells S. Gillett's cigar company on Wellington Street in 1859. I guess in this case the more things changed the more they stayed the same.

I also remember a doubleheader late in the 1958 season when the skies opened, and despite our apparently safe refuge in the bowels of the old ballpark, we were rain soaked. I can't recall going to the stadium in the 1960s other than seeing the old Toronto Rifles football team play a game there in 1965. My brother went down when the Harbour Commission was quickly tearing down the park after the Leafs had left following the 1967 season and he came home with a purloined seat. I also recall going with my friends to a now open field on which the stadium had stood, and we played a ball game there in 1979 shortly before it was covered in townhouses.

Not only may we have been the last to do so on the site where those 1926 Leafs went the distance but a few years before I was at the first Blue Jays game in 1977, sitting in $2 seats in the uncomfortable grandstand bleachers. So you might say I have my own palimpsest.

Those places have largely disappeared, but I'm convinced the cheering for the home team remembered in those long-ago times, as well as the ballplaying moments, linger somewhere. After all, since we can view the light of stars in the sky that burnt out millions of years ago, who is to say the echoes of our own baseball stories don't have a similar resonance. Doug Fox has painted that world for us to revel in. Let the enjoyment begin!

*William Humber is a Canadian baseball historian recognized by his induction into the Canadian Baseball Hall of Fame in St. Marys, Ontario, in 2018 and his installation as a Member of the Order of Canada in 2021. His latest book, **Old Ontario at Bat: Baseball's Unheralded Ancestry**, was published by the Centre for Canadian Baseball Research in 2024.*

CHAPTER 1
THE TOAST OF
THE MINORS

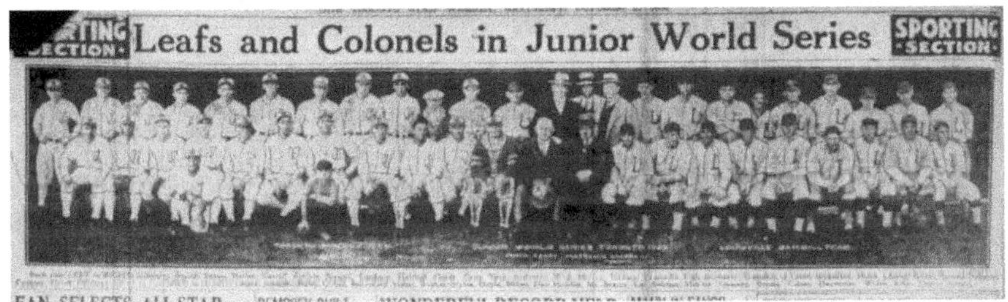

1926 Toronto Star *photo, Junior World Series.*

As Dan Howley made his way to a late September game at Maple Leaf Stadium on the city's waterfront, he no doubt was reflecting on the highly successful season experienced by his Toronto Maple Leafs ballclub in 1926. Leaving from his then-midtown apartment in Toronto's Avenue Road and St. Clair Avenue West area, Howley would likely have had his suitcase in hand while taking the Bathurst streetcar down to the ballpark, as the team would be leaving the city immediately after the game. The Leafs were playing Louisville in the 1926 Junior World Series, the Minor League Baseball championship for the highest AA level.* The first four games were played in Toronto; the Series would shift to Kentucky for the remainder of the best-of-nine set.

In the fourth season of his second go-round as manager of the International League's Toronto Maple Leafs, Howley had seen considerable change both on and off the field. Originally sent to the city in 1923 to help nurture and develop the handful of prospects his employer, the Detroit Tigers, sent to Toronto for some final seasoning as part of their working agreement, Howley had become the face of the franchise. He had taken over a moribund club mired in the bottom half of the International League's standings and attendance, turning it into an outfit capable of challenging the mighty Baltimore Orioles, winners of seven IL pennants in a row. Under Howley's guidance, a sprinkling of Detroit prospects were combined with players acquired from his own informal network of scouts and contacts, and Toronto became the toast of the minors, a city suggested by many to be a Major League city in waiting.

Over his 21 years in baseball, Howley had seen the role of manager change in several ways since he was a young catcher playing in the Class B New England League. Most teams in the minors and majors employed a "player-manager," often a star player who directed the team's on-field strategy. A player-manager was also a way for teams to boost attendance and save money by having one man fill both roles. But as baseball transitioned from the dead-ball to the live-ball era in 1920, the increasing complexity of the game, along with the dual demands of playing and managing at the same time, caused teams to employ a full-time manager. Even Howley served as a player-manager as late as 1918, albeit in a reserve role, but he was the last of a dying breed. The job of a big-league manager had become more complex, as teaching skills, personnel management, leadership, team chemistry and morale, deployment of players, and in-game strategies had made the position far more demanding.

---

* The Little World Series technically became the Junior World Series in 1932, but most press references used the Junior World Series moniker.

As the 1920s dawned, baseball entered its Golden Age, thanks to mass communications, economic prosperity following World War I, and slugging stars like Babe Ruth. During this time, managers became celebrities in their own right; Miller Huggins of the Yankees, Wilbert Robinson of the Dodgers, John McGraw of the Giants, and Connie Mack of the Athletics were as well-known as their players. In fact, newspaper reporters referred to their teams by the manager's name as often as they did the team's nickname; hence the "Hugmen," the Brooklyn Robins, "Mackmen," and "McGraw's Giants." That status applied to veteran minor-league bench bosses like Howley as well. Toronto beat reporters took to calling the ballclub "The Howleyites," as often as they did "the Leafs," in their dispatches.

The 1920s were a time of significant transformation in the demographics and economy to the country in general, and Toronto in particular. Canada had fought alongside Great Britain in World War I, but the end of the War marked the beginning of the split between the Mother Country and her former colony. Canada was starting to flex its muscles on the world stage diplomatically and economically. The country was making advances in medicine, literature, academia, the arts, transportation, and technology, and nowhere was this more evident than in Toronto. By virtue of its central location, the city was becoming a major manufacturing, financial, and transportation hub. Jobs were plentiful in the Toronto of the Roaring Twenties, and a wave of newcomers from around the world was filling those employment opportunities, changing the face of the city in the process.

Canadians were feeling justifiably proud of their country. Two decades earlier, Prime Minister Wilfrid Laurier predicted in a speech in downtown Toronto that, with its bountiful resources, "the Twentieth Century will belong to Canada." The War had slightly derailed Laurier's prophecy, but there was no doubt that by the 1920s the country was booming, finding new markets for its products and lessening its economic ties with Britain in the process.

Howley's team had clinched the International League pennant several weeks earlier. The club had played inconsistent ball for much of the first half of the season, disappointing hopeful fans making the trek to Maple Leaf Stadium, the sparkling new ballpark built in just six months on the Lake Ontario shoreline. Howley himself crafted a team reliant on pitching and defense, and the veteran baseball man knew it would take time for the club to come together. His patience was rewarded when they went on a tear in the second half of the season, ending the Orioles' reign in a pennant race that was all but decided by Labour Day.

During his streetcar ride, Howley likely had time to reflect on the changes he had seen in Toronto since his arrival back in the city in 1923. Howley lived in the city year-round; as a native New Englander, he was more than used to Toronto's winters. He even became an avid hockey fan, as Torontonians had fallen under the spell of the fastest sport on ice. As far back as spring training, Howley, road secretary Bill O'Hara*, and the Leafs' trainer Tim Daly had talked about the game so much that, "many of the players who had never witnessed a game (got) all worked up over the winter pastime."[1]

Even during Howley's four years in the city, Toronto had grown. With more women entering the workforce, Howley no doubt would have noticed their presence on his daily commute. Major construction projects downtown were changing the city skyline almost monthly. Prohibition, which firmly held Ontario in its grip when Howley arrived in 1923, was weakening. With more leisure time and money in their pockets than ever before, many of the city's half-million residents were looking for entertainment; the city's movie theaters, concert halls, and sports stadiums had never been so busy.

The Leafs' torrid play at the end of the season—losing only six games from the start of August to the end of September—failed to shatter attendance records at their new home, as had been expected; fans didn't seem to buy into the team until late in the season, and the Leafs "were appreciated everywhere but in their home town."[2] But the baseball world had taken note of what was happening in Toronto.

---

* Toronto native Bill O'Hara was a former MLB centre fielder with the New York Giants and (briefly) the St. Louis Cardinals in 1909-1910. In World War I, he won the Military Cross for using his outfielder's arm to throw grenades at the enemy from a distance.

Big-league scouts had been following the team since late August, seeking to pluck some of the Leafs' stars for the next season. Howley had been presented with offers for several of his players, so as the team rushed to Union Station after the final home game of the season, he knew this would be the last road trip for this group. But what few people knew was that Howley was the object of desire for several teams making changes in the dugout, and this was probably going to be his last time on the road as a Maple Leaf as well. "Howley is a pretty capable, safe, and sane sort of man to be directing a ball club," observed the "Bible of Baseball," *The Sporting News*.[3]

CHAPTER 2
THE CITY GAME

The second Hanlan's Point Stadium.

WHILE TORONTO HAS BEEN KNOWN FIRST AND FOREMOST AS A HOCKEY town, there was a time—several decades long—when baseball was the biggest game in town.

Baseball itself has a long history in Canada, with the first recorded game taking place in the Southwestern Ontario farming village of

Beachville in 1838.[1] While there is considerable skepticism among baseball historians as to the credibility of an eyewitness account of the game published some fifty years after it supposedly took place, there is little doubt that the great American pastime had long since crossed the border into the province by the mid-1800s.

In the 1850s, according to the *Toronto Globe*, a baseball team was practicing Monday afternoons on the University of Toronto grounds.[2] But the game was slow to make inroads with Torontonians; lacrosse, the country's national sport, and cricket, a staple among the city's predominant British population, were regarded as being far more favourable sporting pursuits. Baseball players were considered to be of questionable character. "Baseball is just a sandlot sport, usually played by undesirables,"[3] said a writer of the time. Steadfast British Empirists were somewhat suspicious of the rowdy game from the south.

Nonetheless, the game slowly gained popularity, and by the 1870s, Toronto had two teams, one dubbed "Dauntless" and the other "The Clippers." The Dauntless received permission to play a game on the sacred grounds of the Toronto Cricket Club. The Clippers were the stronger side and were given permission by the city to practice in Queen's Park, the site of the provincial legislature. In 1876, the Clippers joined the Canadian Professional Baseball League. The league lasted only one season, but by then baseball had firmly taken root in the city.

By the 1880s, baseball had eclipsed cricket in popularity, mainly because fans had discovered it was much easier to bet on. By 1885, a group of Toronto businessmen met at a local hotel to discuss putting together another team to represent the city. The following year, construction of the first park built for baseball in the city was taking place east of downtown on eight acres of land near Queen Street on the east banks overlooking the Don River. With a covered grandstand and seating for 2,000 spectators, the facility became known as Sunlight Park, because of its proximity to the Lever Brothers extensive Sunlight Soap Works factory. The park would be home to an International Association (which ultimately became the International

League) club that Toronto papers referred to alternately as the Canucks or the Torontos.

By 1887, the team was firmly entrenched in the hearts of Toronto sports fans, and management sought to reward their loyalty with a contending club. To that end, they brought in several high-profile American players, the most prominent being Edward "Cannonball" Crane, a man whose skills on the field were surpassed only by his appetite for food, drink, and good times off it. Crane won 33 games for the Torontos while leading the league in hitting with a .428 average (walks counted as hits at that time) in the 102-game schedule. He pitched in and won both ends of a doubleheader to clinch the league championship on the final day of the season.

After several years' absence caused by the folding of the International League in the middle of the 1890 season, Toronto returned to professional play in the late 1890s, this time in the Eastern League. By 1897, the team was purchased from its original owners by the Toronto Ferry Company and moved to a newly built stadium on Hanlan's Point in the Toronto Islands, a chain of 15 small islands just off the city's waterfront. The Ferry Company, run by a young Toronto businessman named Lol Solman, also owned a hotel and amusement park on the same island. Solman also sponsored a lacrosse team that moved to the Point. For 50 cents, a Toronto sports fan could buy a ticket to watch either team play, with a ferry boat ride from the docks at the foot of Bay Street thrown in.

The wooden ballpark succumbed to fire twice, the first time in 1903 and again in 1909. The second fire was extensive, destroying the hotel (which was not rebuilt) and the amusement park. Solman, whose Ferry Company had sold the team back to its ownership group, rebuilt the ballpark, and the Maple Leafs—as the team became known by 1902—was its principal tenant. When Ed Barrow, later the architect of the first Yankees dynasty of the 1920s and '30s, came to town to manage the club in 1900, the team moved to a park on the mainland for several seasons, but eventually returned to its Island home.

Over the next twenty years, the team would become the dominant outfit in the Toronto sports pages. With hockey still very much a seasonal sport, lacrosse struggling to maintain its toehold with the sporting public, and rugby football still years away from gaining widespread acceptance, baseball was king in the city. Lol Solman's 18,000-seat ballpark was often filled to near capacity from June until September. The team was successful on the field, bringing home five pennants between 1902 and 1918.

By 1920, lacrosse still may have been Canada's national sport, but baseball was far and away the most popular game in Toronto.

CHAPTER 3
HOWLING DAN

Dan Howley with the Philadelphia Phillies, 1913 season. (Library of Congress, LC-DIG-ggbain-12270.)

DANIEL PHILLIP HOWLEY WAS A BASEBALL LIFER, CRASH DAVIS LONG before Annie Savoy ended his baseball wanderings on the silver screen in the classic baseball movie, *Bull Durham*.

The son of a Nova Scotian transplant, Howley was born and raised in East Weymouth, Massachusetts, located south of Boston. He signed his first professional contract close to home with New Bedford of the Class B New England League in 1905, but Howley lived somewhat of a peripatetic existence in his first half dozen years in pro baseball, making friends of fans, players, umpires, and writers alike along the way, playing for teams in Grand Rapids, Michigan; Indianapolis; and Utica, New York. At six feet tall and just over 200 pounds, Howley became the proverbial backup catcher, lauded for his receiving skills and ability to handle a pitching staff. But he never was able to hit enough to land a first-string role; in his one and only shot at the big leagues, Howley was released by the Philadelphia Phillies after managing only four hits in 32 at-bats as a third stringer in 1913.

Still, Howley had made an impression in his short time in the big leagues. Howley was "full of the old paprika and hot tamale stuff that puts life in the game, and is valuable behind the windpad,"[1] a "Philly scribe" told the *Elmira (NY) Star-Gazette*. After being let go by the Phillies, Howley landed with Montreal of the International League. Despite his Canadian heritage, Dan was less than pleased with the 15 percent cut to his $400/month salary that came with the demotion north of the border and initially refused to report to *la belle province*. But he was lured back with a promise to serve as a player-coach with the Royals; the following season, he was named player-manager. And so began a tenure that would see him lead teams in Canada often over the next three decades.

The first World War created manpower shortages across baseball. Canada was not immune from that effect, and when the International League reorganized and shortened its schedule for the 1917 season, Montreal was left out. Between the Royals and his hockey club Montreal Wanderers, owner Sam Lichtenhein estimated he had lost over $150,000 over the previous five years and had no interest in continuing.[2] The decision didn't come until the calendar rolled over to 1918, and Howley was looking for work.

But Dan wasn't out of work for long. Boston Red Sox (and former Leaf) manager Ed Barrow had long admired Howley's work, offering him a job working with the Sox pitchers and catchers in spring training. And before the Red Sox camp was more than a few weeks old, Barrow gave Howley another assignment: chaperoning Babe Ruth, Barrow's talented and fun-loving prodigy.

Barrow was in the process of converting Ruth from the mound to the outfield, to keep his bat in the lineup every day. Ruth at first balked at the assignment, possibly because having to play on a daily basis, rather than every fourth day, put a serious crimp in his night-time extracurricular activities. Howley was given the task of keeping a lid on Ruth's carousing. "Don't worry, Manager. I'll put an iron ring through his nose if I have to," he told Barrow.[3]

But Howley "proved to be no match for Ruth, who continued to flout his manager's rules."[4] Shortly into their roommate arrangement, Ruth stayed out all night; Barrow gave up waiting for him at 4 a.m. In order to both prove his point and deliver a message, he put Ruth in the lineup for that day's game. Ruth, predictably, went hitless. That evening, Barrow gave the hotel porter two dollars to tell him when Ruth came in; Barrow told the porter to wake him if necessary.

Sure enough, Babe took part in another all-nighter, strolling into the hotel at 6 a.m. The porter scurried up to tell Barrow, who headed for Ruth and Howley's room in his slippers and housecoat. When he got the room, there was a light on under the door; when Barrow knocked, the light suddenly went out. The door was not locked, so Barrow went in to find Howley hiding in the bathroom, and Ruth lying in bed, smoking a pipe.

"Why Babe, do you always smoke in bed?" asked Barrow.

"Sure," replied Ruth smoothly, "It's very relaxing, helps me get back to sleep."

Barrow wasn't buying it, tearing off the bed covers to reveal a fully dressed Babe. The gig was up. "You're a fine citizen, Babe!" Barrow bellowed. He stormed out of the room, yelling, "I'll see you at the ballpark!"

Later that day, as the players (including Ruth) gathered in the Sox's clubhouse prior to that day's game, Barrow stormed in and slammed the door shut. Rolling up his sleeves (Barrow, like Connie Mack, managed in street clothes), the manager told the players to leave, because he and Babe had some unfinished business. Barrow was never one to back down from a physical confrontation and had boxed in his younger days. He was giving up a few inches and close to 30 years to Ruth, but the Babe knew this was a battle he could not win and quietly left the clubhouse with his teammates.

Moments later, Ruth sidled up to Barrow in the dugout and asked if he was in the lineup that day. "No, Babe," retorted Barrow. "Not today, not tomorrow, either. Get out of my sight." And with that, Ruth slunk back to the clubhouse. But he and Barrow worked out a deal later that day. Ruth promised to leave a note at the hotel front desk with the time he came in from his evening's fun; Barrow, in turn, vowed not to put Ruth in the lineup if the arrival was close to sunrise. The arrangement, from that point on, worked well for both.[5]

One person the deal did not work out for was Howley. Barrow let him go on the eve of Boston's Opening Day game.

Again, Howley was not out of work for long, however, as there was a managerial opening in Toronto, where player-manager Nap Lajoie's contract was bought by Brooklyn. Despite having little time to prepare for the season and inheriting only two players from the previous year's International League pennant winners, Dan set out to defend the title in a war-shortened 1918 season. The Toronto press felt there was considerable reason for optimism with his arrival.

"Howley is a very aggressive manager, a good catcher, and a comedian thrown into the bargain," noted the *Globe*. "He puts all kinds of 'pep' into his team and gets a lot out of his men."[6] Penciling himself into the lineup in the second games of doubleheaders to give the Leafs' regular catcher a breather, the backup backstop guided the Leafs to an 88-39 record, and another IL crown.

An observer couldn't help but think that Howley, hired to manage Toronto after the Royals had folded after the 1917 season,* would be a lock to return to run the Leafs for the 1919 season. But Howley, who had feuded with Maple Leafs President James McCaffery all season

---

* The Royals suspended operations after their ballpark burnt down.

long on matters of strategy and player personnel, was let go at the end of the season. McCaffrey claimed that Howley was still technically under contract to the Montreal club's owner—even though the club had ceased operations. McCaffrey also believed that it was best to change managers on an annual basis, so Howley's supposed contractual ties gave him a convenient excuse to look for another field boss. Howley was gone from Toronto, but he certainly was not forgotten by the fans or press. "He didn't receive a word of praise for his clever handling of the team," observed the *Toronto Globe*, "but was politely informed by President McCaffery that he ought to feel glad that he finished at the head of a championship ball club."[7]

Baseball lifer Howley wasn't out of work for long after McCaffrey let him go. After his brief stint with the Red Sox, Dan caught on with the Detroit Tigers and soon became Tigers' player-manager Ty Cobb's right-hand man. Howley had the team's pitchers throw live batting practice to the hitters, an unheard-of practice at the time, which helped the Tigers finish first in the American League in batting in 1921.

When Detroit later signed a working agreement with Toronto to send some of their top prospects there for some final minor-league seasoning,* Cobb dispatched his most trusted lieutenant to return to the shores of Lake Ontario prior to the 1923 season to manage the team. Howley had already developed a following around the International League as a result of his time with Montreal and his previous stint in Toronto. He had a fondness for clothing, often found away from the park in three-piece suits replete with fedora and spats; reporters in other International League cities took to calling him "Dapper Dan," for his sartorial splendour. Along the way in his baseball travels, Howley also acquired the sobriquet "Howling Dan," but a *New York Times* sportswriter said he should be called, "Orator Dan," because "he never yells or howls, but discourses fluently at all hours of the day and night."[8]

---

* This was before the days of formal working agreements between MLB teams and MiLB affiliates; players were assigned on a more casual basis.

As a player and a manager, Howley had spent considerable time in a baseball dugout. Perhaps because he saw so little action when he was a player, Howley became a keen observer of the game. Not only did he learn baseball strategy, but he also developed the skills to help players learn the fundamentals. In his decade-plus as a manager, his teams were always well-schooled in the finer aspects of the game. His catchers knew how to handle pitchers, being able to work with them on days when they didn't have their best stuff. His hitters were well-drilled; they put balls in play, drew walks, bunted, ran the bases, and knew how to execute the hit-and-run. Howley was considered a master of what writers then called "scientific baseball," the ability to manufacture runs without a lineup full of sluggers. Howley also knew how to handle his players—his teams made few mental mistakes on the playing field, but when one did, Howley refrained from singling them out either in the locker room or in front of the press for their transgression. He became known as a "player's manager," long before the term came into general use; legions of players had the best years of their careers under his tutelage.

CHAPTER 4
THE KING OF WEEKENDS

Born in Toronto and educated in its public schools, Solman was a master entrepreneur and impresario, catering to workers with burgeoning wealth and leisure time as the 19th century gave way to the 20th and the city became a railway, manufacturing, and financial hub. More people had money in their pockets looking for entertainment, and Solman was adept at finding ways to help them spend it.

After a brief stint in Detroit learning the ins and outs of the mail-order business, Solman returned to Toronto in the 1890s to work for world champion rower Ned Hanlan, who owned the hotel on Hanlan's Point, the most westerly of the three main islands off Toronto's waterfront. Shortly after Solman started his employment, Hanlan sold the hotel to the Toronto Ferry Company, which promptly enlarged the hotel, built an amusement park, and constructed a stadium on ten acres of landfill on the northern edge of the island. Solman stayed on through the transition, managing the hotel at first, later the entirety of the island's operations, and eventually the ferry company himself.

*Toronto Maple Leafs' President Lol Solman and his ever-present
cigar.*

As amateur sports were slowly but surely giving way to professionals, Hanlan's Point Stadium was one of the busiest venues in the city. In 1902, the facility hosted 174 baseball games, 68 cricket matches, 38 football games, and 6 lacrosse contests. When the stadium burned down, a replacement rose on its ashes in months. In 1914, a young prodigy named George "Babe" Ruth (Howley's future roommate) hit his first professional home run over the right-field wall as a member of the minor-league Providence Grays.*

To help promote the use of his stadium, Solman lobbied to join the

---

* This would be the only homer hit by Ruth in the minor leagues. It did not land in Lake Ontario, as legend would have it.

board of directors of his two biggest occupants, the Leafs and the Tecumseh Lacrosse Club. It wasn't long before Solman became prominent in the operations of the Leafs. "During the life of J.J. McCaffery," said the *Buffalo News*, "that buoyant gentleman was the nominal president and cut quite a swath at baseball meetings." But the real brains of the operation, according to the paper, was Solman, "the man who pulled the reins and drove the cart…(and) said little but did much."[1]

But Solman was not content with his role as a seasonal operations manager. In 1905, he headed a syndicate that built the Royal Alexandra Theatre, now the crown jewel of Toronto's theatre district. In 1912, he was part of the group that funded and built the Arena Gardens, the first artificial ice arena in the soon-to-be hockey-mad city; the Blueshirts, the building's principal tenant, brought home the city's first Stanley Cup two years later. Solman promoted boxing cards, wrestling bouts, cycling races, and tennis matches, turning the building into what the *Daily Star* called a "sporting cathedral." In 1916, the ever-enterprising Solman pushed the Toronto City Council to redevelop the city's western beaches; six years later, Sunnyside Amusement Park opened for business, with Solman's brother the president and Solman himself the main shareholder. As far as entertainment was concerned, Solman was everyone and everywhere all at once.

Solman's generosity was known far and wide. He operated a Yonge Street restaurant near the waterfront that barely broke even in the winter months with the ferry service shuttered, but it provided employment for many of his summer workers. When a rising theatre actor who had left Toronto for bigger and better things in New York City passed away suddenly before reaching stardom, Solman reportedly paid all expenses for the return of her remains and subsequent funeral.

Crowds still flocked to Hanlan's Point as World War I approached, but having rebuilt his wooden stadium twice, Solman knew it was likely only a matter of time before the latest iteration of the ballpark went up in flames once more. He also came to realize that with an increasing number of families owning an automobile, fans were starting to grow weary of taking the ferry out to the island when they could simply just drive to a ballpark located on the mainland. The journey just to board the ferry could be hazardous, as fans had to cross an increasingly busy main set of railway tracks to get to the docks; on Saturday and holiday games, a big crowd would have to wait for an hour or more after the game for the return ferry ride. Solman knew that as the city grew, he would need a more permanent and accessible home for his ballclub.

CHAPTER 5
THE MIGHTY ORIOLES

THE JOB OF A BASEBALL MANAGER IN THE FIRST SEVERAL DECADES OF THE last century was a multifaceted one. Front offices were not staffed with Senior Vice Presidents, Directors of Scouting, General Managers, or Senior Analysts. Teams at both the major-league and upper minor-league levels typically had an owner, a business manager (who took care of finances, payroll, and travel arrangements), and a manager running the entire operation. The manager shouldered much of the burden of finding, signing, and developing players. And there were few better in the business—big league or minor—than Baltimore's Jack Dunn.

A former pitcher who reached the majors with Brooklyn in 1897, the athletic and versatile Dunn was able to prolong his career as a position player after injuring his arm. As his career wound down, Dunn became a player-manager, eventually buying the International League Baltimore franchise from his former Brooklyn manager.

It was while at the helm of the Orioles that Dunn gained acclaim as one of baseball's best operators. He cultivated a vast network of official and unofficial scouts for the Orioles, composed of former teammates, players, umpires, and even fans. One of the first players he signed was a local boy, a huge, raw, and somewhat troubled left-handed pitcher from a reformatory school by the name of George

Ruth. A year later, facing competition for fans from the new Federal League Baltimore team (which built a ballpark right across the street from the Orioles), Dunn was forced to sell his prized prodigy, his "young Babe," as reporters called him, to the Red Sox. "He always regretted that," observed baseball historian Bill James, "and from then on swore that he would never sell a star player unless he could replace him."[1] Dunn would hang onto another local southpaw named Lefty Grove, who some say is the greatest pitcher of all time, for much longer.

Dunn could see the coming war with Major League Baseball as the 1920s approached, and he was determined not to give in. He refused any and all offers of working agreements with big-league clubs: "He felt that for the minor leagues to sell their best players to the majors would ultimately lead to the destruction of the minors."[2] Some argued that Dunn's refusal to sell his stars deprived Major League fans of seeing the best players, but "Dunn never accepted any of that nonsense, and by 1920 there was no doubt in anyone's mind that his team was as good as any in the 'major leagues.'"[3] Dunn was popular with his players, and he treated them well. The Orioles' payroll was the largest in the minors, and his team always stayed at the best hotels on the road.[4]

With Grove as the ace of his rotation, Dunn methodically built a team that was to dominate the International League for the first half of the 1920s. After finishing third behind the Leafs in 1918, Dunn's Orioles won 100 games the following year, taking the pennant by eight games over the same Toronto club. Baltimore would win the next six consecutive league pennants, capturing the Junior World Series, the championship of minor-league baseball, three times.

The 1920 Toronto club set a franchise record with 108 wins, but finished second to the pennant-winning Orioles, who were embarking on a streak of dominance that proved to be unmatched by any team at any level in the game's history. In the end, 1920 proved to be the high-water mark for the Leafs under James McCaffery's leadership; with the team president in failing health, the club struggled on the field and at the gate after that season. Toronto fans were getting frustrated by the Orioles' run of dominance. With the pennant race decided every year often by midsummer, attendance started to decline around the league, and McCaffery found himself in something of a bind: even if he wanted to go out and purchase players to compete with the Orioles (newspaper reporters were not always entirely sure), the loss of revenue rendered him unable to go after the biggest names. Over the next two seasons, Toronto finished well back of Baltimore, registering distant fourth- and fifth-place finishes. There was considerable grumbling and resentment of Dunn's success throughout the International League, including Toronto. "It is not a good thing for one club to monopolize the honors," wrote W.A, Hewitt in the *Toronto Star* after the O's clinched the 1925 pennant in Toronto, "and Baltimore's success has been quite a detriment to the International League."[5] Dunn was so confident that his club would clinch against the Leafs that he went off on a fishing trip to Northern Ontario while the Orioles captured yet another pennant.

When McCaffery passed away in 1922, Solman stepped out of the shadows to become the head of the organization. Toronto was changing, and Solman knew the team had outgrown its operations at Hanlan's Point. A new, more accessible facility was needed, preferably near downtown. And bold measures would need to be taken to both fill a new ballpark and put an end to the Orioles' dynasty.

CHAPTER 6
THE CHANGING PERSPECTIVE OF THE CITY

HAD IT NOT MET THE WRECKER'S BALL IN THE MIDDLE OF THE DECADE, A baseball fan sitting in the third-base seats at Hanlan's Point Stadium would barely recognize the Toronto skyline in 1930 from the one that existed only a decade earlier. The city would arguably undergo more changes in those ten years than at any other point in its history. The 1920 view from that grandstand would mostly consist of spires from The City of Churches, as Toronto was known. A decade later, a virtual forest of commercial buildings would obscure all but the tallest of spires. Even City Hall, a Romanesque sandstone edifice at the top of Bay Street, which was one of the tallest non-ecclesiastical buildings when it opened at the turn of the century, had long since disappeared from view.

Prohibition, which had been ushered into being with the Ontario Temperance Act of 1916, had withstood many challenges, but was still in full effect across the province as the decade began. But even with that legislation in place, Ontarians could still get access to alcohol. The sale of liquor was illegal, but not its manufacture, and a considerable amount of it produced for the export market found its way into many local speakeasies. Those looking to quench their thirst could find the answer with their doctor and local drugstore; over 650,000 prescriptions for alcohol were written by Ontario doctors in 1920 alone. And if booze was hard to come by for some, drugs like cocaine and marijuana were sometimes available instead.

The Roaring Twenties may have been louder in Toronto than in any other Canadian city. Montreal, by virtue of being older, may have been the financial centre of the country, but Toronto was rapidly becoming its industrial and transportation capital. Many newcomers were attracted to the city, including an aspiring young writer from Michigan named Ernest Hemingway, who penned reports and columns for the *Toronto Daily Star* before seeking greater literary inspiration in Paris. Somewhat disappointed by his time in Toronto (although he penned over 170 articles for the *Star*), Hemingway later wrote in a poem called "I Like Canadians," "Canadians don't believe in Literature, and think Art has been exaggerated."[1] Historian Frank Underhill agreed, observing that in the 1920s, Canadians read newspapers, not books.[2] With four daily newspapers of record in the city, it was hard to argue with that sentiment.

The left-leaning *Globe* and its right-wing rival *Mail and Empire* did circulation battle in the morning, as did the *Star* and the *Telegram* in the evenings. The *Globe* called itself "Canada's National Newspaper," a self-proclaimed title it still uses today. It was "Canada's great Liberal paper, solid and drab," according to Canadian historian Mark Bourrie, "as dry as the liquor prohibition tracts and church news that it ran on its editorial pages."[3] The *Globe* was owned by William Jaffray, a deeply religious man firmly stuck in the Victorian era. No lingerie or underwear ads were permitted in his newspaper, and he led an unsuccessful one-man crusade to ban horse racing results in all Canadian publications. The *Mail and Empire*, despite its right-leaning editorial views, was quite progressive for its time, hiring female reporters. The *Mail and Empire* boasted a larger circulation than that of the *Globe*, which would result in the latter taking over the former in the next decade.

The *Star* (founded by printers who lost their jobs with the *Toronto News* because of a labour dispute) was the progressive and independent afternoon voice of the city. Publisher Joseph "Holy Joe" Atkinson's father died when he was young; his mother, with eight children to feed, began to take in boarders, many of whom were part of the nation's fledgling union movement. It was at the Atkinson family dinner table that Joe's social activism was born. The *Telegram* was the favoured publication of both Conservatives and blue-collar workers. Publisher John Ross Robertson was a sports purist and decried the growth of professional sports early in the century (the trophy for the championship of the top junior hockey league in Ontario still bears his name). But in 1926, Robertson was in declining health, and while his paper had the largest circulation in the city, the *Star* was gaining quickly. None of the four major dailies in Toronto the Good published a Sunday edition, although the *Star* included the *Star Weekly* as a supplement to its Saturday edition. The Lord's Act of 1906 prohibited the publication and distribution of newspapers on the Sabbath; the *Star Weekly* was an attempt to get around that law.

With radio still in its infancy, and television still years away, Torontonians learned about the city, province, country, and world around them through their favourite newspaper. The *Star* had a daily radio column, listing programs and time for local stations (which, unlike today, did not broadcast all day long), as well as American stations that could be heard the previous evening. Atkinson was an early radio pioneer in the city, launching CFCA in 1922; a year later, a *Star* reporter called the third period of a hockey game at the Arena Gardens, the first live hockey broadcast in history, one that would shortly vault the sport into the upper realm of a national audience in terms of popularity. Radio may have been more for hobbyists at that point (approximately 1,000 crystal radio enthusiasts listened to the *Star*'s first broadcast), but its days as a dominant medium were coming.

With grain pouring in from the newly settled Canadian (and American) west, minerals and timber from Northern Ontario, and several rail lines converging in Toronto, the city was a hive of activity. Industry was booming, and that 1920 Hanlan's Point spectator would have no doubt seen a tremendous growth in the number of smoke-stacks along the city's waterfront just several years later. Abundant and cheap hydroelectricity from the newly opened plant at Niagara Falls helped power the boom. Refrigerators were replacing ice boxes, electric ranges took over from woodstoves, and electric streetlights lit up the buzzing city. More women were working than ever before, building on the economic independence many had built during the War, when the manufacturing workforce was overwhelmingly female.

Union Station. (City of Toronto Archives, Fonds 1244, Item 5045.)

The 1920s saw the creation of the Toronto Transit Commission (TTC), a conglomeration of private and public transit lines resulting in the expansion of existing streetcar lines. That, coupled with the explosion of automobile sales (the vehicle of choice being the McLaughlin-Buick, built locally with an American General Motors engine), led to a boom in the outlying sleepy villages, transformed into bustling suburbs. The '20s witnessed the building of Union Station—still Canada's busiest, largest, and most opulent train depot—and across from it, the Royal York hotel, a 1,000-room edifice with its own hospital, would rise later in the decade. Motion pictures, the latest entertainment fad, were taking over the city. Solman, seeing this entertainment trend developing, hedged his bets by becoming a vice president of Loew's Canadian movie theatre operations.

But not only the physical face of Toronto was changing. The population of the city, which had swelled by 33 percent from a decade earlier to over a half million people by 1920, was becoming increasingly diverse; in the 1921 Canadian Census, 62 percent of Toronto residents were born in Canada, and 32 percent hailed from the British Isles. The country itself, with British institutions and leanings dating back over a century, was becoming increasingly multicultural in the aftermath of World War I. A trickle of Italian and Asian immigrants before the War turned into a veritable flood in the Twenties—according to the 1931 Canadian census, almost two in five workers in Toronto were foreign born. At the same time, while the United States' investment in Canada was outpacing that of Britain by 1922, many Torontonians joined the estimated one million Canadians (representing about 10 percent of the population at the time) in heading south of the border to chase the American Dream.

A new Canadian identity was born in the years following World War I. While Union Jacks aplenty flew about Toronto in the early days of the '20s, British ties were weakening. The growing National Hockey League was imported south of the border, but the game maintained its strong Canadian background, with almost all the players, coaches, and officials coming from the Great White North. In 1920, an exhibition at the Art Gallery of Toronto (later Ontario) featured the exciting new work of a group of local artists showcasing the rugged beauty of the Canadian wilderness. Using broad brush strokes, vivid colours, and unique style, the Group of Seven caused Canadians to come to look at and appreciate the vastness of their country in a whole new prideful way. The Group members were first drawn to the wilderness of Algonquin Park in Canadian Shield country several hours north of Toronto before stretching the length and breadth of the country. "In capturing the spirit of Algonquin, the Group of Seven opened a new chapter in the growth of Canadian political self-consciousness," wrote Canadian art historian Joan Murray. "They paved the way to a consciousness of the national environment; they were 'environmentalists' who did not know the word."[4]

In 1923, two University of Toronto medical researchers named Frederick Banting and Charles Best (with the help of James Collip, now largely forgotten) discovered and purified insulin, creating a life-changing treatment for diabetic patients, winning the pair the Nobel Prize. A year later, a fellow U of T staffer, Professor Harold Innis, took part in an epic canoe trip across the country as fieldwork for his opus *The Fur Trade in Canada*, the first comprehensive economic history of the country not written by a British academic. Prime Minister William Lyon Mackenzie King, grandson of the leader of a short-lived Rebellion in Canada nearly a century earlier, represented a rural riding just outside of Toronto, sweeping to victory in 1921. King's first term was marked by severing of several long-standing ties with Britain, as Canada sought to have its own voice heard in international affairs. For the first time, women voted in the 1921 federal election; five women ran for Parliament, and one of them, Ontarian Agnes McPhail, won a seat.

Near the geographic heart of the city, a Gothic Revival castle called Casa Loma ("hill house" in Spanish) was nearing completion atop an old pre-Ice Age shoreline in the middle of the city. With 98 rooms, 21 fireplaces, an elevator, a kitchen featuring an oven big enough to roast an ox, a great hall with a 60-foot ceiling, an underground 800-foot tunnel to its stables, and five acres of gardens, Casa Loma's $3.5-million construction cost had all but bankrupted its builder, financier Sir Henry Pellatt. Pellatt walked away from the mansion and the city seized it for unpaid property taxes in 1923, but it remained a source of wonderment and civic pride for Torontonians.

All the home, factory, and office tower construction in the city created a virtual mountain of fill that had to be relocated somewhere. With growth limited to only three directions because of Lake Ontario, the waterfront was a logical destination. Front Street, named so because it ran along a terrace winding up from Lake Ontario, was soon to be almost a half kilometre away from the water, as hundreds of thousands of hectares of earth were both dumped from construction and dredged up from the harbour, facilitating shipping.

It was on this reclaimed land that Solman dreamed of building a new more permanent ballpark, a large concrete-and-steel stadium supplanting the outdated one on the Island. It would be easily visible for that spectator sitting at Hanlan's Point. The new park would also be the crown jewel of the waterfront, one that even might one day attract a big-league team, a state-of-the-art edifice to symbolize Toronto's status as an up-and-coming world-class city.

CHAPTER 7
HOWLING DAN RETURNS

WHEN DAN HOWLEY CAME TO TORONTO WITH HIS DETROIT TIGERS for a late August 1922 exhibition game against the Leafs, the local press treated the occasion like the return of the prodigal son. The game itself seemed secondary to Howley's visit, judging by the headlines in the *Globe* and *Daily Star*. With the Leafs a dozen games under .500 and headed for a fifth-place finish, reporters knew big changes were in store, and with the former Toronto pilot in town, rumours naturally started that he was going to take over the team the following season with Solman now in charge.

Solman wasted little time in confirming those rumours, bringing Howley back to the city as soon as the season had ended. Solman also negotiated a working agreement with Tigers owner Walter Briggs Sr. to supply the Toronto team with young prospects needing further minor-league seasoning. Toronto was not exactly a Detroit farm club, as the modern farm system still years away, but it was a step many high-level minor-league clubs were taking to ensure a steady stream of decent players. But both Howley and Solman had considerable reconstruction jobs ahead of them.

The day after Howley arrived in October to meet the press, he met with his former boss Ty Cobb. Cobb was in town waiting on a train the next day to take him on his annual hunting trip in Northern

Ontario, and he and Howley met to talk about possible players for the Leafs. Solman, meanwhile, was fielding questions about a possible new home for the team. For the time being, he played coy, as the City Council was debating building a bridge from the mainland to traverse the short gap over to Hanlan's Point. But the Leafs had all but outgrown Hanlan's Point, and Solman was quietly making inquiries about that newly infilled land along the waterfront.

With only a few months to rebuild his team, Howley's 1923 team was not a contender, but still showed improvement, ten wins better than the previous edition of the club. The Orioles had the pennant pretty much sewn up by August, but with Howley at the helm, Toronto's attendance improved by several hundred fans per game. The season was very much about laying a foundation for the future. The return of Howling Dan had given fans reason to hope better days were ahead.

Baseball was undergoing a huge transformation at both the major- and minor-league levels as the 1920s dawned. The 1919 Black Sox scandal was the culmination of a decade of constant allegations of game-fixing and players associating with known gamblers; Commissioner Judge Kennesaw Mountain Landis had cracked down severely, banning for life several players implicated. The death of Cleveland's Ray Chapman from a pitch thrown by New York's Carl Mays resulted in rule changes increasing the number of fresh baseballs put into play and banning pitches like the spitball. Foul balls landing in the stands did not have to be returned by fans. Because balls were now much brighter and less misshapen after innings of use, there was an explosion of offence, and hitters who swung from the heels were now in demand; Babe Ruth's 54 home runs in 1920 were more than that of any other American League team.

At the minor-league level, changes were taking place that would see those teams gradually become more subservient to MLB needs. "By a long series of actions, agreements, and rewards," wrote Bill James, "the minor leagues were reduced in tiny degrees from entirely independent sovereignties, existing only to serve the needs of major league baseball."[1] Prior to 1920, the manager and the owner formed the bulk of a big-league team's front office. But when St. Louis Manager Branch Rickey was booted from the Cardinals dugout to the front office, the new position of General Manager was born. Rickey's official title was Business Manager, but the restless Rickey could not help sticking his nose into the Cards' player personnel matters. With the team having fallen on tough times in the early 1920s, Rickey convinced club President Sam Breadon to begin buying up clubs in the low minors. This helped the clubs sidestep the bidding wars that often took place involving the top prospects at the upper levels. As those players matured, Rickey could either use them in the Cards lineup or sell them off to other teams. The term "farm system" came into use as Rickey bought or had controlling interest in as many as 33 teams by the late 1930s (much to the chagrin of Landis, who was very much against "syndicate baseball"). Sharp minor-league operators like Baltimore's Jack Dunn refused to entertain any thoughts of a draft of top prospects, as had been proposed at that time by big-league clubs. During the 1920s, times were changing for minor-league teams, but as far as many of them were concerned, they were in competition with Major League Baseball for fans. Indeed, in those pre-television times, minor-league baseball was the only live version of the professional game most fans could reasonably see. Modern fans might think that Dunn held on to future 300-game winner and Hall of Famer Lefty Grove for several years in order to drive up his value and wonder why a pitcher who had won 96 games over four minor-league seasons wasn't "promoted," but "...there was no structure for him to get 'called up'....the major leagues didn't have anything to do with it," James wrote. "They were keeping him to draw crowds. He was *just playing baseball.*"[2]

So while the Leafs had an agreement with the Tigers for Detroit for players, there certainly were no guarantees as to their quantity and quality. Howley would need to beat the bushes and utilize his network of contacts (many of them former teammates or players) to construct his roster. For the 1924 season, he laid in some foundational pieces. Howley himself was not averse to hopping a train south of the border for recruitment forays. The challenge would not only be finding players, but it would also involve the right kind of players. That is, generally veteran players MLB teams had decided didn't fit the bill but would still be at a point in their careers where they could still play at a high level. It would take several seasons to put the puzzle pieces together to oust the juggernaut Orioles.

CHAPTER 8
TORONTO ON THE MOVE

As the middle of the Roaring Twenties approached, Toronto was very much a city in a hurry. The establishment of the Toronto Transit Commission (TTC) at the start of the decade brought about a consolidation of the patchwork of existing private transit systems, standardized fares within the city limits, ushered in a flurry of streetcar track rehabilitation, and launched construction of new lines to outlying communities that would soon become part of the metropolis.

Automobile sales soared in the first half of the decade. According to *Might's* city directory, there were 32,000 cars and 6,200 trucks in the city in 1921. Just four years later, there were 63,000 cars and 8,500 trucks. In 1918, there were fewer than 130 kilometers of all-surface highways; a decade later, that figure had climbed to just under 4,000.[1] The Ontario government introduced a tax on gasoline in 1925 to help finance construction of this burgeoning network.

The public electrification of Ontario, led by Member of Provincial Parliament Sir Adam Beck, introduced a bevy of time-saving home appliances. Quite simply, Torontonians had more leisure time than ever before, and most had the means to pursue it. Toronto was a city very much on the move.

With efficiency changing lives, city dwellers were too impatient to wait for Lol Solman's small fleet of plodding ferry boats to the Toronto Islands. Weekend lineups at Hanlan's Point would queue after the Leafs game was over. Even though, in those pre-floodlight days, games would usually be finished by 5:30 p.m., a standing-room-only crowd would see fans still waiting for the shuttle back to the mainland hours later. And, paradoxically, as the city grew, the Islands became even more popular until crowds started to diminish by the middle of the decade. As baseball and malaprop icon Yogi Berra would say about a popular restaurant years later, "nobody goes there anymore—it's too crowded." The pennant-winning 1920 Maple Leafs averaged almost 2,700 fans per game. Four years later, the club drew half that many. And Solman's ferries, with fewer passengers each season, were beginning to lose money. For the team president, the signs to move the ballclub over to the waterfront were obvious. His hope was for a downtown site, one which was accessible by the city's burgeoning public transportation system.

Solman's first hope for a new stadium was one built by the city. He approached the city council in the fall of 1922 with a proposal for a civic ballpark, the $255,000 cost and management of the facility to be borne by the taxpayers. Councilors then put the issue to a public referendum on New Year's Day 1923. After 47,000 Torontonians cast ballots on the question, the result was clear: 55 percent voted no. Solman would spend much of the next two-and-a-half years negotiating with the city on a revised plan.

CHAPTER 9
THE LEAFS TAKE SHAPE

Assembling a minor-league roster in the 1920s was a complex process. A working agreement, like the Leafs had with the Tigers, was no guarantee of securing a roster full of top-flight players that fans wanted to see. Howley certainly leaned heavily on his personal friendship with Cobb to form the core of the lineup. In order to fill out the roster, he needed to beat the bushes, and while Howley had become a year-round resident of the city, he was seen frequently at Union Station waiting to board a train to some cross-border destination, where he would bang the recruitment drum.

While Solman was in the early stages of a new ballpark plan, Howley was given a building project of his own: to overhaul the Leafs roster. Inheriting a 1922 team finishing in fifth with a 76-88 record (a whopping 42 games back of the first-place Orioles), Howley quickly took a wrecking ball to the roster, bringing back only a half dozen players for 1923. With only a few months to rebuild his team, Howley's 1923 team finished well back in the standings. The Leafs came in fifth, ten wins better than the previous edition of the club. The Orioles had the pennant pretty much sewn up by August, but with Howley at the helm, Toronto's attendance improved by several hundred fans per game. The season was very much about laying a foundation for the future.

The return of Howling Dan had given fans reason to hope better days were ahead.

Building for the future, Howley added a pair of players to his first team who would become key members by 1926.

Jess "Slow Motion" Doyle with the Vernon Tigers. He became Howley's most dependable starter down the stretch.

Jess "Slow Motion" Doyle was, as his nickname would suggest, a soft-tossing southpaw from Tennessee who jumped into prominence on the strength of a 26-win season for Greenville of the Class C South Atlantic League in 1920. The Yankees signed Doyle and sent him to Atlanta of the Class A Southern Association for the 1921 campaign. Following a strong performance with the Crackers, Doyle jumped all the way to the high-calibre Pacific Coast League, winning 20 games for Vernon in 1922. The Yanks tried to send him back to Vernon the next season but ran afoul of the option rules of the day, and Commissioner Landis declared Doyle a free agent. The Leafs swooped in and picked up his rights in time for the '23 team, and he became a rotation stalwart, winning 15 games.

Illinoisan Otis Miller was a slick-fielding, light-hitting middle infielder who had made a reputation as a sensational defensive player in his pro debut with Saginaw of the Class B MINT (Michigan-Ontario) League in 1922. The Tigers thought enough of him—thanks likely to Howley's lobbying—to promote him from Class B to the Class AA International League for 1923. Babe Ruth and his upper-cut swing was all the rage and produced many imitators, but many hitters (having grown up in the Deadball Era) were still contact-oriented, walking as often as they struck out, working the count, and putting balls in play. Howley preferred pitchers who worked quickly, pitched on the margins of the strike zone and got ahead in the count, which tended to produce a lot of groundball contact. Up-the-middle defense was of paramount importance as a result—not just players who could field balls hit their way but could make the quick throw or pivot to start the double play or deftly snag errant throws from the catcher to tag out would-be base stealers. Miller was that kind of player, and with Howley working with him on the hitting side, he soon became an important part of the Leafs' lineup. Howley platooned Miller in his first two years with the team, and he responded by hitting .329 in 1924.

The 1923 Maple Leafs managed to finish two games over .500 but were 30 games behind the Orioles. Howley knew that gap would not get closed overnight, so for the 1924 season, he continued to acquire players who would become key contributors once the team was ready to contend for a pennant.

Wally "Lefty" Stewart in a later stint with the St. Louis Browns. He provided a solid one-two punch with Owen Carroll at the top of the Leafs' rotation.

Wally "Lefty" Stewart reached the big leagues with the Tigers before he turned 21, but after a brief trial was returned to the minors. He struggled with Syracuse of the International League in 1922 and demoted to the Southern League for the 1923 season, having lost much of his previous top prospect luster. Stewart rediscovered his fastball command, however, and was sent to Toronto before the 1924 season for some final touches.

Frank "Flash" Gilhooley was a speedy minor-league veteran who made his Major League debut with the Cardinals in 1911. Dealt to the Yankees in the middle of the decade, the outfielder showed considerable promise, but injuries derailed his career. Traded to the Red Sox in 1919, Gilhooley, like Howley had the year before, roomed with Babe Ruth. Limited to playing only every fourth day when Ruth trotted in from right field to take his regular turn on the mound, Gilhooley asked the Sox owner to send him back to the minors, where he would play more. "I'm only 26 years old. I can't sit and watch. I want to play the game. I'll never get a chance while Babe is here. I was very happy in Buffalo, so why don't you send me back there?"[1]

When he returned to the International League, Howley kept a close eye on Gilhooley, who had played for him in Montreal (and later married a girl he met there) in 1913. He was the prototypical, get-on-base leadoff hitter, who could reach via a hit, walk, or bunt single. He was regarded as one of the best players in all of minor-league baseball, but as he was approaching 30, his days as a prospect were behind him. On defense, despite his injury history, he was still a ballhawk patrolling centre field. When Howley purchased his rights from International League rival Reading, he finally got his man: a proven table-setter and everyday centre fielder.

Frank Gilhooley, an International League vet with big-league
experience, was a sparkplug for the 1926 Leafs, hitting leadoff and
playing centre field.

Having cut his baseball teeth as a player and manager during the Deadball Era, Dan Howley had a preferred type of ballplayer—one who could get on base, with speed a factor both on the bases and in the field. West Virginia grad Herman Layne more than fit that bill. The corner outfielder had a smash debut with Bristol of the Class D Appalachian League in 1922, catching the attention of many big-league teams. The Tigers signed him to a contract, and by 1924, he was in Toronto. Not a long ball hitter, Layne took advantage of his speed on both sides of the ball, playing a rangy centre field, and turning many hits in the gap into doubles and triples

Claude Satterfield was a two-way product of the University of Georgia whose contract Howley purchased from Augusta of the Sally League late in the 1923 season. A right-handed pitcher and left-handed hitter, Satterfield played in the outfield for Augusta in between regular turns on the mound. With the Leafs, Howley had him concentrate more on pitching, using him as a spot starter and mop-up reliever, as well as an effective late-inning pinch hitter. Satterfield took to Toronto right away, living in the city in the offseason, coaching and refereeing amateur basketball in his spare time.

With the new additions, Howley's 1924 team arrived as contenders ahead of schedule. Sharing Georgia spring-training facilities with the parent Tigers, Dapper Dan got a first-hand look at the players not able to make the big club's final cuts, and he led the Blue and White to a 98-win season, a 17-game improvement over the previous season. But the Leafs finished a distant second, 19 games behind Baltimore, and the crowds at Hanlan's Point reflected that in the final months of the season. With the pennant race truly decided not long after Dominion Day (as Canada's July 1 birthday was then known), Toronto drew an average of just over 1,200 fans, the lowest total since the team had moved to the Islands sixteen years earlier. While Solman was no doubt concerned about the lack of interest in his team, he knew that as he made plans for a new ballpark, Howley was assembling a team that could knock the Orioles off their perch.

CHAPTER 10
THE STADIUM DEBATE

Despite the setback of the referendum on the new stadium a year earlier, Solman continued to lobby town officials and City Council members as the calendar turned to 1924. Ty Cobb was certainly on board when the Tigers came to Hanlan's Point for an exhibition game in July.

"With grounds anywhere but where you are," Cobb told Solman in front of an audience of local reporters, "the chances of your city getting in the major leagues some day will be considerably enhanced."[1] Not long after that, the Toronto Harbour Commission was given permission by the city to enter discussions with Solman on the purchase of land along the lakeshore.

Baseball had been played in the city on the mainland before. The Toronto club played at Hanlan's Point in the 1890s, but when Ed Barrow was hired to manage the team in 1900, he made the team's "Maple Leaf" nickname official, clad them in uniforms with a stylized "T" over a blue maple leaf, and raised funds for a ballpark in the west end (an area of the city known today as Liberty Village), calling it Diamond Park. The team played there for several seasons before returning to the Island.

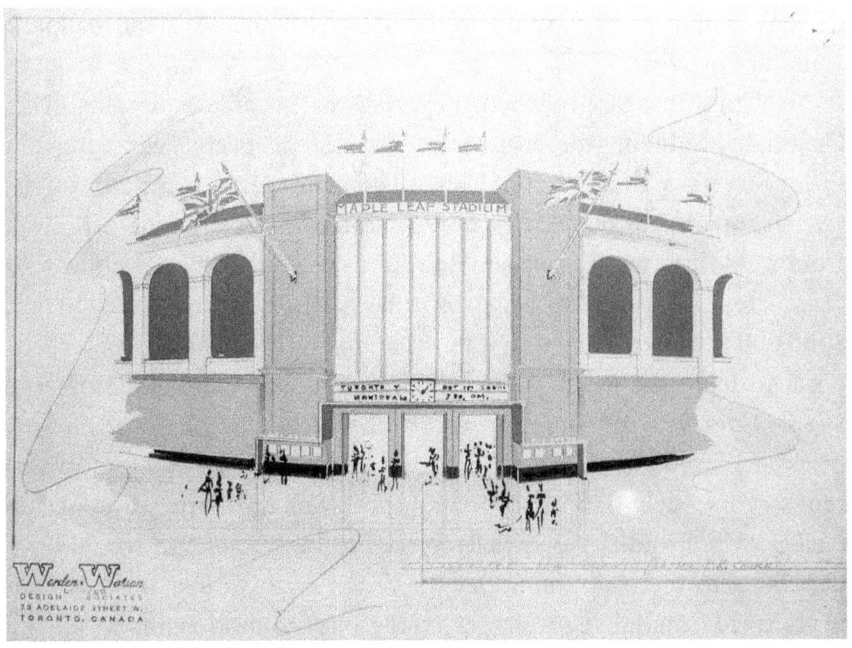

Rendering of proposed Maple Leaf Stadium. (City of Toronto Archives, Fonds 1257, Series 1057, Item 645.)

Solman likely had big-league dreams when he formulated his stadium plan. In early December 1922, the cash-strapped Red Sox entertained an offer from a syndicate headed by Solman.* He offered Boston $1.25 million to move the team to Toronto. Sox President Harry Frazee reportedly offered Solman first chance on the franchise.[2] The proposal was quickly shot down at a meeting of American League owners a week later, but Hanlan's Point, in Solman's mind, had served its purpose; if Toronto wanted to one day be in the big leagues, a big-league stadium was needed. While many Torontonians would need transit to reach a new park, the rise in automobile sales in

---

* This was not the first time Toronto had hoped to land a big-league team. When Western League President Ban Johnson announced his intention to turn his loop into the American League (challenging the monopoly of the National League) for the 1901 season, Ed Barrow, then the manager and majority shareholder of the Leafs, had hoped Johnson would add Toronto. In the end, Johnson added four American East Coast cities to broaden the league's appeal to fans.

the city would require space for parking, which the island ballpark could not provide.

As Christmas approached, negotiations became more involved. Originally, Solman wanted to purchase city property near York and Front Streets, a block west of Yonge (the main north-south thorough-fare in town), and not much more than a line drive to the gap away from a stadium with a retractable roof that would be built almost 70 years later. The property was said to be worth between $350,000 and $400,000. Solman balked at the price and submitted a counterpro-posal to lease the land from the city for fifteen years, guaranteeing $25,000 per year in rent, plus a certain percentage of ticket sales. A week later, the city came back with a demand of $40,000 in annual rent to cover debt and interest charges, as well as depreciation on the facility, which the city originally agreed to build. Solman would have the rights to the stadium, under the terms of this offer, on dates the Leafs were scheduled to play, with the city holding rights to all the other days.

Early in the 1925 New Year, the city let Solman know that the York Street site was no longer available. A new steam plant providing heat to downtown businesses was to be constructed there. A few weeks later, Solman presented a new offer to city council, prompting criticism from the local papers. Solman agreed to amend his proposal, by which the Maple Leafs would have exclusive rights to the stadium. Amateur sports and other events could only be held with the club's approval. Solman offered a guaranteed annual payment to the city but didn't provide specifics. And rather than put this to another plebiscite, Solman suggested that the Harbour Commission would vote on this offer.

The *Daily Star* was wary of the debt the Sunnyside Pavilion had incurred on the opening of the facility three years earlier—when bathers showed they were unwilling to swim in the cold waters of Lake Ontario, a heated pool (at great expense) had to be built. Both the debt and the pool had to be built with public funds, and the *Star* was less than thrilled with Solman's original submission:

If the latest proposition is to be entertained at all (and many could not see why it would be, in view of the vote of 1923)…and a stadium built with civic funds for the professional baseball project of a private company, the people of Toronto have the right to know what exactly is being done with their money before the deal is consummated. In any such deal the city and its investment must be amply protected.…Mr Solman's baseball franchise may be worth a lot of money, but it is not something the city can seize and realize on in case of default.…If Mr Solman and his company would invest a few hundred thousand dollars of their own money in a stadium built on harbour lands, the public would have greater confidence.…the (latest) stadium proposal has caused justifiable uneasiness among those who know how easily guarantees can go wrong.[3]

With York Street out of the question, the City Council and the Harbour Commission started to nudge Solman west, in the direction of Bathurst Street, about 3 kilometres (just under two miles) away on parkland built atop more reclaimed shoreline. Solman was reluctant to entertain this move at first because of the lack of roads and transit to the area. But city officials convinced him that the city was growing in that direction, and that the stadium would be accessible for fans by the time it opened. The city originally offered to build the ballpark, in return for a $100,000 deposit from Solman that would be refunded at the end of fifteen years if he lived up to his obligations. The team would have exclusive concession rights for all events in the stadium, with 10 percent going back to the city. Solman was to agree, under these terms, to have the club pay all taxes other than municipal property tax. Fifteen cents for the sale of each seat under the covered section of the stadium would go back to the city, and ten cents for each uncovered seat. Interestingly, a clause was included that the team would play all its home games in the stadium, even if it was to move to another league.

One-time Toronto Mayor Tommy Church, one of five members of the Harbour Commission board, was firmly in Solman's corner, vociferously arguing against this latest proposal from the city. He lobbied for a deal that would include a $90,000 deposit from Solman, two-thirds of which would be refunded in three years. Negotiations dragged on through the winter and spring, and even after Solman offered to have the Leafs pay for the stadium, the Harbour Commission still could not come to an agreement. At the end of August, the commissioners held what the *Star* described as a "stormy session," but could not come to a consensus that would see Solman lease the Bathurst Street property from the city. Solman had been willing to pay rent to the city of 5 percent an acre on land valued at $10,000 per acre, on a total parcel of 15 acres. But the property had recently undergone a reevaluation, and the commissioners wanted to upgrade the valuation to $15,000/acre. Solman apparently agreed to this, but the commissioners still could not come to a unanimous decision. "It is understood," said the *Star*, "that the commissioners seriously disagreed on the matter, and the whole thing is 'up in the air.'"[4]

By August, sensing that the deal would not go through unless he agreed to build the ballpark, Solman announced the formation of a company that would finance its construction. This seemed to break the logjam at council, and the city agreed to the lease the property so Solman. The prophecy of Cobb (and many others) was about to be realized: baseball was returning to the mainland

A week later, the commission finally agreed to move forward with the lease of the property to Solman. A 42-year lease was granted, "of a stadium for stadium purposes only." An option for seven acres adjacent to the property, for purposes of parking, was approved until the end of July the following year. The annual rent was settled upon at 5 percent per acre on a valuation of $15,000, which worked out to about $750/acre. In 21 years, the property was to be re-valued.

Construction was to begin shortly after that, and Solman had budgeted a cost of $300,000—financed by the team—and a completion date of late April 1926. Site preparation began almost immediately, and the stadium began to rise from the reclaimed land in early December.

Solman had initially commissioned noted Toronto architectural firm Chapman and Oxley to build a 35,000-seat stadium with a covered grandstand from the left-field to right-field foul poles. But with costs for the concrete and steel structure (creating a fire resistant facility, unlike its predecessors on the Island) spiraling, the seating was cut back to 20,000. Still, Solman envisioned another sporting palace like his Arena; plans were quickly made to host football (both the Canadian and American versions) and lacrosse games, high-school sports, concerts, and even boxing matches. The sparkling new park, completed in just five months, offered a view of the Lake Ontario waterfront, but that reduced capacity would come back to haunt future owners of the club with dreams of luring a struggling existing MLB franchise to the city.

CHAPTER 11

SILENT CHARLIE AND MORE PIECES OF THE PUZZLE

For the second year in a row, the Tigers invited the Leafs to share their Georgia spring-training facilities.

Howley's relationship with Ty Cobb—and likely his club's remarkable 1924 turnaround—helped land one player for the 1925 Leafs that should have launched the Toronto bench boss over the moon.

Charlie Gehringer was a second baseman from the University of Michigan sent over the border to London of the MINT League to begin his pro career, impressing in the southwestern Ontario city enough that Cobb called him up to Detroit for the final week of the 1924 season. But it was obvious from his brief Tigers trial that while Gehringer was close to big league-ready, he needed some more time in the minors, and the Dan Howley Finishing School was just the place for the last stage of his big-league apprenticeship. Gehringer would be among the International League leaders in home runs, batting average, and runs batted in at the end of the 1925 season. He would go on to a 19-year Hall of Fame career featuring over 2,800 hits (he failed to hit .300 in only three of his sixteen full seasons), one batting title, a Most Valuable Player Award, and a World Series championship. In 90 World Series at bats, he struck out only once. He has been considered one of the game's best second basemen of all time, and certainly was the best prospect to pass through Toronto. The soft-spoken Central Michigan farm boy would later become known as "The Mechanical Man." "Wind him up in the spring," said future Hall of Famer Lefty Gomez, "and he goes all summer. He hits .330 or .340, then you turn him off in the fall."[1]

Howley's main additions in 1925 were on offence. First baseman Mickey Heath had dominated Class D ball in 1924 but struggled in his debut International League season with Toronto the following year, hitting only .225. Howley had great faith in the youngster, though, and worked him into 123 games. But that low batting average had Howley concerned enough to secure the contract of Dale Alexander, a 6'3", 200-pound slugger who had torn up the South Atlantic League in 1925. The Sally League may have been several notches below the International, and Alexander was no match for Heath with the glove. But Howley, knowing his team would be challenged to score runs, thought Alexander was worth bringing to spring training.

Georgia native Cleo Carlyle spent a couple of years in college before signing with Charlotte of the Class B South Atlantic League in 1924. He batted .355 with 14 HRs in 127 games that season and was signed by the Tigers in the offseason. Cobb invited him to spring training, telling reporters that he was one of the best-looking prospects he had seen in years. After impressing that spring, Carlyle was sent to Toronto for some fine-tuning.

With many puzzle pieces in place, Howley's 1925 club was able to improve on its 98-win of the season before by one game. A better road record (the team played close to .800 ball at home, but only .400 on the road) may have propelled the Leafs to break the Orioles' streak; a late season slump didn't help, either. More importantly, there was something resembling a pennant race in the International League for the first time in a half decade. It wasn't necessarily a tight race—the second-place Leafs finished six games back of Baltimore—but for once the pennant wasn't decided by July. One bright spot for the Howleyites came near the end of the season, when they won their final two meetings with the Orioles to take the season series, the first time an International League opponent had done so in seven years.

Even though Howley would lose his top player (Gehringer),

pitcher (28-game-winner Myles Thomas), and fan favourite Joe Kelly (who led the team in round-trippers with 29) at the end of the season, with the gap between to Leafs and Orioles closing and a new water-front stadium taking shape, there was plenty of optimism in Toronto for the 1926 season.

After the 1925 season ended, a Canadian federal election was held at the end of October. Prime Minister Mackenzie King's Liberal Party managed to win only 100 seats, with King losing his own Ontario riding. Arthur Meighen's Conservatives topped the polls with 115 seats but was eight seats short of a House of Commons majority. Governor-General Lord Byng, the representative of the British Crown in Canada's constitutional monarchy, asked Meighen to form a government. But King had the support of the Progressive and Labour parties, who with their combined seats effectively held the balance of power, and Meighen's government was quickly defeated on a vote of non-confidence in the House. Under parliamentary tradi-tion, Byng turned to King, and the Liberals once again formed a government, albeit a minority one. A year later, King's government fell under the weight of scandal, and a constitutional crisis was brewing.[2]

CHAPTER 12
MAPLE LEAF STADIUM RISES ON THE WATERFRONT

After Christmas 1925, the stadium price tag began to climb, reaching almost $750,000 by the time the park was ready for play. Eager to unload his ferry company to help pay the extra cost, behind the scenes Solman was lobbying certain city officials and council members to get the city to agree to a purchase price in excess of $400,000. In the end, just weeks before the stadium was to open, the city and Solman reached a deal for $337,500, but not before bribery charges had been leveled against him. A former alderman named Fred Burgess alleged that Solman told him that any price tag above $300,000 would allow him to redeem the company's bonds and preferred shares, and that would allow him to "buy" enough members of council to swing the vote of the sale in his favour. Burgess claimed that Solman admitted that he had bribed the city comptroller and one alderman, and for $2,000 figured he could "get" two more. Burgess pushed council for a judicial investigation into the matter. The mayor, likely mindful of Solman's power and influence, hemmed and hawed before council voted to go ahead with the inquiry. Amid considerable public skepticism, the "harbour scandal" eventually went away.

A sign heralding the future Maple Leaf Stadium. (City of Toronto Archives, Fonds 1266, Item 6161.)

Solman, the architects, and the engineers building the stadium followed the lead of the company that built the Buffalo ballpark a year earlier, installing a drainage system for the playing field in the fall before construction of the grandstand started and the first snows fell. Solman personally oversaw much of the construction, arriving by 8 a.m. every morning, and staying until the last worker left. There was a buzz in the city as the ballpark slowly rose from the reclaimed land along the Lake Ontario shoreline.

Early in the New Year, there was a work stoppage one day when several carpenters and two engineers were taken off the job site. Solman said that he had put a clause in the construction contract for only union labour to be used to build the stadium and said that a dispute between the two associations representing the workers was responsible. The secretary of the Toronto building trades council said that while Solman had put in the agreement to use union workers, he refused to pay union wages, and in some cases had hired nonunion workers for some jobs on the project. Solman met with union reps the next day and agreed to pay union wages, which no doubt led to a final price tag far exceeding Solman's initial budget.[1]

As early as mid-January, the stadium was coming along well. The *Buffalo News* reported that "all piling work had been finished" for the grandstand, and that an official from Syracuse who visited the site was "astounded by the progress already made." The Syracuse official gushed about the stadium, "which he described as being one of the best in any league, major or minor."[2]

In February, Howley and Leafs' business manager Art Lehman traveled to New York City for the annual International League scheduling meetings. The pair had managed to secure a late April start to allow for last-minute finishing touches to be applied to the facility and had obtained home dates for all Canadian holidays. The *Star* may have been critical of the stadium proposal and the debate around it, but the paper's sports section—beat writer Charlie Good in particular —was fully on board.

"Lol Solman was more than pleased with the work of his agents, and he anticipates the greatest season in the history of baseball locally," Good wrote. As for the stadium construction, which by mid-February was running behind schedule, Good advised that fans would be fine with it once they saw the finished product. "The stadium might not be complete," Good opined, "but when finishing touches are added, it will make the front of the stadium look like the average man's conception of a palace in Spain." The fifty tons of marble dust workers applied to the stadium's street-facing facade would make fans glad the team was back on the mainland and forget "any trifling inconvenience which they might be subjected to in the early days of the campaign."[3]

By mid-March, the structure of the grandstand was complete, and was starting to get filled in with structures and seats.

Long before construction was complete, Solman was busy adding events to the Maple Leaf Stadium calendar. While the team was on the road in mid-May, a World Bantamweight boxing championship—a prestigious event—was scheduled. The New York Yankees, featuring

Babe Ruth and Lou Gehrig, would come to town on September 19 for an exhibition game with the Leafs. Other exhibition games with the Tigers and Senators were proposed, with dates to be arranged. When the Leafs were out of town, elite amateur teams could use the stadium. In the fall, a provincial high-school championship track meet would be held, and games involving teams from the Ontario Rugby Football Union—a precursor to the modern Canadian Football League—would take place after the conclusion of the Leafs' season.

Attendance at Maple Leaf Stadium in its first year of operation fell short of expectations, the long walk from the last streetcar stop being one of the main reasons. This was the walkway over Bathurst Street. (Toronto Star Weekly, May 15, 1926.

As March turned to April, construction took on a dawn-til-dusk, then round-the-clock pace of operations. The Leafs would open the season with two weeks of games on the road, which Solman had anticipated. As the middle of the month approached, seats still had to be installed, the infield rolled, and a small set of bleachers in left field were yet to be built. Streetcar tracks close to the stadium would not be constructed until the following year, but a new bridge over the railway tracks had been erected at the Bathurst Street line's southern terminus, where the street cars would end their journey before heading back north. The city installed a sidewalk to take patrons from the streetcar to the ballpark. Already, fans were referring to the ballpark as the "Fleet Street Flats," for the name of the road fronting the stadium.

CHAPTER 13
THE HOWLEYITES TAKE THEIR FINAL SHAPE

Howley was putting in the final pieces of the roster as 1926 dawned. He had graduated more players to the big leagues than any other AA* club but had the core of his lineup mostly intact. Contracts for returning players were sent out. Both Solman and Howley were initially concerned about the slow response from the veterans in mailing back signed deals. Lefty Stewart, who had initially briefly held out when he was first obtained by Toronto, was among the early 1926 holdouts. After Jack Dunn finally got the price he wanted for Lefty Grove ($103,000, from Connie Mack's Philadelphia Athletics), Stewart was in a much better bargaining position. With 45 wins over the previous two seasons, even Howley thought Stewart was the more valuable hurler. Solman quickly agreed to Stewart's demand for a raise while granting his wish to start the first game in Maple Leaf Stadium.

Howley wanted his pitchers to report to Georgia for spring training by the last week of February, and the position players a week later. Unlike his previous three springs, which were sometimes more of an open audition for jobs, Howley wanted a pared-down version of camp, with most roster spots decided before spring training broke in

---

* AA was then the highest minor-league classification.

early April. He was still in talks with the Yankees on the return for Myles Thomas, ace of his 1925 staff. Toronto papers speculated that George Pipgras, a hard-throwing but control-challenged prospect who was the prize of the New York system and would later become a stalwart in the Yankees rotation, might come to Toronto. But despite his Toronto connections, Yankees GM Ed Barrow—who, in addition to once managing the Leafs, also married a local woman and ran a downtown hotel for several years when he took some time off from baseball—showed no sympathy for his adopted hometown, sending Pipgras to St. Paul of the American Association. Another name bandied about was that of Walter Beall; no less than Babe Ruth had said he had the best curveball he'd ever faced. But Beall did not become a Leaf, and one must wonder if that's when Howley began to sour on working agreements and deals with big-league clubs. Thomas, who had command problems of his own when he came to the Leafs, had his delivery lengthened—Howley thought he was short-arming the ball—and starred for Toronto. That the club got next to nothing back (player-wise) in return must have been a bitter pill for Howley to swallow.

Spring training opened minus a couple of bodies Howley knew he would be counting on. Flash Gilhooley had an appendectomy in early February and would be delayed two weeks before he was ready to suit up. Collegian Vic Sorrell had caught scouts' eyes with 26 wins in a semi-pro league in 1925, and Solman/Howley outbid many suitors to get Sorrell's signature on a contract, but he wouldn't be reporting to Toronto until his university classes at Wake Forest finished in late May.

Additions to the Leafs roster for the upcoming season included:

RHP Joe Maley was signed by the Yankees after a stellar 1924 season in the Class B Virginia State League, pitching at Buffalo in 1925. According to the *Star*, he was overused by the Bisons, which partly explained his 11-18 record. Sold by the Yankees to Atlanta of the Southern Association after the season, the Leafs managed to secure his release from the Crackers, signing him for the 1926 season. Howley planned to use the 6'3" stringbean pitcher in a swingman role.

Jim Faulkner was a left-handed pitcher originally signed by the Leafs prior to the 1924 season. He couldn't crack Howley's lineup, and was loaned to International League rival Jersey City for the next two seasons. Faulkner was unhappy about essentially being "farmed out" to an International League also-ran: the Skeeters finished dead last in 1924, losing 111 games. The Skeeters were only marginally better the following year, but Faulkner managed to win 17 games for a team that lost 92. When Howley attempted to bring him to Toronto for 1926, Faulkner initially balked, still slighted by his exile to the International League wilderness for two seasons. Faulkner always seemed to save his best outings for Toronto; when told by Howley on the Skeeters' last visit to Hanlan's Point of the Leafs' interest in him, according to the *Star*, "the pitcher stated that he was not burning up with eagerness to either play in Toronto or under Howley's management." At the same time the paper said, "his childish attitude did not make a hit with either Howley or President Solman."[1] Rumours abounded that Howley was looking to deal Faulkner not long after acquiring him, with the lowly Boston Braves the club most prominently mentioned. Either Howley and Faulkner mended fences, or the southpaw decided to sign with Toronto in the hopes that his pitching would land him a big-league job, because he reported on time for spring training.

Third base had been held down for much of the 1925 season by Andy Harrington, viewed by many as the Tigers' third baseman of the future. But he strained his shoulder in the second half, while also suffering a "pulled groin" (as diagnosed by the Leafs' trainer, Tim Daly) in spring training. Howley had already been toying with the idea of shifting Harrington to second in order to save his arm, but the injury, combined with a severe cold he picked up in spring training, meant that Howley had an immediate need for a man to play the hot corner, a search that would continue after the season opened.

As insurance against Harrington's injuries, Howley obtained light-hitting infielder Carl Schmehl, a wizard with the glove. Schmehl had played for Minneapolis of the American Association the previous season, signing with San Francisco of the Pacific Coast League for 1926. But Schmehl's wife had to return home before the season began to care for an ailing relative, taking their children with her. Homesick, Schmehl asked the Tigers to post him closer to home, and he was made available to Toronto.

Clyde Manion had been a dependable backup catcher for the Tigers for several years before Howley was able to obtain him for the 1925 Leafs. His performance on both sides of the plate that season led Cobb to want him back the following year, so Howley was once again on the hunt for a primary backstop. He swung for the fences when he made a contract offer to Steve O'Neill, a 15-year big-league veteran who, at 35 and with almost 1,600 major-league games behind him, was approaching the end of his career. But O'Neill was highly regarded defensively and for his work calling games and was not a bad Deadball Era hitter. From 1915 to 1924, he had been one of the most durable catchers in the game; he caught 149 of 154 games in leading Cleveland to a 1920 World Series title. O'Neill had served as a backup for the Yankees in 1925 and was much in demand by other teams for that role, but he chose the chance to both play regularly and for Dan Howley in deciding to sign with the Leafs. O'Neill would prove to be one of Howley's most important offseason acquisitions.

Howley's second-most important roster upgrade came in the form of Owen "Ownie" Carroll. Carroll had starred at Holy Cross for four seasons and was regarded as one of the greatest college pitchers of all time. Howley had offered him a contract after his freshman season, but Carroll opted to stay in school. He made his big-league debut shortly after signing with the Tigers at the conclusion of his collegiate career in 1925 but was deemed in need of more seasoning in

Owen Carroll was sent back to Toronto for more seasoning in 1926 and quickly became the Leafs' ace.

the minors. Howley once again finally had his man. A year in Toronto would be the final touch-ups to his command and pitching skills. Howley wasted no time in installing Carroll at the top of his pitching rotation with Stewart, Faulkner, Satterfield, and Doyle.

CHAPTER 14
SPRING TRAINING APPROACHES

Carl Hubbell as a New York Giant. Deprived of his signature pitch per Ty Cobb's decree, Hubbell was the last man on the Leafs' pitching staff.

As spring training neared, the return for Myles Thomas from the Yankees had still not been settled. The Toronto press was not pleased. "Negotiations between the New York American League Baseball Club and the Toronto club in the past have not been favourable to Toronto," said the *Globe*. "In fact, there has been a disposition on the part of the Leafs not to deal with the Hugmen [the nickname reporters gave the Yankees after their manager, Miller Huggins].”[1] In his final turn with the Leafs a decade later, Howley said he wanted the Leafs to have as much homegrown talent as possible, lessening their reliance on affiliation with a big-league club. The intractability of the Yankees likely nudged him in that direction.

Ty Cobb was many things, but a great talent evaluator he perhaps was not. His Tigers had signed a left-hander from Oklahoma named Carl Hubbell, who had won 17 games in the Class A Western League in 1925.[2] Hubbell's signature pitch was the screwball, better known then as the fadeaway. Because it broke in the opposite direction of a curveball, away from right-handed hitters, it was a highly effective pitch against them. Hubbell had discovered his by accident when he was experimenting with different grips on his sinker. He used the pitch in Western League games and was instantly tantalized with its results, to the extent that he began to feel the strain of it in his throwing shoulder. Between starts he lifted weights and went everywhere with a rubber ball that he squeezed repeatedly to strengthen his arm and fingers, which helped relieve the stress on his shoulder.

The screwball/fadeaway could be a very difficult pitch to command because of the unnatural throwing motion it involved. There were many who felt the pitch was too hard on a pitcher (even though the legendary Christy Mathewson had used it to win 373 big league games), and after seeing it in action in spring training in 1926, Cobb was firmly in that club. Howley, at first, was very excited to have Hubbell for the upcoming season, telling local reporters that he thought Hubball and Owen Carroll could combine for 40 wins,[3] but his enthusiasm was dampened when he learned via telegram from Cobb just after camp broke that Hubbell was forbidden to use the pitch. Cobb's usual treatment with rookies was to ignore them; “Hubbell could not recall speaking to him about his fadeaway—or anything else—that spring.”[4] A Tigers coach who had once played with a pitcher who hurt his arm throwing the pitch put the bug in Cobb's ear that the untested rookie with the odd pitch would be better served working on his other pitches. Howley broke the bad news to Hubbell before the season opener. Cobb, who had a future

Hall of Famer right under his nose but couldn't see it, would resign before season's end, and Howley had a pitcher he could only use in long relief and mop-up situations.

Two players not in training camp had Toronto connections, but their signings were probably an attempt to drum up ticket sales before the season started.

Babe Dye was an accomplished player in both baseball and hockey, although the latter was his strongest sport. The Hamilton native made his debut in the fledgling National Hockey League with the Toronto St. Pats in 1919. Not blessed with great speed on the ice, Dye terrorized NHL goalies with his quick, accurate shot. Dye led the league in goals on three occasions, and in total points twice. With Dye starring on the top line, the St. Pats won the Stanley Cup in 1923.

But Dye's sporting accomplishments were not limited to the ice. Originally signed by the Red Sox, he was sold to Buffalo in 1921 and starred for the Leafs' crosslake rivals for several seasons. "Dye is surely a nifty baseball player, a good hitter, reliable outfielder, and speedy on the basepaths," *The Sporting News* noted.[5] Dye hit over .300 in his first three seasons with the Bisons, and even though his average dipped to .294 in 1925, Howley still thought the fleet centre fielder would be a good fit in the Leafs lineup, especially given the advanced age of Flash Gilhooley.

However, the physical toll of playing two sports had taken its toll on Dye by the time he became a baseball Maple Leaf.* The St. Pats finished in sixth place in the then-seven-team NHL in 1925-26, missing the playoffs. A back injury Dye suffered that year not only delayed his arrival at spring training until the end of March, it also had the St. Pats quietly shopping him around to other NHL teams, believing he was past his prime as a hockey player.

While Dye was a legitimate player, the signing of multisport local star Lionel Conacher was most likely an attempt to generate headlines and spark baseball interest in the depths of winter. Nicknamed the "Big Train," Conacher was an established NHL star, had won a Grey

---

* The hockey team would take that name in the following season.

Cup with the Toronto Argonauts, and held provincial wrestling and boxing championships—he even sparred with World Heavyweight Champ Jack Dempsey.

But baseball was Conacher's least accomplished sport; his time in the boxing ring, hockey rink, and gridiron may not have given him the time to develop his skills. He did play semi-pro ball in Toronto between seasons, but his background in the sport was limited, given his other athletic pursuits. However, if there's one thing Howley loved, it was a challenge. Missing a chunk of spring training while his Pittsburgh Pirates (who finished a surprising third in their first NHL season) took part in the Stanley Cup playoffs likely had a huge negative impact on Conacher's development on the diamond, as the skills sessions Howley likely had in mind for his talented-but-raw player were few as a result. Nonetheless, he created some media buzz for the Leafs at a time of the year when hockey dominated the sports pages.

Starry Athlete Signs With the Leafs

CONACHER SIGNING HIS TORONTO BASEBALL CONTRACT

Local baseball history was made yesterday when Lionel Conacher, football, hockey and lacrosse star, accepted terms to play with the Leafs. Conny may or may not make good, but Mr. Howley is of the opinion that an athlete of his calibre apart from being a box office asset, should be useful to the club as a player. Conacher is no stranger to the diamond game, having starred with the Hillcrests and other local clubs. The big fellow himself is confident that he will hold his own in class A.A. company. In the above picture Conacher is shown signing his contract with Manager Howley and Cecil (Babe) Dye, also of the Leafs, and a Toronto boy, looking on. Picture by the Alexandra Studio.

Multisport star and local hero Lionel "Big Train" Conacher was signed mainly as a box office attraction. Toronto Star, *January 30, 1926.*

CHAPTER 15
THE LEAFS HEAD NORTH

THE LEAFS BROKE CAMP ON MARCH 31. THE LOCAL AUGUSTA KIWANIS club held a barbecue with many local notables and celebrities in attendance hoping to pay tribute to the Leafs and Tigers, but Howley's club was on a train headed to Atlanta, as the team prepared to open the season April 14 in Reading, playing 10 games against other minor-league teams on their way north.

The roster Howley took north from Georgia was just a few over the 20-man limit; most competitions for jobs had long been decided, but there were still a few battles he wanted to see before settling on a final lineup. Slugger Dale Alexander was thought by many to have the inside track on the first-base job, but a case of the mumps sidelined him for most of training camp, and incumbent Mickey Heath had made the most of the opportunity by hitting well.

One of the players Howley brought along for the winding trip to Reading was Lionel Conacher, who had reported just a few days earlier. Reports from the exhibition junket before the season said that in batting practice, Conacher had "rattled" line drives off the centre- and right-field fences. "Naturally," reported the *Star*, "he has yet to look at any curves."[1]

Maple Leaf Stadium, March 1929. (City of Toronto Archives, Fonds 1231, Item 465.)

Dye was brought along on the trip, but his workload was restricted due to his back injury. This more than likely would doom his status in the long term, as Howley seemed intent on going with a set roster, with Herman Layne, Cleo Carlyle, and maybe Frank Gilhooley (still in Georgia recovering from an appendectomy) patrolling the outfield. All in all, the Leafs had a number of walking wounded: Harrington's recovery was going slower than had been anticipated, and Owen Carroll had tripped and badly sprained an ankle walking into the ballpark. Jim Faulkner appeared to be going through a dead arm period. Layne and Carlyle both reported ailments. The weather had not been cooperative, either, with some of the fields the Leafs visited not ready for play. Howley had a tough task of resting his regulars but still fielding a competitive club.

Still, as the club prepared to board a "rattler" to Atlanta, Howley was pleased with the group he was breaking camp with. "I think that we are going to get somewhere this season," he told the Toronto *Star Weekly*, a weekend supplement to the *Star*. "My players, with two or three exceptions, are leaving Georgia in better physical condition than any that I have ever managed." Howley was very confident in the hurlers he was taking north, indicating he would rely only on a handful of pitchers. "We finished second in the last two campaigns, and I have a better balanced pitching staff than ever before. I have or will have six pitchers who will win consistently for me."[2]

"Howley is gambling strongly," wrote the *Star Weekly*, "on Stewart, Carroll, Hubbell, Faulkner, Maley, and the twirlers he hopes to get." Carroll, in particular, "the Toronto skipper thinks, will have little difficulty in putting over 25 victories."[3]

Howley would not have Jess Doyle at the start of the season. The southpaw had struggled with Detroit the previous season, and Howley had reason to believe he would be available, but Doyle had shown enough to Cobb to earn a spot on the Tigers' Opening Day roster.

Howley had hoped to start the season with a stronger infield, but injuries meant that his starting four would be something of a patchwork lineup. "The loss of Charlie Gehringer," said the *Star Weekly*, "was a severe one to start with." But, the *Weekly* said, "There is every reason to believe that the outfield of the Leafs will be stronger than last season."[4] Gone was slugger Joe Kelly, but "Herman Layne and Cleo Carlyle, with experience gained last season, will play more finished baseball, and their hitting should show improvement."[5] Kelly took advantage of Hanlan Point's short lakeside right-field porch, and Howley likely knew the defensively limited pull hitter would be out of place in the more spacious Maple Leaf Stadium outfield.

When the Leafs stopped in Charlotte, North Carolina (Alexander's team the previous season) on their way north, a finally healthy Dale Alexander banged out two hits, one a lengthy home run, and with that the deal between Toronto and his former club to secure his services saw the price tag suddenly go up. With the Charlotte owner demanding cash—"a considerable sum, at that,"[6] said the *Globe*—and Heath in return for the slugger, when the Leafs' train pulled out of Charlotte the next evening, Alexander wasn't a passenger.

As the Leafs were gearing up for their final spring training tune ups, the Stanley Cup playoffs took place in the first week of April. The Montreal Maroons, in only their second season of existence, defeated the Ottawa Senators in a two-game, total-goals playoff to decide the National Hockey League championship. The Victoria Cougars, winner of the Western League, would head across country to take on the Maroons, with all games to be played in Montreal's new arena, the Forum.

With five future Hall of Famers in their lineup, the Maroons easily took the best-of-five series from the Cougars in four games. The Western League folded soon after, and from that point on the Stanley Cup became the sole possession of the NHL. The league, which had added its first U.S.-based team (Boston) two years earlier, and another (New York Americans) the following season, was, like Toronto, on the verge of major changes, which included borrowing their baseball cousin's nickname.

The last two exhibition games were in Waterbury, Connecticut, and Howley had to be wondering if the final tuneup was worth it against the defending Eastern League champs. The Leafs dropped both games to the lower-level club, and Otis Miller tweaked his shoulder in the cold weather making a throw from the hole at short-stop. With snowflakes appearing from time to time, the team report-edly went through the motions in the second match, which was completed in an hour and a half—Waterbury fans who braved the wintry weather to attend the game speculated that the Leafs played like they had a train to catch. Howley unveiled his likely starting lineup at Reading in two days' time:

Gilhooley or Dye CF
Harrington 3B
Carlyle RF
Lane LF
Miller SS
Heath 1B

Schmehl 2B
O'Neill C
Stewart P

Meanwhile, International League beat reporters were predicting that 1926 would bring an end to Baltimore's run of dominance. The 1925 club was weakened by the sale of Lefty Grove to Connie Mack's Philadelphia A's, but the Orioles did manage to eke out a pennant win over the second-place Leafs on the last weekend of the season, earning Baltimore its sixth trip to the Junior World Series, where they captured their third minor-league crown over Louisville. In addition to an improved Toronto squad, reporters noted that Jersey City, Syracuse, and Newark rosters had been bolstered as well.

Baltimore's path to the pennant would be a tough one. Orioles' owner/manager Jack Dunn had seen his health decline after the death of his son Jack Jr. The younger Dunn, a former O's player, served as his father's co-manager and team secretary but had died of pneumonia in 1923. Dunn Sr. had been under a doctor's care for several years because of a coronary condition. Dunn was not one to give up easily. At the age of nine, his arm was run over by a boxcar when he was playing at a local railway yard. Doctors said his life was at risk unless the arm was amputated; Dunn refused, but the arm was deformed as a result, and he couldn't lift it above his head. By 1926, worn down by the passing of his son, the baseball wars, and his health issues, it seemed his desire for the game was waning.

In Toronto, there was plenty of optimism about the upcoming season. "Dan Howley's Toronto team," gushed the *Globe*, "looms as the best assembled across the Canadian border since the Maple Leafs won pennants in 1917 and 1918."[7] The *Star Weekly* favoured the Orioles to win, reasoning that manager Dunn's pitching staff "is one of the best he's had in two seasons, since the departure of Lefty Grove for the Athletics."[8]

On the eve of the Reading season opener, Howley received word in New York (where he had the team stay for two days after the

Waterbury debacle) that Gilhooley was ready to play, and on his way to Pennsylvania to join the club. Howley told reporters at the team's hotel that he planned on starting Gilhooley over Dye in the opener. He also had a message for Toronto fans: "You are going to have a team worth cheering for, and one that will do credit to the wonderful new stadium that is being built by President Solman."[9]

CHAPTER 16
MAPLE LEAF STADIUM
NEARS COMPLETION

WHILE THE LEAFS PREPARED TO TAKE ON READING, MAPLE LEAF Stadium was nearing completion, and Solman was entertaining visitors and reporters on tours. Workers scrambled to install "orchestra chairs, in which the fans will watch games in comfort this season," according to *Globe* sports editor Frederick Wilson. The drainage system installed the previous fall left the playing field "dry as a board," in Wilson's words. Over 16,000 square feet of sod had been transported from a former park in Scarborough, in the east end, which was giving way to a housing development for the growing city. "Already it is showing green," observed Wilson, no small feat for early spring in Toronto. The infield consisted of loam and burnt moulding sand, which was the preferred mix of big-league groundskeepers. "The whole playing surface is as smooth as a billiard table," gushed Wilson. Everything about Maple Leaf Stadium seemed to say Major League, albeit on a smaller scale.[1]

Ticket sales were brisk in the weeks before the game, and W.A. Hewitt, sports editor of the *Star*, opined that if the weatherman cooperated, the International League single-game attendance record would be broken on Opening Day.[2] In the weeks before the game, fans were invited to win a suit by sending in their best guess of the final turnstile count. This ad ran in all the papers.

1926

Clothier and Leafs' superfan Roth Eaton's promotion prior to the Leaf's 1926 Home
Opener. From the Toronto Star.

For one day, the eyes of much of the baseball world would be on Toronto, and for a city that aspired to one day be world class, Opening Day was emerging as a breakthrough event, a chance for the city to be displayed on a continent-wide stage.

The local media was quite likely distracted by the upcoming Opening Day, but the biggest story in Canadian sports—if not North America—in the last week of April was the incredible Boston Marathon victory of Cape Bretoner Johnny Miles. The 20-year-old son of Welsh immigrants was coached by his father, Willi, and had never competed beyond 10 kilometres. He trained by running behind the wagon while delivering groceries for a local store. Miles showed up to Boston in a homemade singlet (with a Maple Leaf bearing the initials "NS") and 98-cent running shoes, his transportation to the event paid for by fundraising neighbours. The unknown Nova Scotian and his father walked the course a couple of days before the race but got lost, which left him stiff and sore, and his father had to ask a policeman for directions. "Tell your son just to follow the crowd," was the officer's advice when he learned that Johnny would be running the race.[3] The senior Miles cooked his son a steak the night before the marathon, advising him to stay as close as he could to the two race favourites, local runner Clarence DeMar (a four-time Boston winner, and current holder of the world marathon record) and Albin Stenroos of Finland, the defending Olympic champion.

DeMar and Stenroos broke away from the pack about five miles into the race, with Miles following close behind. At about the ten-mile mark, Stenroos made his move; Miles managed to move with him, but DeMar fell back into the pack. Stenroos slowly pulled away from Miles, but trying to put the upstart young Canadian away came at a price. By the time the pair entered the famous Newton Hills section in the course's final miles, Miles knew he could outlast Stenroos when he caught up to him on the last hill. "When we came to Heartbreak Hill," Miles said in 1996 on the Boston Marathon's 100th anniversary,* "I looked at Stenroos and his eyes were sunken, his face was

---

* Miles lived to be 97, passing away in 2003.

kind of pulled in, and I figured this was the time to pass him. I was afraid to look behind me again for fear he was coming."[4]

The press and movie cameras mobbed Miles as he crossed the finishing line, an astonishing 400 yards ahead of Stenroos. He finished in a time of 2:25:40, just over four minutes ahead of DeMar's course and world record. It was one of the greatest Boston Marathon upsets of all time. The day before the Marathon, he told one of the race officials, "I didn't come all the way from Nova Scotia to finish 2nd," according to the *Brooklyn Eagle*.[5]

It's curious that the Toronto papers didn't make a bigger deal of Miles' win. One had to dig 11 pages into the *Star* before finding the headline "CANADIAN GROCERY BOY WINS BOSTON MARATHON," atop a wire service article. While Miles was feted throughout the Boston area in the days after his surprising victory, the Toronto papers paid only scant attention. Perhaps there was no small amount of local bias. "The synod of Nova Scotia passed a resolution congratulating young Johnny Miles in winning the Boston marathon," huffed *Star* legendary sports columnist Lou Marsh. "History does not reveal the fact that any synod or church body congratulated [Ontarian] Tom Longboat when he won it."[6] Other than running a wire service story about Miles being feted at a banquet in his hometown, there was little mention of his win in the *Globe*. Hewitt in the *Star* wrote what amounted to a passing paragraph about Miles, paying more attention to whether he could represent Canada at the next Olympics by virtue of his British birth—he could, and he wanted to carry Canada's flag in Los Angeles.[7]

Scaffolding on west side of Maple Leaf Stadium. (City of Toronto Archives, Globe and Mail fonds, Fonds 1266, Item 7685.)

CHAPTER 17
SEASON OPENER

The team gathers on Opening Day. (City of Toronto Archives, Globe and Mail Fonds, Fonds 1266, Item 7698.)

On a cold, blustery mid-April Wednesday, the Leafs took to the field against Reading in a season-opener that almost didn't happen.

An injunction had been threatened by the Reading club's former owners against William Ashton of Baltimore, who had taken over the franchise in the offseason. Ashton, it was charged, did not receive permission to use the field at Lauer's Park, owned by a wealthy brewer who had died several months earlier. But consent was obtained minutes before the game's scheduled start.

The Leafs took the field "resplendent in new road uniforms of University of Toronto blue trimmed with a light shade of grey," according to the *Globe*. "There is an Old English 'T' on the breast, and the green maple leaves on a black background on sleeves, and cap very natty."[1] Only 3,500 Reading fans braved the weather, which Toronto won handily by an 8-2 score. Lefty Stewart went the distance for the win, and Steve O'Neill drove in two runs with a pair of doubles.

Toronto took the second game of the series, 6-1. Owen Carroll, in his International League debut, pitched a complete game and struck out nine, but his erratic control was on display, as he walked five batters and hit three. Cleo Carlyle hit the first Leafs' home run of the year, but the victory came at a cost. Andy Harrington, starting at third, injured his shoulder on a throw across the diamond, and Carroll re-injured his ankle sliding into second. With a series coming up in Baltimore on Sunday, Howley had to be concerned.

Toronto won the following day, with Jim Faulkner scattering five hits in a 4-3 victory, and topped Reading in the series finale 14-3 on getaway day for a four-game sweep. Early in the season, the 4-0 Leafs were in first place heading into the series with their archrivals, the Orioles.

Howley had likely circled the Sunday afternoon doubleheader in Baltimore back in February when the Leafs schedule was set. Toronto came into town on a high but came crashing back to earth when the O's swept the double bill. Lefty Stewart took the loss in the Leafs' 6-1 drubbing by Baltimore in the opener, while Carl Hubbell, who started the second game—minus his best pitch—failed to get out of the first inning, giving up three runs and four hits enroute to an 8-6 loss, although the Leafs had fought back twice to tie the game. Baltimore, who had taken three games from Buffalo, was back in their familiar spot atop the standings with a 5-0 record.

Cold weather and wet grounds forced the postponement of the final two games of the series, and the Leafs headed off to Newark. With Opening Day at Maple Leaf Stadium now a week away, W.A. Hewitt of the *Star* took his readers on a tour of the shiny new ball-park, calling it "the last word in modern baseball construction." The grandstand, he wrote, "practically surrounds the diamond in V-fash-ion." The scoreboard and flagpole were in straightaway centre field, and the infield had held up well over the winter, "but will require plenty of rolling to make it as true as the Island playing field."[2] Perhaps as a tribute to the club's 30 years across the harbour, the grandstand would look onto the Toronto Islands, with Lake Ontario behind it. The two things fans would not see would be Sunday base-ball (banned until the late 1940s), or beer for sale, which would not happen until the Toronto Blue Jays were in their sixth season down the Lakeshore at Exhibition Stadium 1982. Charlie Good of the *Star* noted the diamond's vast outfield dimensions. "The outfield will take some covering," he noted, "and there should be some sensational catches in the roomy spaces in left and centre during the summer. Frank Gilhooley, who can go far and wide for fly balls, should be in his glory."[3]

Toronto handed Newark their first loss of the season, 7-6 in 10 innings, in the series opener in classic Howley small-ball fashion. Faulkner, the Leafs' starting pitcher, had his struggles, twice giving up runs to allow the home team to tie the game. The teams were tied at five at the end of nine innings and headed off to extras. Gilhooley led off the inning by reaching on an error; even approaching his mid-30s, his speed was still a threat, and with that in mind, the Newark second baseman bobbled Gilhooley's grounder, and Toronto had the leadoff man aboard. Mickey Heath sacrificed Gilhooley to second, then Gilhooley easily strolled home with the go-ahead run on Carlyle's double. Toronto added another run, which turned out to be fortunate, because Faulkner gave one run back to Newark in the home half of the tenth before taking a line drive off his shin. Joe

Maley finished the game, and Faulkner got the win, despite giving up 19 hits.

Howley raved to a local reporter about his team. "The so-called experts picked us to finish seventh last year," he enthused, "and we fooled 'em. We've got a better team this year, and we will fool them again." About Owen Carroll, a Newark boy, he said, "He's a big-league pitcher right now, but one year with this team is just what he needs." Of Carl Schmehl, another local product, Howley told the reporter, "(he) won't hit much, but he'll knock down a million base hits."[4]

About 5,000 fans were in attendance the next day to cheer on hometown boy Carroll as the Leafs routed the Bears 13-4. Howley gave Gilhooley the day off, and his replacement Babe Dye made an impact, collecting a pair of doubles and driving in four runs. The win assured the Leafs, now 6-2 on the young season, would arrive home with a winning record.

In the next game, a 17-13 slugfest won by the Leafs, the game was stopped by the umpire because Maley had been applying resin to the ball. The resin bag had been a source of controversy for several years. Use of it dated back to the late 1800s, but was popularized in the 1914 World Series, when each pitcher carried their own resin bag to the mound; the trend quickly caught on. But among the many changes made in the aftermath of the death of Cleveland's Ray Chapman as the result of being hit by a pitch in 1920 was the banning of all foreign substances on the ball. Pitchers began to concoct their own version of grip-enhancing resin, which sometimes included pine tar. The practice got out of hand, so the National League brought the bag back in 1925, standardizing its use across baseball. There was controversy about its use in the World Series, so the MLB Rules Committee adopted its use for the 1926 season, only to have the American League opt out less than a month after play began. The umpire took the resin bag from Maley, and he was allowed to remain in the game.

Newark took the final game of the series, 11-5, but the Leafs lost more than the game. Leslie Beck was a right-handed pitcher who had pitched close to home in the Nebraska State League for a couple of seasons when the Tigers bought his contract in 1924. He failed to show up for spring training, possibly because of a dispute over a bonus. Sent by the Tigers to a Texas League club, he returned home to Hastings, Nebraska, before even appearing in a game. After showing some promise with Denver in the Western League, Detroit sent him to Toronto. Howley, in the manner of the day, brought him along slowly, and probably planned to ease him onto the Leafs pitching staff. Newspaper reports of the spring of 1926 tabbed Beck as an up-and-coming prospect, but he didn't start a game until April 4 and was out of it soon after giving up four runs in the fourth inning. The *Star* didn't make a big deal out of the outing, noting that as it was his first start, "there was some excuse for his failure to go the route...with decent support, he might have escaped unscathed."[5]

That poor start must have weighed on Beck, or perhaps he was frustrated at the limited opportunities he'd had. Maybe even there was some homesickness, but when Beck didn't appear at the park that afternoon, Howley checked with the hotel to see if they had any clue as to his whereabouts. Hotel staff did not see him, and it looked like Beck had jumped the club, without a word to anyone. The *Globe* called Beck "a temperamental individual," an "eccentric flinger" after news of his departure reached Toronto.[6] Beck had gone to the Newark station and boarded a train for the Midwest, taking him out of organized baseball for good. A few weeks later, he was pitching for a semi-pro outfit in his Nebraska hometown of Hastings. Beck never pitched professionally again.

That was not the only bad news Howley had for the press that day. Earlier, Reading Manager Frank "Shag" Shaughnessy phoned Howley in his hotel room to tell him Reading management had fired him.[7] Born in Illinois, Shaughnessy came to Canada in the early 1910s and was a legendary figure in three sports, well-respected by fans and the press alike in his home country. It was up to Howley, who no doubt knew of Shaughnessy's popularity north of the border, to break the news to reporters. In the doubleheader played that Sunday afternoon in Jersey City, the Leafs' final stop on their road trip, Toronto split with the Skeeters, Carroll getting the W in the second game. On

Monday, April 25, Maley went the distance as the Leafs easily won, 6-1.

The club boarded a train headed north for Canada immediately after the game, and as they rumbled home for a nearly month-long homestand, Howley had to be both happy with the club's 9-4 start (given their woes on the road the year before) and looking forward to seeing the finished ballpark.

CHAPTER 18
BASEBALL ON THE MAINLAND

The day before Maple Leafs Stadium was to open, the *Globe* enthused about the new mainland park ("Fans Dream Realized—Baseball on the Mainland" was the headline) and Toronto's future. "No more ferryboats, no more police lines," read the cover of a souvenir insert, "the dinner will be warm and ready for you when you get home." The cheerleading continued as the cover encouraged fans to "Get right in behind Dan Howley and the Leafs, and we'll show the world what kind of ball town Toronto is." "When you look around the mammoth Stadium," the souvenir said, "we are inclined to speculate on the question of Toronto in the major leagues." The insert, which documented Toronto's lengthy professional baseball history, also revealed that Massachusetts native Howley was a rabid hockey fan.[1]

As Maple Leaf Stadium readied for opening, the *Globe* lauded the work of the engineers, who decided in the winter months to save time (and as a result, money) by precasting the concrete for the grandstand indoors. It was reported 150 carpenters were employed for the winter in building the forms for the concrete, and as many as 300 labourers were hired to help maneuver the castings into place.

Maple Leaf Stadium construction, April 1926. (City of Toronto archives, Fonds 1548, Series 393, Item 20393a.)

The Leafs came home on the heels of the most successful first road trip of the season in team history. The *Mail and Empire* noted that Howley was "dubious about the trip," as "Western clubs are always at a disadvantage owing to lack of batting practice on the road, at a time when they need it the most." While the players were anxious to see the new stadium, the *Mail and Empire* said that "the ballplayers will always have fond memories of the Island grounds," which were said to be "among the best in the circuit." "This spring," the paper added, "more than one of the Leaf regulars expressed regret that the beautiful grounds could not be transferred to Fleet Street."[2]

Howley had his players work out on the new field, pronouncing it ready for play. Over 1,000 fans were on hand to watch the team emerge from their dugout in their new home uniforms with cream flannel trimmed with black. The whole team was present, even Claude Satterfield and Herman Layne, who left the team's Toronto-bound train in Buffalo to drive Layne's car, which he had left in the Queen City before departing for spring training, on to Toronto. The

Star said the players after their first looks at the park were "filled with amazement at its magnitude." Howley was "flabbergasted at the size of the stand [and] greatly smitten with the roominess of its field." Howley even went as far as to say that Maple Leaf Stadium was superior to the new ballpark built in Los Angeles for the Pacific Coast League Angels. Wrigley Field, named after the chewing gum magnate who also owned the Chicago Cubs, was called the "Wrigley's Million Dollar Palace." Not only was Maple Leaf Stadium better, Howley said, but "'Few in the majors are half as good,' he soliloquized as his eyes rolled heavenward.[3]

J. Henry Brown, Woodstock, is greeted by Dan Howley. (City of Toronto Archives, Globe and Mail fonds, Fonds 1266, Item 5075.)

Plans were made for fans and notable officials as well. International League President J. Conway Toole would attend the game. J. Henry Brown from Woodstock, who had been in attendance for every Leafs home opener save one since 1885, had his tickets and would be in the grandstand. And the grand old man of the game itself, Commissioner Judge Kennesaw Mountain Landis, would be there. Landis said he had long since retired from ceremonial first-pitch duties, but he was open to the idea of Toronto one day having a big-league team to call its own. "It is entirely up to your own city," he responded to reporters' broaching the question.[4]

On the eve of the game, there was far more than excitement in the air—plenty of rain was in the forecast. In fact, it rained all night, and with the weatherman calling for north winds, cloudy skies, cool temperatures, and the possibility of a few snowflakes, not even the new infield drainage system could make the field playable, and the game was postponed early in the morning. Solman inspected the grounds not long after daybreak, and with an east wind blowing in the promise of more precipitation, decided to make the call. The minor-league attendance record would likely be safe, at least for one day. One positive development that came out of the day was that Solman decided then and there to have tile installed under the outfield on the next Leafs' road trip. "The difference (between the infield and outfield) was so apparent," observed the *Mail and Empire*, "that President Solman will let the contracts immediately for the work."[5]

Landis, who had to leave town that night and would miss the rescheduled opener the next day, examined the stadium from head to toe, "even going to centre field to inspect the flag mast," which stood in play in front of the outfield wall, according to the *Globe*. Landis examined the club's offices, Solman and Howley's offices, clubhouses and umpires' rooms, heating and lighting systems, and even the restaurant and lunch counter. "Absolutely nothing overlooked or forgotten," the *Globe* reported. "As near perfection as possible to have a baseball park."[6]

While the Leafs were less than thrilled with the day off, Reading likely welcomed it. The Keystones limped into Toronto late on Tuesday night, their train delayed en route. Reading had lost nine of their first ten and were competitive in only one of their first four home games against the Leafs. The weather forecast for the rescheduled Opening Day was barely better than the first, but the prospect of clearing skies late in the afternoon (game time was 3 p.m.) provided enough optimism for the game to go ahead. Toronto would send Lefty Stewart, as he was promised, to the mound, while Reading would counter with veteran Jim Marquis. To add indignity to the Keys' tough start, and despite Landis' pronouncement on Maple Leafs Stadium's readiness, the visitor's clubhouse was not completed, forcing opponents to dress for the game at their hotel. Workers literally were scrambling to complete the final touches to the ballpark in the hours before the game. Gates at the ballpark entrance were not installed until close to midnight the day before.

The game started in a drizzle, which—despite the weather forecast—would last for much of the game. "14,000 rabid fans, shivering in the grandstand,"[7] according to the *Mail and Empire*, were in attendance, many sporting umbrellas. With a game-time temperature of 33°F (1°C) that did not promise to move in an upward direction, both the *Globe* and *Star* agreed that if not for the importance of the game and the previous day's cancellation, this contest would likely have been postponed. Much of the projected capacity crowd from the day before opted to stay home and listen to a studio recreation of the game over the *Star*'s CFCA radio station, but there were many honoured guests in the crowd, including the labourers who built the stadium, invited by Solman. The chilly conditions would be echoed 51 one years later as the expansion Toronto Blue Jays took to the field for their home opener.

The players lined up along their respective baselines, then paraded out single file to the flagpole while a band played "The Maple Leaf Forever." Mayor Thomas Foster threw the first pitch to former Mayor Tommy Church, who pantomimed a hitter's action in the right-handed batter's box. The first two of Foster's lobs landed well short of home plate; on the final one, Church mimed a swing and miss to finally bring the Opening Ceremonies to a conclusion.

Howley went with much the same lineup as the one he used in the first two weeks of the season, the only changes being Babe Dye in centre field for a resting Frank Gilhooley, and utilityman Del Capes starting at third in place of the ailing Harrington. Reading got off to a quick start, scoring a run in the top of the first. Toronto failed to score in their half and had trouble mounting any offence against Marquis. Reading added a pair in the sixth, and one more in the seventh while Marquis continued to blank the Leafs. The trickle of the fans out of the ballpark to their warm dinners at home began after the seventh-inning stretch; it turned, much like the day, into a flood by the end of the top of the ninth. Reading had added another run in that frame to build what looked like an insurmountable 5-0 lead, and with the way Marquis continued to stymie the Toronto bats, it looked like a sad ending to Opening Day.

Cleo Carlyle, Toronto's leadoff hitter in the home half of the ninth, had struggled all day with Marquis' offerings. When he squared around to bunt, Marquis was taken by surprise, and he slipped while trying to field the ball along the third-base line, with Carlyle safe at first with a bunt single. The next hitter, Herman Layne, singled to left, and there was some stirring among the handful of soaked fans left in the grand-stand. Otis Miller bounced back to Marquis, who took the sure out at first, allowing the runners to move up a base, but the groundout effectively let a lot of air out of the Leafs' comeback balloon, and more fans headed for the exits. Capes' sacrifice fly to centre field brought Carlyle in to score to spoil Marquis' shutout bid, but now the Leafs were down to their final out, still down by four. Andy Harrington pinch hit for Carl Schmehl and departing fans on the concourse stopped in their tracks when his single up the middle brought in Lane to score from second. The next hitter, Steve O'Neill, singled as well to keep the rally alive. Claude Satterfield, the good-hitting pitcher, had been told by Howley to grab a bat to hit for Joe Maley, who had relieved Lefty Stewart in the 8th; his base hit—the fifth single of the inning for the

Leafs—brought in Harrington to cut the score to 5-3. The lineup turned over to local boy Dye, who drove Toronto's sixth hit of the inning between shortstop and second, scoring O'Neill with the fourth run of the improbable inning, Satterfield moving up to third. Mickey Heath drilled a comebacker that Marquis couldn't handle, and Satterfield scampered home with the tying run.

Carlyle could not keep the inning alive in the Leafs' bat-around comeback inning, but with Owen Carroll coming in from the bullpen, the remaining fans had to be encouraged. Sure enough, Carroll retired Reading in order in the 10th. In the bottom of the inning, Layne drew a leadoff walk and moved up to second on a wild pitch from an exhausted Marquis, who was still in the game for the Keys. Miller laid down a sacrifice bunt to move Layne to third, 90 feet away with the winning run. In the final act of the small ball characterizing so much of the Leafs' season, the next hitter, Capes, hit a dribbler that a water-logged Marquis could not field, and Layne raced across home with the winning run. The Leafs improved to 10-4 on the season with the win. "It was sweet for the Leafs, but sour for the Keys," said the *Star*.[8]

"The opening of the Leafs new home will long live in the minds of those present," noted the *Mail and Empire*, "for seldom has a game commenced in a rainstorm and played throughout for ten innings." With the game turning into something of a waterlogged affair, the *Mail and Empire* hoped none of the players would come down with a cold. "They got their feet wet early in the parade to the flagpole," the paper said, "and in the game that followed picked up more mud than they ever thought possible on a ball field." But the Leafs' come-from-behind win was a reminder to "never leave until the last man is out."[9]

The weather took over on the scheduled third game of the series, creating a Saturday doubleheader. Jim Faulkner was again the victim of a lack of support in the opener, as the Leafs lost 4-3. Carroll won his fifth straight decision in a tight 2-1 game in the nightcap—his five wins were more than any other pitcher in baseball. Solman was incredibly pleased with the attendance, despite the poor weather, telling the *Globe* that the turnstile count for the two dates in the new park surpassed the whole month of April's total on the Island the season before.

CHAPTER 19
OFF TO A COLD START

May did not see much of an improvement in weather conditions along the Lake Ontario shoreline. Cold winds off the lake had kept attendance down below Solman's expectations. The weather broke enough for a sunny Saturday twin bill on the first of May, but the grounds, according to the *Star Weekly*, "still showed the effect of the recent rains, the steam rising from the diamond as the sun got in its work on the wet ground."[1]

And the soggy, chilly weather did not help the club's collective health, as the Maple Leafs stumbled through the first four games of the month, splitting that Saturday doubleheader with Reading and managing only a split of a four-game series with Newark after that. Frank Gilhooley seemed ready for full-time duty, but then hurt his knee and out of the lineup. Babe Dye was sent for X-rays because his troubled back was acting up, Cleo Carlyle was on the limp, Steve O'Neill was out of the lineup with a sore hand, and the only healthy outfielder—Herman Layne—twisted his ankle rounding first in the third inning of a May 4 game with Newark, forcing him to the clubhouse. O'Neill, filling in as bench boss because Howley was out of town, was forced to end the game with an outfield of two pitchers (Owen Carroll and Claude Satterfield) and an infielder (Andy Harrington). Fans clamoured for an appearance of Lionel Conacher, yelling, "Bring in Big Train!" but O'Neill kept the rookie firmly nailed to the end of the Leafs' bench.

Not helping matters: Stewart, for the second outing in a row, was hit hard, lasting only two and two-thirds innings in a start against Newark earlier in the week. Fans had petitioned Solman for later start times given the new location of the stadium, and he agreed to do a trial run, pushing games back from their usual 3 p.m. start time dating back to the Island days, to 3:45. Double-headers would start at 2, instead of the usual 2:30.

On May 5, the Leafs split a Saturday doubleheader with Newark in front of "4,000 frozen fans," in the words of Mike Rodden of the *Globe*, with Howley saving Carroll for the first game of the Baltimore series. With the club slumping and a number of players nursing injuries, the impending arrival of the Orioles was not welcome news. While the Leafs had fallen to a 12-6 record, the O's kept on with their winning ways, leading Toronto by two games. Both teams had won 12, but the Orioles, who had dealt with more postponements, lost only two. The Howleyites were likely itching for a chance to avenge their doubleheader sweep by Baltimore two weeks earlier.

The Baltimore papers were full of anticipation of the upcoming series with Toronto. "Dan Howley will use every trick and all the strategy at his command to pull up with the Orioles," said the *Baltimore Evening Sun*. "Toronto is handicapped to some extent by injuries," noted Jesse Linthicum. "The entire outfield has been on the crippled list, and Howley will not have his full strength on the field."[2] At the same time, the Orioles were missing their ace George Earnshaw, who had more than filled Lefty Groves' spot atop Baltimore's rotation with 29 wins the season before. Having pitched 332 innings in 1925, he was not the same pitcher through the first weeks of the 1926 season.

On the day before Baltimore's arrival, there was some good news and some of the bad variety for the Leafs. Layne was diagnosed with a severe ankle sprain and put in a cast. Howley had been in Detroit finalizing a deal (hence O'Neill taking over manager duties for a day) and was bringing back with him a pair of players. Having decided that he couldn't wait for Harrington's shoulder to recover, Howley convinced Cobb to let him have third baseman Bill Mullen.

Mullen, who had made his MLB debut in 1920 with the St. Louis Browns, had bounced around the minors for several seasons before breaking out with Fort Worth of the Texas League in 1925. The Tigers signed him to a contract and invited him to spring training the following season, but when he was beaten out for Detroit's starting job at third, Howley eagerly accepted him to fill that hole for the Leafs. Jess Doyle, the soft-tossing southpaw who had pitched in Toronto for two seasons before making the Tigers roster in 1925, was sent back to the International League along with Mullen. Both players would play pivotal roles for the club as the season unfolded.

While the Leafs took the first game of the much-anticipated three-game set with Baltimore (Carroll improving his record to 6-0), the visiting Orioles took the second and third games, solidifying their lead atop the standings and dropping the home side into third place, behind the surging Buffalo Bisons, winners of six straight. Controversy dogged the second game before a pitch was even thrown, the temporary left-field bleachers the source. The umpires—following dictates from Major League Baseball—ruled that any ball hit into or over the bleachers would be a home run, instead of a triple, as was the custom. This was not a new phenomenon in the league: Newark, awaiting construction of their own new park, had to open the season in a semi-pro park with a short right field. Even though there was a screen above it, it was an easy task for a left-handed hitter to pull a ball over it, so the ground rule was that any such ball would be a double—the Leafs hit nine of them in their 17-13 win over Newark two weeks earlier.

Howley put up a protest in the pre-game lineup exchange at home plate to go over the park rules—his team's lack of power from that right side was a definite factor, so he was adamant that any ball hit into the bleachers be ruled a triple. Baltimore Manager Dunn, with plenty of pop from that side of the plate in his lineup, was in favour of the home-run rule, and the umpires agreed. Dunn used the ruling to his advantage early in the game with Toronto when Carlyle was slow to get over to a base hit to left by O's slugger Tillie Walker. The ball rolled into the bleachers, and Walker was awarded a home run. The Toronto bench jockeys were on the umpires and the opposition for much of the day after that—there was clearly no love lost between the two sides. Toronto looked clumsy for much of the 6-1 second-game loss, committing five errors.

Doyle and Mullen made their debuts in the third game of the series, but the newcomers could not provide a spark, and the Leafs wasted a fine pitching performance by Doyle as their offence went cold in a 1-0 defeat.

As of Monday morning, May 10, the standings were (per the *Globe*):

Baseball Record

INTERNATIONAL LEAGUE.

	Won.	Lost.	P.C.
Baltimore	16	3	.842
Buffalo	17	8	.680
TORONTO	14	9	.600
Rochester	10	9	.526
Newark	10	13	.435
Syracuse	8	13	.381
Jersey City	8	16	.333
Reading	5	17	.227

Yesterday's Results.

Rochester........7-4 Reading 5-9
Newark........... 5 Syracuse 4
Buffalo........... 8 Jersey City 2
  No other games scheduled.

Saturday's Results.

Baltimore......... 1 Toronto 0
Buffalo........... 4 Jersey City 3
Syracuse.......... 4 Newark 3
Reading........... 8 Rochester 7
  Games today:—Baltimore at Buffalo; Jersey City at Toronto; Reading at Syracuse; Newark at Rochester.

CHAPTER 20
TORONTO'S STUMBLES CONTINUE

THE NEWS HEADLINES OF THE FIRST TWO WEEKS OF MAY demonstrated the profound changes taking place in 1920s telecommunications. The invention and evolution of wireless telegraphy meant that news could reach across the Atlantic almost as soon as it happened. The world was becoming smaller, and nowhere was this reflected more than in Toronto newspapers. A threatened General Strike in Britain saw daily dispatches in the *Star*. "BRITAIN NEARER CIVIL WAR THAN IN CENTURIES" thundered an early May headline. "Proud Parents of Royal Babe" just below featured a photo of the Duke and Duchess of York, celebrating the birth of a baby girl who would become Queen Elizabeth II. Thanks to regular radio transmissions, the *Star* was also following the journey of explorer Richard Byrd and his quest to be the first to fly over the North Pole.[1]

In the sports section, details of a stormy annual meeting of the National Hockey League were reported. Boston owner Charles Adams had made an offer to purchase the players from the defunct Western Hockey League and distribute them as he saw fit. Arguments over proposed expansion sparked rumours of the creation of a rival league, but middle ground and compromises were found.

In Ottawa, news of a growing scandal was starting to grab the nation's attention. It had been revealed earlier that George Boivin, the

Minister of Customs and Excise, had personally interfered with the sentencing of a convicted alcohol smuggler named Moses Aziz. Customs officers raided Aziz' New Brunswick home and found 98 bottles of whiskey and cognac hidden in biscuit boxes and behind a piano, and he was charged and soon convicted of smuggling—for a third time. The conviction should have come with an automatic one-year jail sentence, but Boivin wrote letters to have the punishment reduced. This was widely viewed as evidence of Liberal corruption by the Opposition, which sparked a parliamentary investigation into liquor smuggling in the Customs department. This investigation would eventually bring down Prime Minister King's government.

With perennial also-ran Jersey City in town for the next five games from May 11-13 as part of the extended homestand, the Leafs took four games. In the series-opening doubleheader, Owen Carroll won his seventh in the first game, and Carl Hubbell once again shone in the nightcap, twirling an eight-inning, two-hit shutout. With Buffalo's winning streak finally snapped at 12 games by the front-running Orioles, Toronto was back in second place, three games back. Herman Layne came back into action faster than had initially been anticipated, and W.A. Hewitt of the *Star* told his readers about what made the young phenom Carroll so effective:

> The mystery about Carroll's pitching is his tremendous speed. He is a little fellow and throws the ball with a minimum of effort. He has something more than speed: a good curveball; he has pitching intelligence and good judgement.[2]

The only Leafs loss in the series was in the third game and was easily one of their worst efforts of the season. Toronto committed a whopping eight errors—four in the ninth inning alone, to boot the game away—and hit into four double plays and Maple Leaf Stadium's first triple play in an 8-2 loss to the Skeeters (or, the "Pests," as the local press nicknamed them). The one saving grace in the aftermath of the embarrassing defeat was the return to form of Lefty Stewart, who shut down Jersey the next day. But that loss, combined with a Buffalo win, put Toronto back into third, with the red-hot cross-lake rival Bisons and Manager Bill Clymer coming to town.

Clymer was a career minor-league player and manager—save for all of 11 at-bats in the American Association, then considered a big league, in 1892—with over 3,000 games' experience, including a season playing (in 1900) and managing (1915) the Leafs. "Derby Bill," as the writers called him, was a well-known International League figure, immortalized in Zane Grey's famous short story, "The Redheaded Outfield." Grey, a former ballplayer himself (he had suited up for Toronto's Eastern League entry in 1889), turned to writing short stories when his career ended. "The Redheaded Outfield" was his most famous baseball story. Clymer was referred to as "Reddy Clammer," described as a flashy player "who made circus catches, circus stops, and circus steals, always strutting, posing, talking, arguing, and quarreling."[3] Grey went on to a career as a novelist, mostly writing Westerns. The 85 books he wrote sold over 100 million copies; many were made into movies watched by millions more.

The series was scheduled for four games. The first two would be part of a Saturday (May 15) afternoon doubleheader in Toronto, then the two clubs would head to Union Station for a train and a Sunday afternoon affair in Buffalo. After that game, the teams would retrace their steps for the season finale in Toronto (the ban on Sunday baseball in the city was responsible). With less than a quarter of the schedule played to that point, it would have been hard to call this series a crucial one, but as Baltimore appeared to have rounded back into form, every game lost in the standings at this time of year would be hard to make up down the stretch.

The series could not have gone worse, from a Leafs perspective. Buffalo swept both games of the doubleheader by 8-0 and 8-2 scores, and to make matters worse, the twin bill—which didn't start until 2:15, as per fan requests—didn't finish until 7:30 p.m., and there was plenty of grumbling on the part of those who started the day expecting to go home to that warm dinner. "The Leafs not only fielded poorly," noted the *Star Weekly*, "but were helpless at the bat before the southpaw slants of Pitcher Leverenz, formerly of Boston

Nationals." Toronto committed a season-high four errors in the first game. "The second game did not start until 4:50 and was limited to seven innings. The crowd chafed at the late start," added the *Weekly*. The magazine ran a photo of the temporary walkway that fans had to climb over in order to get to Maple Leaf Stadium.

The Sunday game in Buffalo saw a minor-league record crowd of close to 23,000 fans pack Offermann Stadium, a facility opening just two years earlier. Fans were packed in everywhere, and there was considerable grumbling from disappointed Toronto fans who had made the trek across the border, only to be turned away when tickets sold out. (More than sold out: the listed capacity for the ballpark was 15,012.) The Buffalo park had only one entrance; even those fans who managed to secure either a seat or stood in the overflow roped-off sections along the baselines and around the outfield had to wait in line for hours.

The Leafs had high hopes with the undefeated Owen Carroll on the mound, and after giving up three to Buffalo in the home half of the second, the offence gave Carroll a four-run lead after scoring four in the top of the fourth. Carroll headed to the bottom of the seventh with the Leafs up 7-6, but he gave up a pair of runs to the Bisons, then allowed seven more in a disastrous eighth inning. Perhaps because his bullpen was taxed by two doubleheaders that week, or maybe to teach the young pitcher a lesson, Howley left Carroll in to absorb all the Buffalo onslaught, including 19 hits, as the Bisons extended their lead over Toronto in a 15-7 win. In fairness to the young hurler, Carroll had probably never pitched in such a situation; the overflow crowd that ringed the ball field behind a rope that ran the length of it was just inches away from fair territory.

The Leafs avoided a sweep by taking the series finale at home, 8-3, but they had fallen three games behind the Bisons and four behind the leading Orioles. The home fans at least got to see the International League debut of Lionel Conacher, who came in as a late-inning outfield defensive replacement, but he did not get a turn at bat.

The Buffalo press had some observations about Maple Leaf Stadium in the *Evening News*. "It is all grandstand, built in the shape of a bent-out hairpin," a columnist observed. But he was very critical of the viewing space Lol Solman had set aside for the press:

> But you should see the press box, or rather mouse-trap. It is a screened dug-out, with foot-level below the ground, and vision slightly above it, and with room for about six or eight sardined reporters. It is almost directly below the catcher's position, and a backstop of the posterior beam and elevation of (portly Brooklyn manager and former big league receiver) Wilbert Robinson, say, shuts out about all view except that of said elevation. Second base is seldom seen."[4]

The Buffalo scribe agreed that Maple Leaf Stadium's dimensions were indeed pitcher-friendly, noting, "It takes a real, he-man swat to clear either fence for a homer." Howley must have been pleased with the three long swats his team hit in the 8-3 win over the Bisons in the series finale back at Maple Leaf Stadium. His players may not have shared that view, however. While some had mused about "goin' fishin'" on the scheduled off-day following the game, Howley had ordered a full-team morning practice.

The next club to pull into town would be Syracuse, sitting fifth in the standings, from May 19 to May 22. The opening game was postponed, then Stewart threw a 4-0 shutout in the second game the following day. The rain from the day before continued in the form of a steady stream of obscene epithets from the Syracuse dugout, mainly over the home plate umpire's strike zone. Things reached a head in the home half of the seventh, when the Syracuse manager was ejected, and the whole bench tossed from the game as well. The third contest on May 21 was once again cancelled early in the morning due to rain; that didn't stop Howley—in full uniform himself—from ordering another workout at the stadium.

Saturday's bill (May 22) was supposed to be a doubleheader, but rain delayed batting practice by 40 minutes. The first game was to be a matchup between Faulkner and "the famous" (according to the *Star Weekly*) Duster Mails. The former big leaguer was known for his eccentricity both off and on the mound. During the rain delay before the first contest, Mails and several of his teammates entertained the small crowd with some "comic stuff, including shadow fielding practice, no ball being used," reported the *Weekly*. "Mails played first base and made a decided hit with his make-believe scoops, pick-ups, and one-hand catches."[5] Toronto defeated Mails and his Syracuse club 7-6 in 10 innings, but because of the earlier day, the second game was postponed. Mails was fond of bragging about his exploits. In his final professional game in the Pacific Coast League, Mails was one out away from victory. He called in his outfielders, then proceeded to strike out the final batter of the game. It was his last win in pro ball.[6]

After the shortened doubleheader, for the second weekend in a row, the Leafs logged many miles by rail as a result of Toronto's ordinance banning Sunday sports. Immediately following the win over Syracuse, the team headed to Union Station (several blocks away) for a train bound for Rochester, where they had a Sunday matinee scheduled. At the conclusion of that game (a 10-inning, 7-6 Leafs win), Toronto headed again for the railway station; Rochester joined them for the return trip to Ontario, where the two teams would play the next day as a Victoria Day holiday (May 24) split doubleheader was scheduled: 5,000 fans saw the Leafs win the morning game 8-1, and 9,000 were in attendance for the afternoon match, which Toronto took as well, 13-6, extending the home side's winning streak to six games. Rochester snapped the streak the next day with a 6-3 win. Carroll became undone in the sixth inning when Carlyle booted a ball hit to the outfield. The ball rolled under the stands and the base umpire waved the hitter, who by then had reached third base, home. "It unsettled Carroll, who was inclined to be wild," said the *Rochester Democrat and Chronicle* of the visitors' four-run sixth inning. The Leafs closed out the homestand on a winning note with a walkoff 9-8 triumph.

Toronto was about to head out on a lengthy road trip. Over the next month, all but three of their games would be on the road. One of those home dates would feature an exhibition game against the two-time defending American League champs Washington Senators.

Despite finishing the month at Maple Leaf Stadium with a 15-9 record, there was a feeling among many that the Leafs were somewhat less than the sum of their parts, particularly with the bats. W.A. Hewitt in the *Star* lamented the Leafs' anemic lineup. "Even in victory, the Leafs have not looked like a first class team to the fans," he wrote in late May as the homestand wrapped up. "They lack color and a real punch. There are too many .260 hitters and not enough .300 clubs in the lineup." Howley probably concurred, as he had already begun to beat the bushes to try to find some more pop for his light-hitting lineup, which stood sixth in the International League in hitting, ahead only of lowly Jersey City and Reading.

Howley made numerous inquiries and thought he had a chance at landing Fred Merkle, a 15-year Major League veteran who was still productive in the twilight of his career. History had not been kind to Merkle; as the youngest player in the National League in 1908, he made what the papers called a "boneheaded play" in a crucial late-season September game involving his New York Giants and the Chicago Cubs. The Giants appeared to have walked the game off when Al Bridwell, with two out and runners on first and third, slashed a single up the middle, scoring the runner from third. The apparent victory would have clinched the pennant for the Giants, except for the fact that the runner on first—Merkle—did not touch second, as Giants' fans swarmed the field in celebration. After the victory party had moved to the Giants' clubhouse, Cubs second baseman Johnny Evers retrieved the game ball—and there is considerable doubt that it was actually that—and convinced the umpires to rule Merkle out, negating the run. Since there was no chance of continuing the game, the decision was made to rule it a 1-1 tie, with a replay ordered. The Cubs won the replay, as well as the National League title, and Merkle's inability to touch second—which almost all players did in such situations—had cost his team the pennant. The event overshadowed an otherwise solid big-league career: Merkle was well regarded as a player, and Giants' legendary Manager John McGraw consulted him often on strategy. Merkle went to the World

Series five times as a player but didn't play for a single winner despite his long and distinguished career.

Merkle spent several seasons playing for Rochester in the early 1920s before signing with the Yankees for the stretch run in 1925. Howley tried to convince Merkle to come to Toronto, but the former big leaguer had landed a scouting job with the Giants, and said he wasn't interested.

Howley did land an offensive upgrade when he acquired Otis Lawry, a versatile infielder/outfielder. Lawry had been a stalwart in the Orioles lineup for four seasons; Manager Dunn often left Lawry in charge of the team when he went on scouting trips. But the two had a falling out in 1924, and prior to the next season, Dunn banished him to the International League wilderness by selling his contract to Jersey City. Lawry refused to report and went home to Maine (where the North Carolinian had played his college ball and married a local young woman) to play semi-pro ball. Howley was able to obtain his contract and had plans to replace Schmehl at second, but Lawry would need some time to play himself into shape.

As of May 26, the Leafs still found themselves in third place, per the *Toronto Star*:

INTERNATIONAL LEAGUE

	Won.	Lost.	P.C.
Baltimore	26	9	.743
Buffalo	29	12	.707
Toronto	25	14	.641
Newark	19	21	.475
Rochester	17	19	.472
Syracuse	14	22	.389
Jersey City	15	26	.366
Reading	8	30	.211

—Yesterday's Results—

Toronto	9	Rochester	8
Baltimore	6	Reading	1
Jersey City	5	Newark	4
Buffalo	12	Syracuse	10

CHAPTER 21
SIGNS OF A TURNAROUND

Taking to the road seemed to be a magic tonic for the Leafs, as they took five of seven games in Syracuse and Rochester. Lefty Stewart's shutout in the series finale was a masterpiece, showing he had shrugged off a dead arm period of a few weeks earlier.

Steve O'Neill took over managing duties during the Syracuse series while Dan Howley went to Detroit to try to convince Ty Cobb and the Tigers management to give him an outfielder. But he almost came away from the Motor City having lost Steve O'Neill, who Cobb had initially requested when his regular catcher broke his leg. At first, Howley and Solman reluctantly agreed. O'Neill was under contract to Toronto, but the unofficial terms of a working agreement with a big-league team in the 1920s often included helping the MLB club out in case of emergency. But Solman and his skipper had no intention of letting O'Neill go without a fight. His work with the young Carroll, Stewart, and Faulkner was obvious, as was his ability to call a game, his defensive work behind the plate, and even his bat. The veteran backstop had clearly become a foundational piece of the team. So Solman asked Cobb for Clyde Manion, Detroit's backup receiver for several seasons before being loaned to Toronto for the 1925 season. Cobb, likely fearing that O'Neill's legs might not stand up to a regular American League workload, wanted the former big leaguer as a backup to Manion. But given Toronto's asking price (and likely his relationship with Howley) Cobb backed down and instead accepted a young Toronto catching prospect playing in the West Virginia League named Ray Hayworth.

At the same time as this transaction took place, fans in Detroit were calling for the Tigers to call up Lefty Stewart—Hewitt of the *Star* even reported that a Detroit paper had run an article calling for his promotion. The problem was that Stewart was under contract to the Leafs and was not Tigers property to call up. The Tigers probably did not inquire about his services; they knew Toronto's return demand— in terms of money and/or players—would be exorbitant, a reminder that minor-league teams still had some independence from their big-league partners. Besides, the Leafs were "in the market to buy, not sell." It was also rumoured that Cobb was on the verge of calling up Owen Carroll, but "Cobb quickly spiked that rumor, and said he had no such intention."[1]

Toronto's pitching staff was bolstered at the end of May by the return of prospect Vic Sorrell. The Wake Forest grad had contracted a severe case of the mumps toward the end of training camp and had only returned to training a few weeks earlier. With Carroll, Stewart, and the young Sorrell on his roster, Howley had three of the top pitching prospects in all of baseball under his tutelage.

Toronto swept the four-game series in Syracuse, stretching their win streak to seven games. The Leafs had their run snapped in the first game of a Sunday twin bill at Rochester on May 31; Buffalo had jumped into first place by taking a pair of games against Syracuse, and Baltimore surprisingly was swept in a doubleheader by last place Reading. The Leafs suffered a rainout in the first game, followed by an 11-10 loss to Rochester, a game in which the home team had spotted Toronto a 10-0 lead. The train ride back to Ontario for the exhibition game against Washington and the mini homestand must have been a long and somber trip.

Toronto was absolutely abuzz with the arrival of their big-league visitors. Washington had won their first American League pennant and World Series in 1924, becoming the first championship team to receive an invitation to the White House. Pitching great Walter Johnson led the league in wins, winning percentage, shutouts, and strikeouts, and won the Most Valuable Player award. The Senators won the World Series in dramatic fashion in a 12-inning Game 7 over the Giants. Johnson, nearing the end of a Hall of Fame career, lost his two starts in the series, but came on to get the win in relief in that final game. The Senators featured young slugger Goose Goslin and second baseman Bucky Harris, who also doubled as the Sens' manager. The Senators repeated their pennant-winning ways in 1925 but lost the World Series to Pittsburgh in seven games. Two Washington coaches—Nick Altrock and Al Schacht—had developed a between-innings comedy routine that was a hit with the fans, and a fixture at home games. Schact would don a top hat and tails and sometimes ate a fine meal at home plate with the visiting team took their warmup tosses. Altrock, who had pitched for the Leafs two decades earlier, was quite a character: "He was hard to handle, but (Leafs manager Ed) Barrow kept him in his place,"[2] wrote Charlie Good in the *Toronto Star Weekly*. In Altrock's routine, he would pretend to wrestle himself, and on occasion appear to spike his own leg. The pair had a number of routines they would perform during rain delays. The two had washed out as pitchers, but their act allowed the "Crown Princes of Baseball" to remain in the game.

Toronto fans had hoped to finally see a glimpse of the Big Train— not necessarily the local version, Lionel Conacher, who some thought might be put into the Leafs lineup. Walter Johnson was the true Big Train, a pitcher who had won 20 games an incredible ten years in a row and a handful of wins away from 400, a plateau reached only by the legendary Cy Young. But Johnson had apparently pulled a muscle in his back earlier that week and would not be available to face even a couple of hitters. In the top of the ninth, the Leafs faithful had started chanting his name, and Altrock pulled a publicity-shy Johnson out of the Senators dugout to doff his cap.

Prior to the game, Howley had announced Carl Hubbell as his starter. It was Owen Carroll's scheduled day to pitch, but Howley had a pennant to pursue—with league-leading Buffalo coming to town the next day—so it made sense to save his ace and use the last man on his staff. Catcher Steve O'Neill warmed up Hubbell on the sidelines before the game, and when Hubbell mixed in a few screwballs, O'Neill asked him if he could use it in the game. Hubbell readily agreed, and Howley either okayed it, or preferred not to know. Staked to a four-run lead thanks to Mickey Heath's inside-the-park first-inning grand slam to the deepest part of the cavernous park—the centre field scoreboard—Hubbell was brilliant against the AL champs, who were befuddled by his secret weapon. He pitched the Leafs to a 6-1 victory, allowing only five hits and one unearned run, "(displaying) an assortment of shoots and slants that had the erstwhile World's champions sashaying back to the dugout almost as quickly as they had appeared."[3]

Before the first Buffalo game the following day, Howley updated the press on the progress of Andy Harrington, who had been expected to be a middle-of-the-order bat for the Leafs until his shoulder troubles flared up. Harrington had been to see a specialist in Detroit, Howley told reporters, but part of his recovery orders involved no throwing until the weather warmed up; he would be limited to pinch-hitting duties only. The Leafs then blasted Buffalo, knocking the Bisons into second place behind idle Baltimore. Carroll picked up his ninth win of the season. "That's the kind of ball he pitched in Buffalo, but they beat him 15-7,"[4] Howley said after the game, suggesting his pitcher had been the victim of some bad luck.

The next day, Howley's club made the standings atop the International League even tighter by sweeping a doubleheader from the Bisons at Maple Leaf Stadium, starting with an easy 9-0 win in the opener. Herman Layne was the star of the second game, belting the longest home run hit in the park to date and making three outstanding running catches in the outfield. Layne was the difference in the 3-2 Toronto victory. With no Sunday ball in Toronto, the series once again shifted to Buffalo for the final game.

"What a race! What a race!" raved Charlie Good in the *Star*. "Sunday's scramble at Buffalo was another one of those hair-raising toe-to-toe tilts which have marked most of the games between the

Clymerites and the Howleyites this spring,"[5] he wrote about the contest, which Buffalo won 4-3 on a walk-off sacrifice fly. The Buffalo win, combined with Baltimore surprisingly losing a pair of games to Newark, put the western New Yorkers back atop the standings on Monday morning with a two-and-a-half game lead on both the Orioles and Leafs.

CHAPTER 22
DOES BASEBALL MAKE GIRLS MASCULINE?

"DOES BASEBALL HURT MORALS OF GIRLS WHO PLAY THE GAME?" asked the *Star Weekly* in their end of May issue. "Women wear clothes like men," started the article, "carry on businesses like men, cut their hair like men—and now they play like men."[1]

While change was definitely in the air in 1926 Toronto, white males still dominated the city's elite, and churches exerted tremendous influence over many aspects of everyone else's life. The demographics were changing, but the British—specifically Victorian—influence was still obvious.

"There used to be two kinds of games, women's games and men's games," lamented the *Weekly*, but those days were clearly gone. "It was only ten years ago that Torontonians were shocked as they read newspaper accounts of the first league games of the Commercial Ladies Softball Association." A decade later there were over 1,000 registered female ballplayers in the city, representing some 45 clubs. Toronto, in the eyes of the magazine, had gone "mad" over women's baseball. "On May 24 a crowd of six thousand fans cheered themselves hoarse, when Supremes of the Major Ladies' League triumphed over the visiting St Catharines team at Sunnyside."

With sales of baseball equipment to women having doubled at a downtown sporting goods store, the *Star Weekly* had to ask if this was in the best interests of the fairer sex. "Now if girls are playing ball in such numbers," the magazine asked somewhat rhetorically, "the questions naturally arise....Is the game too strenuous for them? Does baseball make girls masculine? How does it affect their morality?"

The *Star Weekly* consulted several "experts" on the matter. The first, "a well-known religious educationist and church worker in the city," not surprisingly answered, "Baseball is not a girl's game." The unnamed (male) authority, who had coached and organized "every conceivable kind of girls' and boys' sports," did not allow girls to take up baseball. "There is too much profanity and smoking among girl ball players," he alleged, "and the coarse language the girls use is most objectionable."

"The girl baseball player," this morality police official continued, "is not the kind of girl that men admire. Your really athletic girl is not attractive. That is not the type that men want to marry." But the issue went far beyond that, according to this individual. "...the trouble with this women's baseball is that there is too much playing to the grandstand. The coarse language and the rough play of the girls is really due to the fans who egg them on."

Another "expert," one Al. Dickey, described as "closely connected with the sport, especially in inter-church ball," didn't know about morality, but women, in his words, "seem to be poorer sports than men." That manifested itself, according to Dickey, into a "tendency for rough play because girls take a thing like baseball far more seriously than men do."

To their credit, the author of the article did contact Miss Mabel Ray, "president of the Women's Softball Association, as well as secretary of the Women's Amateur Athletic Federation of Canada," for her thoughts on these comments. Her response: "Applesauce."

"The standard of morals has not been lowered by baseball," Ray countered. She said she had never seen a girl smoking on a baseball diamond, and that "rough language" would not be tolerated. Ray even revealed that on her own team, players were forbidden to chew gum. "It is simply rubbish to talk of softball making girls rough and masculine," she opined. "It's just a game and a game that teaches girls fair play."

As Toronto headed out on the rest of their road trip, the Lionel Conacher experiment appeared to be coming to an end. Conacher was left in Toronto to play with a local semi-pro team managed by local sporting figure Harry Deacon. Deacon's All-Stars had an exhibition game scheduled with the Buffalo Colored Giants of the Negro National League while the Leafs were on the road that month. Newark, a pushover for the Leafs when they met earlier in the season, was slowly creeping into the pennant race, having won 14 of their previous 21 games. The Leafs entered New Jersey as the hottest team in the league, though, having taken 15 of their last 19. Baltimore was only 12-9 in that stretch, and it looked like an honest-to-goodness race for the first time in ages was shaping up. Orioles fans were largely underwhelmed by the prospects of a pennant race; at a recent home game, only 600 fans showed up for the raising of the flag to mark their 1925 league title.

A big challenge was coming up for Toronto: 20 games in 15 days on the road were next up. Luckily, Jersey City and Reading were on the schedule, but so was a hard-charging Newark club. The trip would culminate with six games in four days in Baltimore.

All International League games were wiped out by rain on Monday, June 6, and Tuesday became twin bill day. The Leafs took both ends of their doubleheader with Newark by 10-7 and 6-3 scores. Hubbell, likely minus his out pitch, was ineffective in the opener, but the Toronto offence bailed him out. While the doubleheader was being played, a Wild West show was taking place in the lot behind right field at the Newark ballpark.

With "war whoops and pistol shots," a special dispatch to the *Globe* reported, "the right field bleacher fans were able to stand up and view the proceedings, and they forgot all about the ball game."[2] With 16 runs scored on the day, the Leaf bats provided some loud entertainment as well.

The next day was Owen Carroll Day, as over 20 social, fraternal, and civic groups came out to pay tribute to their local son. Before the game, Carroll was provided with a cheque for $200 from various boosters in a pre-game ceremony at home plate. Two giant horseshoe-shaped floral emblems were given to Carroll as well, and Carl Schmehl, a fan favourite when he played in Newark, was given $100 in gold and silver coins. Ten thousand Bears fans became Leaf rooters for a day, and Carroll didn't disappoint, tossing a four-hit shutout in an 8-0 Toronto romp, improving his record to 10-1. With the win, the Leafs finally moved up in the standings into second place as Buffalo dropped both of their games to Jersey City. Hewitt of the *Star* was effusive in his praise of Howley the next day:

> Manager Dan Howley has to be given credit for having the courage of his convictions in nothing else. When the Leafs were wobbling he refused to make any changes in his line-up, even when some of his athletes were not hitting anything like their weight, and recent developments have shown that his judgement was sound. Schmehl, Miller, and Carlyle are playing fine ball all around, while Mickey Heath is batting better than at any time since he became a member of the club.[3]

The Leafs completed the four-game sweep of the series when they downed Newark 8-2 the next day. Howley had been tempted to hold newcomer Vic Sorrell back and give him his first start in the final game of the Buffalo series but opted to let him make his International League debut in the final Newark game. Sorrell walked five, but he pitched out of jams to pick up the win. "Though it was his first game," said the *Globe*, "Sorrell worked with the coolness and finesse of a hardened veteran."[4] After the game, the Leafs made the short trip to Jersey City looking to extend their four-game winning streak. Toronto and Baltimore were now tied with 37 wins, but the Orioles were in first by virtue of their two-game advantage in the loss column. Beginning with the 1920 season, the Orioles usually had a lead approaching double digits by this point in the schedule. Not only was the International League having a pennant race for the first time in a half dozen years, multiple teams were involved.

CHAPTER 23
SHINBONE

Ball teams in the first two decades of the last century often had a mascot—in human form, as opposed to the costumed characters like the Phillie Phanatic of today. "Lefthanders, hunchbacks, and cross-eyed people were all considered lucky," wrote baseball historian Harold Seymour in his book *Baseball: The Golden Age.* "Touching a hunchback was popularly believed to bring good luck."[1] Baseball players, being a superstitious lot, took to any and all things they thought would bring them good fortune on the diamond.

The Philadelphia Athletics adopted a young man named Louis Van Zelt, who had become hunchbacked as a result of a childhood accident. When the Athletics won a World Series shortly after Van Zelt joined the team, he became a fixture in the Athletics' dugout. "In the day-to-day, Van Zelt was on hand for pretty much every home game and many road games. Prior to each game, players would walk over and rub his hunchback for good luck."[2] The A's would make three more trips to the World Series—winning two of them—after Van Zelt joined the team, and he became a fixture in the Philadelphia dugout. When the mascot died of kidney failure several years later, the A's finished dead last, staying there for several seasons.

Babe Ruth had his own personal mascot, a young man named Eddie Bennett. Born in Brooklyn, Bennett suffered a serious spinal injury as an infant and as a result was left disfigured. Both of his parents died in the 1918 influenza pandemic. While attending a White Sox-Giants game at the Polo Grounds in 1919, Sox outfielder Happy Felsch noticed both Bennett's deformity and his ear-to-ear smile.

Felsch, like so many players of his day, believed rubbing Bennett's hunchback would bring him good luck. Felsch called several of his teammates over to partake in the charm ritual, and so the story goes, he enjoyed a good day at the plate in a White Sox win. As a result, he and teammate Eddie Cicotte convinced their manager, Kid Gleason, to take the teenager on as a mascot and bat boy.

The White Sox, with Bennett along for the ride, won the American League pennant and faced Cincinnati in the 1919 World Series, an ill-fated affair that saw Felsch, Cicotte, and six of their teammates banned for life as a result of being accused of throwing the Series in a gambling scandal that rocked the game.

Bennett found himself out of baseball after the 1919 Series, but not for long. Attending a game at Ebbets Field, members of the Brooklyn Robins noticed him in the stands and took him on as their personal good luck charm. The Robins won the National League pennant and took two of the first three games of the World Series against the Indians. But Bennett was left at home when the best-of-nine Series shifted to Cleveland for the next four games, with the home side sweeping the Robins to win the World Championship. Fingers were pointed at Bennett, according to researcher Peter Morris of the Society for American Baseball Research (SABR). "Bennett, it was said," wrote Morris, "had been distraught at being left behind and put a curse on the Robins, resulting in the team's collapse."[3]

Bennett was let go by Brooklyn, but one supposes that hunchback mascots were in demand, when no less an outfit than the Yankees hired him a year later. He became the most famous batboy in America as the Yanks headed into their glory years, and his closest friend on the team was a fellow orphan, Babe Ruth. Bennett was with the Bronx Bombers for nearly twelve years and saw them win seven pennants and four World Series.

Ty Cobb had befriended a young homeless African-American boy he had found in the Navin Field stands named L'il Rastus. Cobb brought him into the clubhouse, fed him, and made him the team's batboy. The club soon went on a winning streak, and the players thought Rastus was the talisman who had brought them good fortune. Cobb became the boy's protector, eventually taking him back to Georgia with him, where he hired the boy as a servant. The gesture seemed very much in line with Cobb's character.

Racial prejudice was casually accepted by white society in those days. When the Tigers travelled, Cobb had to hide Rasmus under his bunk on the train and sneak him into the whites-only hotel the club stayed in. Several clubs had black trainers at the time—the best known was Doc Buckner of the White Sox, whose physiotherapy skills the Sox players swore by. But like Rasmus, travel for Buckner and his brethren was difficult, to say the least. And as for Cobb, who had many altercations with people of colour, Anthony Papalas wrote in the *Baseball Research Journal (1984)*, "Cobb did appreciate blacks like L'il Rastus…who accepted their racial inferiority, but he was extremely hostile to those who showed some measure of independence."[4]

When the Leafs arrived in Newark, a Black gentleman identified only as Shinbone joined the club. Shinbone and Howley went back to the latter's time managing Hartford in the Eastern League at the start of the decade. Shinbone had become a mascot of sorts for Howley, serving as bat boy for the Hartford club and dancing for the entertainment of the fans between innings. The description of Shinbone in the *Globe* was full of the racial bias of the time; "Charlestoning Darkie" was perhaps the mildest term used. Shinbone was "quoted" in the article in pidgin.[5] Howley invited Shinbone to join the team in Newark, but the dugout was as far as blacks would be allowed in organized baseball for another 20 years.

After sweeping Newark, the Leafs may have thought next-to-last place Jersey City would be an easy touch, but the Skeeters surprised the visitors in the first game of the series on June 11, 5-1. Toronto would leave with only a split in the series, helped by Owen Carroll winning his 11th game in the second game of Sunday's doubleheader. Howley had to be concerned with the performance of Jess Doyle, who had struggled in his past several starts and failed to get out of the second inning of the series finale.

As the Leafs headed off to Reading, Howley dropped Carroll off at home in Newark to rest up for his start opening a showdown series with the Orioles starting on Saturday. Hewitt of the *Star* noted that balls were flying out of International League parks at a record pace. With just a third of the schedule down, 306 long balls were hit, threatening the league high of 777. Buffalo's early-season success was likely due to their league-leading 42 homers. Tillie Walker, despite having been out of Baltimore's lineup for the past ten days, was the leader with 19. Howley told reporters that Babe Dye, who had been out of action for several weeks, would join Lionel Conacher in an exhibition game involving the Colored Giants of Buffalo as the Leafs were opening against Baltimore. With the Leafs on a roll, there was already talk of the p-word in Toronto. "Neither the champions or Bisons," wrote Charlie Good, "has a staff comparable to that possessed by the Leafs…is it any wonder, under the circumstances, Messrs. Solman and Howley, and Co. are beginning to talk pennant?"[6]

Toronto banged out 19 hits in easily taking the first game of the Reading series 10-1 on June 16. But Baltimore continued to win, taking out Buffalo, which was starting to fall behind the pace-setting Orioles and Leafs. "Manager Clymer of the Bisons," critiqued Hewitt in his *Star* column, "has probably found out that you can 'ride' some of the players all the time, some players some of the time, but not all of the players all of the time."[7] But the Bisons rebounded, taking a pair from Baltimore the following day. The Leafs had a shot at a share of first place with a win in the second game with Reading. Howley decided to go with Hubbell, who struggled and left in the fourth enroute to a 6-2 Toronto loss. Dan Howley "howled considerably in the clubhouse after the unexpected downfall," reported the *Globe*.[8]

CHAPTER 24
ORIOLES FANS ARE "PENNANT SORE"

"DEMAND SHAKE-UP IN CUSTOMS DEPARTMENT" WAS THE headline atop the fold in the *Star* the next day, June 18, as the Leafs prepared to take on the Keystones once more. The scandal involving Prime Minister King's government's handling of the bribing of customs officials had been a hot topic in Ottawa. Reports from Parliament Hill indicated that the Opposition Conservatives would move to censure the Members of Parliament involved, a rebuke that could revoke some of their legislative privileges and reflect badly on the government. With a minority that was fragile to begin with, King could ill afford such a move. Speculation about a nonconfidence motion in the House of Commons, which could topple King, was already in the air.

In the game played that day, the Leafs topped the Keys 3-1, moving to within a half game of the idle Orioles on the eve of their showdown. Toronto had lost four of five to Baltimore to this point in the season, but as they left Pennsylvania, Howley and crew had to be optimistic about their chances. Toronto had taken 11 of 14 on the road trip to date. The Orioles were wary of the Leafs' recent road success and Howley's "million dollar pitching staff," in the words of the *Baltimore Evening Sun.* "Dan has the best pitching staff in the league….and

Baltimore will know it has been in some tough battles once the Leafs depart," the *Sun* added.[1]

One thing about the O's-Leafs series was for certain: Dan Howley brought fans to the ballpark. "Although the games will bring out the fans," wrote a Baltimore sportswriter, "the appearance of Dan Howley, one of the most popular managers also will bring them out, 'The Orioles!' his familiar cry on the coaching lines, has made a hit with Baltimore rooters."[2]

Jack Dunn.

The series was of such importance that the league assigned three umpires to work the games instead of the usual two. And the *Globe* thought the series important enough to send their sports editor, Fred Wilson, to cover it. "Howley, with a big string of capable pitchers," he wrote before leaving for Maryland, "and a team imbued with a winning spirit, is likely to be bad medicine for Jack Dunn."[3] The series got off to a successful start for the visitors when the Leafs swept the Saturday, June 19 doubleheader,

nudging the Orioles out of first in the process. But the victory came with a cost: in the opener, Owen Carroll took a line drive off the ankle and had to be carried off the field.

Baltimore returned the favour and regained the league lead the following day, taking both games of another twin bill from the Leafs on Father's Day. Baltimore hit seven home runs on the day, six of them in an 11-1 second-game romp. The long ball was the difference on the day; Baltimore hit six home runs, the Leafs none. "There would have been a different tale to tell if at least one of the games had been played at Leaf Stadium," Wilson lamented. "Balls that looped over the wire screens atop the walls and dropped exasperatingly into the foreshortened bleachers…should have been ordinary outfield outs."[4]

Baltimore lost shortstop Dick Porter, one of their leading hitters, when he collapsed on the field in the first game of Saturday's twin bill. He was later diagnosed with appendicitis; his loss would be a huge blow to the Orioles. Wilson commented on the small Baltimore crowds in the *Globe*. Fewer than 4,000 attended on Saturday, and fewer than 10,000 on Sunday. Wilson attributed the small crowds down to a multitude of reasons: Baltimore fans being "pennant sore," after seven years of domination; the racing season ramping up at nearby tracks like Bowie and Pimlico; and maybe Baltimore, having failed at big-league ball in the past, "did not want minor league ball."[5]

After being absent for the Jersey City series, Shinbone mysteriously reappeared in Baltimore. The *Globe* said Shinbone "came to town not as a passenger, but as 'merchandise,'"[6] suggesting he stowed away on a freight train headed for Maryland. The *Globe* once again quoted him in pidgin. According to the *Baltimore Evening Sun*, Shinbone was a "drummer in New York in a nightclub in the winter season, and a past master of the Charleston art." The *Sun* claimed Shinbone "wished himself on the Howleyites in Newark, and immediately brought the team good luck." But after the Orioles took the Sunday twin bill, the paper said his job, "wasn't so solid this morning."[7]

Owen Carroll, who hung in to pick up his 12th win despite taking the line drive off the ankle, was sent back to Toronto the next day to rest and get treatment. Howley would be missing his best starter for this crucial series.

Toronto dropped the fifth game of the series, 7-3, on Monday to Baltimore, wasting a fine pitching performance by Claude Satterfield, who had pitched well on the road trip, and was rapidly gaining Howley's confidence. Both the *Star* and *Globe* suggested the Leafs were unlucky in the loss; many of Baltimore's hits were of the seeing-eye variety, while Toronto hit several sharp balls right at fielders, resulting in several rally-killing double plays.

Jim Faulkner took to the mound in the final game of the series the next day, starting in place of Carroll. The Leafs would return home from the 20-game road trip assured of being no lower than second place in the standings, but a win would put them back within two-

and-a-half games of Baltimore. But despite outhitting their hosts by a 2-1 margin, the Leafs dropped the sixth and final game of the series on Tuesday, 4-3. Toronto's offensive woes returned. After scoring 10 runs in the opener, the Leafs managed to score only 11 times in the next five games. In the series finale, they hit into three double plays with the tying run on second. The loss gave the Orioles a bit of a cushion of three-and-a-half games as they headed out on the road themselves. Despite losing the last four games, given his club's struggles away from home the previous year, Howley must have felt satisfied with the 12-7 record his club compiled as they boarded their train home, especially with Baltimore visiting red-hot Newark, who had won 12 straight since being swept by Toronto earlier in the month.

Rochester came into town next for four games, beginning on June 23. But thunderstorms swept in off the lake just minutes before game time, and the first contest was postponed. While they waited out the delay at the start of the game, several Leaf players told reporters in the clubhouse that despite losing four of six to Baltimore, the Orioles "failed to strike fear in the hearts of the Howleyites," according to the *Globe*. The players "freely stated…that the Orioles have passed the peak of their greatness and will find it very hard to win on the road."[8]

In another corner of the clubhouse, Howley was holding court with another group of writers. He praised the play of Steve O'Neill (despite the veteran getting only one hit in the Baltimore series), and according to the *Globe*, Howley said, "he would not trade O'Neill for any catcher outside the majors."[9] The eventual postponement of the day's game meant that Howley had to put off for a day continuing his experiment of replacing the light bat of Schmehl with that of utility man Otis Lawry. Lawry had impressed at the plate in Baltimore, and Howley was desperate to inject some life into the Leafs' offence.

Home cooking was definitely not the tonic that cured the Leafs, as they extended their losing streak with a 5-2 loss to Rochester on June 24. Jim Bagby Sr. was on the mound for the visitors, recently acquired by Rochester after being released by Atlanta of the Southern League. Bagby was once Cleveland's ace, winning 31 games for the 1920

World Series winners. But after pitching over 1,500 innings in his first five seasons, Bagby was never the same and had bounced around the minors for several seasons. Before the game, he did enjoy catching up with his catcher from those glory days on Lake Erie, one Steve O'Neill. Seeking his 13th win, Carroll was hit hard by Rochester, and the *Globe* reported that the score flattered Carroll's efforts. He made his regularly scheduled start after being hit by that line drive in Baltimore, but it obviously hampered his delivery.

Toronto took the second game of the series behind a strong outing by Stewart but dropped both ends of the Saturday doubleheader before a disappointing crowd of only 4,000 fans. "Dan Howley had it all planned to southpaw the Tribe into submission,"[10] wrote the *Rochester Democrat and Chronicle,* but the visitors knocked Faulkner out of the box in the fourth, enroute to a 21-hit, 12-5 win. Doyle fared slightly better in the nightcap, withstanding a two-run ninth-inning Rochester rally to triumph 4-3.

When the Leafs lost in Buffalo the following day, Toronto had dropped eight of their past nine and fell into third place behind the stumbling Bisons, who themselves were being called "the blundering herd," by local reporters. Late in the Buffalo game, with Howley having been tossed earlier, O'Neill put Lionel Conacher in to pinch hit in the eighth inning; in his first professional plate appearance, he grounded out weakly to the pitcher. Perhaps Toronto fans were feeling like they had seen it all before and feared once again their hometown heroes were going to fall short in the pennant race. Toronto entered June with high hopes buoyed by winning four games in Newark, but a six-game losing streak to end the month dropped their record to 15-16 over the past 30 days.

CHAPTER 25

NOT A "SEMBLANCE OF A SMILE" ON JACK DUNN'S "CAREWORN FACE"

CARRYING SHEEDY OFF FIELD AFTER HE WAS HURT

An incident which took most of the joy out of the first game yesterday occurred when Clayton Sheedy, hard hitting right fielder of the Balti- more club, ducked into a high inside pitch delivered by Owen Carroll and was knocked out. The above picture shows Sheedy being carried off the field by his troubled team mates. The injury was not as serious as was at first thought and the able athlete in all probability will be able to leave the hospital to-day.

1920s onfield medical treatment. Toronto Star *photo.*

WHILE THE LEAFS WERE PREPARING TO TRY TO BREAK THEIR THREE-game losing streak in Buffalo, Torontonians learned of a constitutional crisis brewing in Ottawa.

The results of the parliamentary inquiry into the corruption in the Customs department led to the censure of Prime Minister King's Liberal government. King desperately tried to cobble together support from the other parties that helped prop up his minority government, but to no avail. So, he visited the Governor General—the representative of the Crown—at his Ottawa mansion to request Parliament be dissolved, and an election be called. Tradition meant that past Governors General had granted such a request in minority situations, but on this occasion, Lord Byng denied the request, feeling that King's minority government of less than a year really had not done much in the way of governing. Byng asked Conservative Opposition leader Arthur Meighen to form a government instead, which was his prerogative—one that had never been used since Confederation almost a half century earlier. This was unprecedented in Canadian politics, but well within parliamentary procedures. The Governor General was normally supposed to be above politics, and King asking for an election would traditionally have been approved. It might seem odd for the Prime Minister of a government rocked by scandal to call an election, but events would later prove that there was method to King's madness. An election campaign was exactly what he wanted.

During the game at Buffalo, Owen Carroll was hit hard for the second outing in a row, and the Leafs' losing streak stretched to four games. The streak stretched to six two days later as June ended, leaving the Leafs in third place, only a game ahead of red-hot fourth place Newark. Tempers flared in the final loss on the 30th, as four Leafs were ejected, Frank "Flash" (as the Toronto papers were regularly calling him) Gilhooley being the first of them. When he was called out on a close play at first in the seventh inning, Gilhooley tossed a chunk of mud at base umpire Hayes, and was "promptly awarded with the order of the tin can,"[1] in the words of the *Buffalo News*'s Don Reed. In the ninth, Howley, backup catcher Lena Styles, and pitcher Jim Faulker were tossed by Hayes over what even Reed said was a "putrid call." Hayes, according to Reed, "was threatening to banish the entire Canadian squad when play resumed."[2] Perhaps the pressure of the pennant race was getting to the Leafs. Howley had complained bitterly to the Toronto press about the umpiring in the series at Baltimore.

But not all the news was bad. Tillie Walker, the IL home-run leader and owner of a .363 batting average, was placed on waivers by Baltimore. At 39, the 13-year big leaguer was on the downside of his career but had been a productive minor leaguer for several years after his time in the bigs ended. Word was that he and Jack Dunn were on the outs. It's curious as to why a slugger of Walker's calibre was available. The Baltimore papers suggested his back had been acting up, and given his age, Dunn wanted to go with a younger and healthier player. There may have been some contract issues as well; even as an aging slugger, Walker still commanded a huge salary, and Dunn was not fond of keeping players with expensive price tags. Howley quickly snapped Walker up, along with pitcher Clarence "Red" Fisher from Buffalo, another former big leaguer. Both players' salaries likely scared other teams away from claiming them. Lol Solman was determined to give Leaf fans a winner, so it seemed.

Reporters learned that Babe Dye would be released to make room for Walker. Toronto fans were saddened to see the local boy not make good, but not surprised. Gilhooley had received most of the playing time in centre field, and Dye's bat did not have enough pop in it for Howley to give him much time in a corner outfield spot. Arriving late to training camp, and with an injured back to boot, did not help his cause.

To cap off an eventful week, the Leafs got back to their winning ways by sweeping a doubleheader from visiting Syracuse in front of a huge Dominion Day crowd. Submariner Clarence Fisher pitched and won the second game. The Leafs also announced the Detroit Tigers would visit in just six days' time; it was widely believed Hubbell would get a chance to show Ty Cobb the mistake he had made.

Meanwhile, in Ottawa, Arthur Meighen's government—which had lasted all of three days—lost a vote of confidence in the House of Commons. Meighen went, hat in hand, to ask Lord Byng to dissolve Parliament for the purposes of calling a federal election; Byng relented, fully springing the trap King had laid. "The great issue as King saw it," wrote historian Randall White, "was that Lord Byng, by refusing to grant (King) an election, he had asked for…had undemocratically interfered in the politics of the self-governing Dominion of Canada."[3] The election would largely be fought on the idea of Canada breaking free from British ties. Here was a British aristocrat—appointed by the British government—taking on Canadian politics, King argued. It was time for Canada, like Toronto, to make its own name for itself, and take its place on the world stage.

The IL standings on the morning of July 2, per the *Baltimore Evening Sun*:

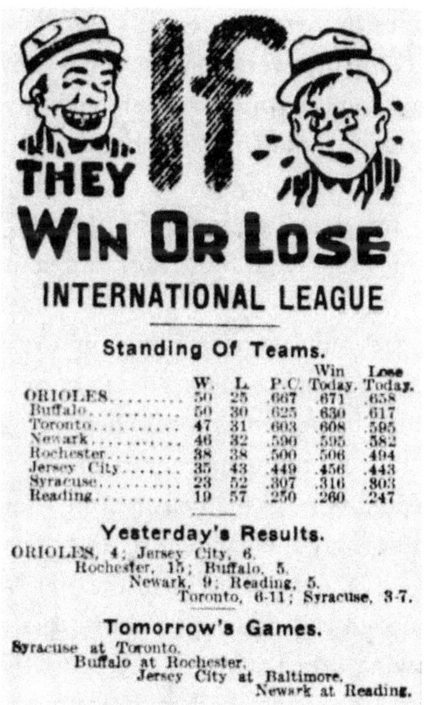

INTERNATIONAL LEAGUE

Standing Of Teams.

	W.	L.	P.C.	Win Today.	Lose Today.
ORIOLES	50	25	.667	.671	.658
Buffalo	50	30	.625	.630	.617
Toronto	47	31	.603	.608	.595
Newark	46	32	.590	.595	.582
Rochester	38	38	.500	.506	.494
Jersey City	35	43	.449	.456	.443
Syracuse	23	52	.307	.316	.303
Reading	19	57	.250	.260	.247

Yesterday's Results.

ORIOLES, 4; Jersey City, 6.
Rochester, 15; Buffalo, 5.
Newark, 9; Reading, 5.
Toronto, 6-11; Syracuse, 3-7.

Tomorrow's Games.

Syracuse at Toronto.
Buffalo at Rochester.
Jersey City at Baltimore.
Newark at Reading.

The Leafs took four of their next six games at home against Syracuse and in Rochester, but could not hold off the hard-charging Newark Bears, winners of 23 of their past 27, and when Toronto split a pair of Sunday games in Rochester on the American July 4 holiday, the Bears slipped past Toronto into third place. And Toronto still did not have the services of Tillie Walker in their lineup. Despite claiming him on waivers, Walker refused initially to report, pointing to an agreement with Dunn that he could not be sold or traded to another club without Walker's permission. Before the July 1 game Walker wired Howley "that the Baltimore club had no right to sell him, and that he was entitled to his unconditional release,"[4] which would make him, in effect, a free agent. Walker likely was hoping for some added compensation, either from the Orioles or the Leafs, before he reported to Toronto. Players had little bargaining power in that era, and Tilley was likely exercising about the only option he had. Howley told reporters he was still hopeful of having Walker in the lineup when the Tigers came to town on the 7th.

As Cobb and company were making their way to Toronto, the Leafs were coming home with Rochester having won three of five. That was good enough to put the Leafs back into third. Newark had vaulted to second in the standings, while Buffalo, who was having troubles with bottom-dwelling Syracuse, dropped to fourth. Only five-and-a-half games separated first from fourth in the International League.

There was considerable hype leading up to the Detroit Tigers game. No fewer than seven former Leafs were on the Tigers' roster, and it was anticipated those names would help bring in a large crowd, as were rumours that Lionel Conacher might finally take the field. One player who wouldn't be available was Andy Harrington, who had undergone a tonsillectomy the day before. In the curious and limited medical knowledge of the day, Hewitt in the *Star* wrote, "Harrington had his tonsils removed yesterday in the hope that the trouble he has had with his throwing arm may be relieved."[5] Otis Miller, who had played well on both sides of the ball at shortstop, had been out since turning his ankle in Rochester, heading to Toronto Western hospital for X-rays while his teammates took batting practice.

The issue of Tillie Walker had finally been settled. He did not report to Toronto right away after being claimed on waivers from Baltimore. "I will not report to Toronto and claim I was unfairly treated," he told the *Baltimore Evening Sun.* Hewitt of the *Star* reported that Walker had sent a telegram to the Leafs saying that since Dunn broke his agreement not to trade Walker without his consent, Toronto would have to deal directly with him. Dunn, for his part, told the press that Walker had failed to keep in good condition, and he had washed his hands of Walker once the Leafs claimed him. "When Toronto claimed him they were automatically charged the $2,500 waiver price," Dunn told reporters, adding, "I do not have to deliver the player, and it is up to the Leafs to get Walker into line," leading one to wonder if that was his plan all along. Walker went home to Tennessee but managed to reach an agreement with Solman and Howley to come to Toronto and was expected to arrive in time to play against the Tigers.

"BENGALS SUBDUED BY HUBBELL," blared the headline in the next day's *Globe.* Hubbell limited the Tigers to three hits—all singles— and struck out six as the Leafs won 5-4. Having tamed yet another big-league team, the lefthander had to wonder just what he could do to gain Ty Cobb's favour. The crowd clamoured for the Detroit player-manager to make an appearance, but he remained glued to the Tigers bench until putting himself into the game as a pinch-runner with two out in the ninth. Detroit was well out of the pennant race, and Cobb was feuding with several of his players, presaging his departure from the Motor City three months later. He did eventually suit up for a game in Maple Leaf Stadium, but in a Philadelphia Athletics' uniform in a late-season exhibition game two years later in the last game the Hall of Famer ever played. With the Tigers' game over, the Howleyites could return to the task of chasing a pennant, with their next 17 games coming at home.

Last place Reading was up next on the Leafs' home dance card, starting on July 8. The Tigers had arrived in Toronto with a surplus of bats, which Cobb gave to his good friend Howley to supplement the Leafs' lumber supply. The Howleyites put the new wickets to good use, scoring 45 runs in four games and sweeping the hapless Keys four straight, including a pair of rain-delayed comeback victories in the Saturday doubleheader. The Reading club had lost 64 of their first 83 games and, not surprisingly, the club was having great difficulty attracting fans. In fact, while Toronto was pounding the Keystones 19-2 on Friday, a special meeting of all International League club presidents was held to discuss the future of both the Reading and Syracuse franchises. It was felt that Syracuse would probably finish the season, as the St. Louis Cardinals had purchased the club five years earlier and had deep enough pockets to withstand the Stars' dismal attendance. The Keys were another matter, though, and there were doubts the franchise—owned by a local syndicate of investors— could make it to season's end.

With Reading out of the way, Toronto enjoyed a day off on Sunday, July 8. Baltimore, with a three-and-a-half game lead on the second-place Leafs in what was shaping up as a crucial four-game set, would be coming to town.

"Star players may come and go," Mike Rodden of the *Globe* started his column off after the Monday twin bill that opened the Leafs-Orioles showdown, "but as long as Jack Dunn is manager, they will take a lot of beating. The visiting pilot walked up and down in the dugout yesterday, and without fear or favour, berated his athletes, and the result was two victories over the Leafs." Clearly, there was no love lost between Dunn and the Toronto press. As for the home side, Rodden continued, "(the Leafs) just to play in the hands of the perennial pennant winners, proceeded to give a fine demonstration of how the game should not be played."[6] Toronto fell to five and a half back of the league leaders by dropping the opener 6-5 in 10 innings (Leafs had a 5-4 lead heading into the ninth) and the second game 4-0. This, despite having their two best starters—Carroll and Stewart—on the mound.

Carroll, who alternated good starts with not-so-good ones over the past several weeks, had even less command of his fastball than usual. After hitting the Orioles' Clayton Sheedy in the head in the first inning, Carroll was very ineffective, as any young pitcher might be in a similar situation. The *Star* wondered why Howley left his young starter in the game:

It would almost appear that there is a condition in Carroll's contract making it compulsory that he should be kept in the box, no matter what happens. Manager Howley would not have hesitated a moment in removing any other pitcher in the first innings yesterday if he had displayed the same erratic tendencies as the ex-collegian did in that fateful chapter. Carroll showed fine courage in continuing in the box after the Sheedy mishap, but perhaps it would have been better for him and the Leafs if he had retired from the scene.[7]

Sheedy was taken for X-rays at Toronto Western, and Carroll headed to the hospital at the conclusion of the game to relay his apologies. Sheedy was released later, with the *Star* showing the medical attitudes of the time: "Fortunately only a slight concussion resulted, and he will be as good as new in a day or so,"[8] as if a fastball to an unhelmeted head was but a flesh wound. Still, there was considerable disappointment among the city's baseball fans at the Leafs dropping the first two games of the important series.

Brooklyn Manager Wilbert Robinson had asked for waivers (later recalled) on ten of his players, and they apparently got the message, as the Dodgers won that day. "MAYBE SOMETHING LIKE THIS WOULD HELP HERE," blared the headline on the *Star* story, hoping for something—anything—to light a fire under the struggling Leafs. In reference to that story, in the *Globe*, Rodden wrote that Leafs fans had all but given up in the second game, and the Maple Leaf Stadium stands were strangely quiet. "The Funeral March of Saul would have been proper under the circumstances," he noted. Rodden also reported that after Tillie Walker, late of the Orioles, had struck out for the second time in the nightcap, falling to one knee in the process, Dunn's "raucous laughter could be heard coming out of the Orioles dugout when Walker fell down."[9] Perhaps pouring some salt on the wound, Dunn signed Babe Dye, released by the Leafs a week earlier, after the second game. Meanwhile, the *Star*, who suggested that President Solman had been more than generous with what was suggested to be a malingering Dye, reported that the Leafs' other local boy,

Conacher, was being used to warm up pitchers, and that Howley was considering converting him into a catcher.[10]

With the pair of losses, Toronto had dropped six straight to the O's, and 8 of 11 games on the year to their archrivals. Buffalo and Newark might be hot on their heels, but the road to the pennant was going to have to go through Baltimore. While it would be hard to call a game in mid-July a "must win," if there was ever a time for a win for the home side, this had to be it. A loss would drop the Leafs 6.5 games back—not an insurmountable lead, but one that would require considerable work and not a small amount of luck to overcome. And Toronto fought back in the third game of the series, pounding the Orioles 18-9. Jess Doyle had spotted the visitors a four-run lead, and Hubbell in relief was not much better, so Howley turned to recent acquisition Clarence Fisher, who shut the door as the Leafs bats came alive. "Jack Dunn," observed Rodden, "with not a semblance of a smile on his careworn face, watched five of his moundsmen shelled."[11]

The Wednesday game was sponsored by the Leafs' Booster Club. With 40 percent of the day's gate being pledged to an association dedicated to bringing major conferences to Toronto, everyone anticipated a record crowd. The results, both on the field and in the stands, fell considerably short, as the Leafs lost 11-1 to the Orioles before a crowd of only 6,600. The boo-birds rained down on the Leafs as the visitors circled the bases. The Leafs, with several banged-up players in their lineup (maybe as a result of Howley riding his regulars so hard), resented the catcalls from the fans. "They (the players) were knocked out," opined Rodden in the *Globe*,

> and the only thing that their dazed minds could understand was the merciless verbal barrage from the grand stand. The players resented this deeply, and it is no secret that for the first time in history that players representing Toronto in the International League prefer to do their playing away from home.[12]

In fairness to the Leafs fans, this was becoming something of a broken record. The team had not won a pennant in seven years, and that the Orioles—to whom the Leafs had now lost 9 of 13—administered a beating on a day that had a considerable build-up in the Toronto papers was a double blow. The new stadium and the new players had brought on high expectations, and now, with the O's threatening to leave Toronto with an even bigger lead than they had arrived—pending the results of the next day's game—the Leafs were falling short.

In the *Star*, Hewitt suggested that the score of the game flattered the visitors, but he acknowledged one of the main reasons attendance was down for the season, according to some of his readers. "Some of the fans are of the opinion that attendance would be greatly increased…if the admission fee was cut down," he reported. "One enthusiast writes that 80 cents for a back seat is too much when it is considered that the tax at the Island was only 75 cents, with a free ride thrown in." Another reader chimed in with complaints about the price of concessions. Then there was Howley's handling of the club. "Several others…advance the opinion that the Leafs would be better off if the connection with Detroit was abandoned. It is the general opinion that there is too much 'babying' of the farmhands."[13]

Winning may not cure everything, but in the case of a ballclub, it certainly takes care of a lot of ills. Howley turned to the veteran Fisher the next day in an attempt to salvage the series and keep Baltimore from extending their lead, and the tall submariner responded in a complete game, 4-3 triumph cutting the Orioles' lead to four-and-a-half games. It was Fisher's third win in as many decisions since coming to the Leafs from Buffalo. "Under the bludgeonings of the Birds our heads are bloodied, but unbowed,"[14] a poetic and upbeat Howley told reporters after the game, likely happy to see the last of the Orioles for a while.

Newark, two-and-a-half games behind the second-place Leafs, but a half-game ahead of the fourth-place Bisons, would be coming to town next. The Bears would not be the pushovers they were a month earlier. But Toronto had their way with Newark, taking three of four in relatively easy fashion. There was a dust-up at home plate in the first game of the series, when the Newark catcher blocked the plate in an attempt to keep Flash Gilhooley from scoring; both benches emptied, as Conacher—no stranger to such gatherings from his other sport—"loomed large in the 'doings',"[15] observed Mike Rodden. Nothing came of the melee, but Rodden wondered in his column if the bad feelings from the incident might spill over to the next time the Leafs visited New Jersey.

A Saturday (July 17) doubleheader was reduced to one game by rain, with Newark taking it, stopping their losing streak to Toronto at six games. The resulting double dip on Monday saw a Toronto sweep; the pair of wins, combined with Baltimore's loss at Buffalo, allowed the Leafs to gain a game and a half on the O's in the standings. After the washed-out second game on Saturday, a contingent of a dozen Leafs, led by Howley, headed north of the city up to Lake Simcoe at the invitation of clothier Roth Eaton, who owned a country estate there near the town of Beaverton on the Lake's eastern shore, for some off-day recreation. On Sunday, the players enjoyed taking part in horseshoes and poker tournaments. Eaton enjoyed kibitzing with the players, Mickey Heath in particular. According to Lou E. Marsh of the *Star*, Heath had gone into Eaton's Beauty Parlor for Males on Friday and picked out a new suit for himself. "Lay that suit aside," he told the cashier, "and I'll hit the sign at the Stadium and get it for nothing."[16] In a promotion for his store, Eaton indeed had a "Hit Sign, Win Suit" advertisement on the outfield wall at the ballpark, a target no player had managed to hit yet, he chided Heath. But Heath had the last laugh, hitting the sign on Monday, and indeed getting a free suit in the process.

Sixth-place Jersey City came to town to finish off the homestand for four games from July 20-23. The team featured a new nickname— the Black Cats—after team and city officials invited fans to come up with a more suitable name than Skeeters. Interestingly, while Rodden referred to the team by their new name, his *Globe* editor Wilson continued to call them the Skeeters.

CHAPTER 26
LEAFS "HANGING ONTO SECOND PLACE BY AN EYELASH"

TORONTO HAD AN EXCELLENT OPPORTUNITY TO GAIN SOME GROUND ON Baltimore against the sixth-place visitors but could only manage a four-game split. After a Friday doubleheader, the Leafs boarded a train bound for Syracuse, and another twin bill the next day.

The Leafs once again had a chance to close the gap with the Orioles over the weekend against the next-to-last-place Stars. But the news the *Toronto Star* carried on Monday was decidedly bad. The headline said it all: ALCOHOL POISON DEATH LIST GROWS TO 31, 15 OF THE VICTIMS FROM ONTARIO CENTRES.

A bootlegger was arrested in Oshawa, just east of Toronto, after reports of a string of deaths along the highway between there and Buffalo. Prohibition was in its final days, and after years of enforced temperance, people were desperate for alcohol in any form. The deaths took place in a 24-hour stretch from Friday to Saturday night.

A bootlegger from nearby Hamilton named Bert D'Angelo was arrested and charged with manslaughter. Two of his assistants would have been charged as well, but both died from drinking the toxic liquor.

Poisonous illegal liquor was quite a problem in the province, one of the unintended (but probably inevitable) effects of Prohibition. Bootlegging was very much a large and organized business; contraband booze was easily shipped under cover of the night at various points along the New York Lake Ontario shoreline and the Niagara River. While there were several publicized gun battles between police and alcohol smugglers, booze flowed quite freely northward across the border. But in the face of increasing government and police crack-downs (police opening fire on unarmed smugglers at Ashbridge's Bay, in the city's east end, became a major scandal), many bootleggers took to making their own alcohol, with lethal effects. Toronto historian Adam Bunch, writing in his *Toronto Time Traveller* newsletter, described the gory details of the July deaths:

> One victim threw up black vomit. A second turned blue. A third foamed at the mouth with a bloody froth. Some died screaming. One woman wondered aloud why the green leaves outside her window had all turned black; her eyesight was going. Many went blind before passing away. By the time it was all over, 45 people had been killed across Ontario and New York State.[1]

The latest poisoning deaths would eventually help spell the end of Prohibition; a December provincial election would see the incumbent Conservatives campaign and win on a promise to establish government-run liquor stores. For over a half century after that, generations of Ontarians were only able to buy wine or liquor at Liquor Control Board of Ontario outlets, where grim-faced clerks would take the order slips filled out by customers, retrieve the product from shelves at the back of the store, then deliver the requested bottle(s) in a brown paper bag.

The news for baseball fans wasn't much better. The Leafs could only manage a split at home against Jersey City, then dropped three in a row to Syracuse, scoring only three runs and leaving 33 runners on base in three games. Luckily, Baltimore had dropped two of three in Jersey City, but the three Toronto losses allowed Newark and Buffalo to move to within a game and a half of the Leafs, while Baltimore's lead over them was now up to five. The Leafs, in Hewitt's words in the *Star*, were "hanging onto 2nd place by an eyelash."[2]

Things went from bad to worse, however, when Newark won on Monday, July 26, while the Leafs were playing an exhibition game against the Chicago White Sox at Auburn, New York. Newark slipped into second, percentage points ahead of the Leafs with the win. Hewitt pointed out that Newark would likely be in first place if not for their difficulties with Toronto. The pall of failed expectations hanging over the club as July was coming to a close was articulated by Hewitt in his Tuesday column:

> The Leafs have been more or less a disappointment all season.…Players who were counted upon to carry the brunt of the attack before the campaign commenced have failed to come through consistently. Cleo Carlyle whose batting was a decided factor last season, has been in and out all season, while Herman Layne has slumped badly on occasions. No club with championship aspirations can afford to carry two men in the infield whose combined batting average is under .200, no matter how well they field their respective positions.[3]

Lefty Stewart offered to pitch on short rest when Toronto returned to Syracuse to finish their series, and Howley eagerly took him up on the offer, as the Leafs' most effective starter for the past month pitched his team to an 8-3 victory. The schedule was about to get a lot tougher, as Toronto headed to Buffalo for a date with the fourth-place Bisons, who would return the favour with a visit to Toronto. Buffalo had fallen off in the season's second half, but they were only percentage points behind the third-place Leafs, giving the Howleyites trouble all season.

Rain forced a postponement of the first game of the Leafs-Bisons series, and a doubleheader was scheduled for the next day—Thursday, July 30. Toronto scored five runs in the top of the ninth to take the first game, 10-5. Ace Owen Carroll, after several failed attempts, picked up his 14th victory. Buffalo took the nightcap, 7-5.

The standings on the morning of July 31, before the Leafs and Bisons tangled in another doubleheader (Toronto was in the middle of a stretch of eight games in five days) in the closest pennant race in years, per the *Toronto Star*:

BASEBALL RESULTS

INTERNATIONAL LEAGUE

	Won.	Lost.	P.C.
Baltimore	68	38	.642
Newark	64	42	.604
Toronto	65	44	.596
Buffalo	63	46	.578
Rochester	54	54	.500
Jersey City	47	60	.439
Syracuse	41	65	.387
Reading	27	80	.252

—Yesterday's Results—
Reading............2-4 Jersey City ...1-3
Syracuse...........12 Rochester 8
No other games played.

Both teams boarded a train for Toronto right after the pair of games for yet another doubleheader at Maple Leaf Stadium on Saturday. And the Leafs finished July on a high, taking both games from the Bisons, nudging out Newark for second place. But their stay there was short; after losing a Sunday game in Rochester, then splitting a pair with Syracuse back at Maple Leaf Stadium on Monday (the Leafs' third in four days), Toronto was back in third. The Sabbath Laws—forcing Toronto to board a train frequently for Sunday doubleheaders elsewhere—were taking a toll on the team. Hewitt, in his column on Tuesday (the *Star* did not publish on Sundays, nor on holidays like the day before), said, "It is asking too much of a team to play five games in three days with a stuffy train trip thrown into the bargain. The Leafs played sleepily in the morning game, and tossed off one they should have won."[4] On three occasions to that point in the season, Toronto had to board a Saturday train for a Sunday game, and the schedule maker had done them no favours with that epic June road trip. The tired group of Leafs sleepwalked through much of the next day's game, a 6-4 loss to Syracuse.

Toronto was grieving that weekend over a canoe tragedy northeast of the city. A group of boys had arrived at a church leadership camp on Balsam Lake, in the heart of Ontario's cottage country. One of the camp's adult directors—a non-swimmer—had asked for volunteers to paddle with him into a nearby town to pick up supplies. They left shortly after dinner in large war canoes, with plans to return in the morning. But once they were out on the Lake, the winds picked up, and the boys—many of whom were inexperienced paddlers—lost control of the huge vessel, which soon overturned in the face of the waves. Lifejackets were not present; several boys clung to the overturned canoe, but could not hang on in the dark, chilly water. Only four of the 15 canoeists made it back to shore safely. On the weekend, the victims were memorialized at a service at St. Paul's Church on Bloor Street in Toronto. The tragedy was North America's worst pleasure craft accident at the time.

With a doubleheader—the end of the grind—scheduled for Wednesday, August 5, and his team about to go on the road for three weeks, Howley decided his team needed a lift. So he called on a friend to help.

CHAPTER 27
A VISITOR GIVES THE LEAFS A LIFT

Dan Howley and J.G. (Jim) Shaw. Photo courtesy Barb Benson.

"RULES AND REGULATIONS WERE IGNORED YESTERDAY," WROTE MIKE Rodden in the *Globe*, "when a man, dressed in civilian clothes, sat in the Toronto dugout and incidentally brought good luck to the Leafs."[1] The gentleman in question was one J.G. (Jim) Shaw, a grain elevator superintendent from Port McNicoll, a Great Lakes grain, rail, freight, and cruise ship hub on Georgian Bay, a two-hour train ride from

Toronto. He was there at the invitation of Howley, whose acquaintance Shaw had made a few years earlier when Rodden arranged a fishing trip of Leafs players and beat reporters to the northern village on an off day.

Shaw, whose travels in his previous career as a grain elevator construction supervisor always included his ball glove, was known as "The finest sportsman on Georgian Bay." He was very active in local ball, coaching several ball teams from little Port McNicoll to provincial titles. Writing about the fishing trip in his column several years later, Rodden said Howley and Shaw "became fast friends right from the start, and that the admiration was mutual."[2] Everyone in the party caught a lot of fish (some 80 bass in all), except Howley, and "there was great merriment thereof, because he had more lures, tackle, and patience than the rest of us combined."[3]

When the party returned to the docks at Port McNicoll that evening, a "mysterious individual approached and announced that he was a warden and that 'Sunday fishin' was agin' the law."[4] The party immediately pointed to Howley as the possessor of the bulk of the day's catch. For a moment, Howley was speechless—truly a rare occasion. The "good natured warden laid the law down, and for a few minutes Daniel probably had visions of resting in a cell,"[5] recalled Rodden, until Shaw advised that it was all just a prank. Howley insisted he knew it was a joke all along, but his red face suggested otherwise.

Howley and Shaw became close friends, and Howley came to rely on the advice of Shaw, who was regarded as an astute baseball man. Howley also felt Shaw's presence would give his team a lift, and it did, as Toronto won both games over Syracuse before heading out on a three-week road trip, with a showdown in Baltimore the first stop. Spirits were no doubt high on the Leafs' car, as the sweep of Syracuse had put them within three-and-a-half games of front-running Baltimore. Fans who could not make it down to the lakeshore were able to listen to the second game on the *Star*'s CFCA radio station; the signal could be heard as far away as Shaw's hometown on Georgian Bay, Napanee near the east end of Lake Ontario, and Upstate New York.

Leafs' broadcasts were becoming quite popular, and while the team wasn't drawing as had been expected, they were developing a strong following across southern Ontario.

It's hard to understand exactly the effect Shaw's presence had on the team. To a modern observer, having a visitor in the dugout during a game is difficult to envision. MLB Rule 3.17 states that only "players, coaches, and authorized officials," are allowed in a dugout during a game, but it was apparently a common practice during the 1920s. Maybe the players saw Shaw as one of those treasured good luck charms. Perhaps Shaw was a calming presence for Howley, who must have been frustrated by his team's inconsistency. A half dozen years later, when Howley was managing the Reds in the big leagues, he sent his ailing slugger, defending National League batting champion and future Hall of Famer Chick Hafey, to Port McNicoll midseason to recuperate with the Shaw family. His two-week stay on the shore of Georgian Bay must have been a powerful tonic for Hafey: over the next two seasons he would appear in more games than at any other point in his career. Whatever the case, Shaw's visit seemed to inspire the team.

Toronto was back in second place, and their fate was in their own hands with a match-up against the Orioles. But having lost 14 of 19 games on the year to the O's, trailing them by three-and-a-half games, meant the Leafs were very much the underdogs. When the two teams last met, Baltimore manager Jack Dunn employed an early form of a shift against his former star Tillie Walker. Whenever the right-handed hitter Walker came up to bat for the Leafs, Dunn would shift his left fielder toward the foul line and his centre fielder in the left-centre gap. Rodden wondered in the *Globe* if Dunn would employ the "two left fielder" defence with the Leafs in town.

Toronto was finally healthy, and Howley scheduled Owen Carroll, who appeared to have turned things around, as his series-opening starter. The Leafs were ready, and "If they lose they have no excuses, although Manager Dan Howley is satisfied that the arbiters will never give the visiting teams any breaks at Baltimore," wrote Rodden of the *Globe*.[6] The umpires would have little to fear from a hostile crowd,

Rodden jabbed, "because few fans attend the games in Dunnville this season."

Before the Leafs boarded their train south, the first rumours of Howley in connection with a big-league managing job came up. "The opinion in general, especially in Detroit," penned Hewitt the morning of the final home doubleheader before the road trip, "that Ty Cobb is a great batsman, and the rumor is going the rounds that Dan Howley is slated to join him as boss of the Bengals. The leader of the Leafs, who is well satisfied with his berth here, says that the story is all applesauce."[7]

While the Leafs were away, Solman had workers remove the troublesome left-field bleachers. Attendance in the temporary stands had been sparse, and they had made for confusing ground rules.

The first game of the series on August 6 was a wild one; four Leaf players and Howley were ejected in a 7-6, 11-inning Toronto triumph. Backup catcher Lena Styles, starting in place of Steve O'Neill, was tossed for arguing balls and strikes with the home plate umpire. O'Neill, who came into the game in Styles' place, was himself thrown out of the game for arguing a called third strike while he batted in the tenth; there was thought that Howley himself might have to come in to catch, but the versatile Carl Schmehl volunteered to don the tools of ignorance and finish the game behind the plate. Owen Carroll was back to his former struggles, and after giving up four runs in the sixth inning was removed for a pinch hitter. But the win reduced Baltimore's lead to two and a half over both the Leafs and Newark, who won that day to keep pace. Despite the win, Hewitt in the *Star* seemed less than thrilled, calling the Leafs a "real fighting crew on the road.

"If only they played with the same spirit at the stadium," he complained, "they would play to thousands instead of hundreds, as has been the case the whole season."[8]

Toronto won the Saturday game and split the Sunday doubleheader. Tensions had been running high since the Friday game (Howley and O'Neill had been fined $25 apiece for their antics), and things reached a head on Saturday. Dunn was ejected for refusing to leave the field after his protest of an umpire's call; bottles were thrown at the men in blue, and two fans entered the field and tried to attack them. League President J. Conway Toole was in attendance on Sunday, and both teams were on their best behaviour.

Newark swept their weekend series and remained in second, just a game back of Baltimore. With the Leafs and Bisons on mini runs, the race was tightening. "Baltimore still hangs onto the lead but by the slenderest of threads, a threatening Newark Bear reaching at the wings of an Oriole," waxed Don B. Reed of the *Buffalo News*. "Just a game between the Bears and the Toronto Maple Leafs, while a half game keeps the thundering herd of Buffalo out of third place."[9] It had been a long time since the league had seen such a logjam atop the standings so late in the season.

Baltimore boss Dunn had hoped Babe Dye would be motivated to take revenge on his old team, but he struggled in the first two games of the series and was benched for the doubleheader. After an off day on Monday, the Orioles would host the resurgent Bisons, while the Leafs promised to have an easier time of things in Reading against the last place Keys. With 91 losses, Reading was on pace to break the International League record for futility. Ownership, in an attempt to recoup some of their losses on the balance sheet, had taken to selling off their top players to other IL teams and not replacing them; at the start of the Leafs' visit, Reading had only 14 players available. Reading manager Hooks Wiltse—a big leaguer at the turn of the century, but 47 years old then—even had to add his name to the lineup at first base for one game.

The fans responded in kind, and with temperatures soaring over 100 degrees F for the week, there were fewer fans in the stands than degrees of mercury on the thermometer. Not surprisingly, Toronto took swept the four-game series (rain washed out the fifth). There were rumours circulating but not proven that Dunn somehow had a piece of ownership in the Reading and Jersey City teams, calling the shots both in terms of rosters and on-field strategy for both. Fans in Toronto were sore that Reading shortstop Hobart "Rabbit" Whitman, who had some pop at the plate, was sold to Buffalo after the Leafs had offered $5,000 for him—more than the Bisons had. "The loss of Whitman is the severest blow the few fans Reading has in the league," noted the *Buffalo News.* Whitman was popular for his hitting, the *News* added, but "a poor runner and weak on mental ball, according to major league scouts."[10]

Toronto writers sensed a conspiracy on the part of Baltimore to keep the Leafs from winning the pennant. "Dunn has had a finger in every International League pie for years," wrote Hewitt in the *Star,* "and judging from recent developments Little Jack Horner from nursery rhyme fame is his only rival at pulling out the plums."[11] Babe Dye, let go by the Orioles, was obtained by Reading to take Whitman's place on the Keys' roster.

Newark kept winning, while the Orioles had their struggles with Buffalo, and as a result on the morning of Thursday, August 13, the Bears were now in first, a half-game ahead of the Leafs, while Baltimore had dropped to third for the first time at such a late date in anyone's memory, just one percentage point behind Toronto. That day's game was wiped out by rain (as was all action in the league that day), made up as part of a doubleheader the next day.

But the Leafs had to fight to beat lowly Reading—in more ways than one. Three games went into extra innings (Carl Hubbell winning the last two with his finest work of the season), but there was an ugly incident in the final game, as tensions boiled over.

The Leafs played no favourite with IL umpires, it seemed, but their rancour was at its highest with Tom Crooke. Crooke had played parts of two seasons with Washington in a 14-year pro career ending in 1918. After his playing days ended, Crooke had worked his way up in the minors before becoming an International League umpire. Howley and Crooke had feuded for much of the season, with Howley claiming bad Crooke calls cost the Leafs two games. In the first game, after Bill Mullen was called out on a close play on the bases, he came up swinging at Crooke—but missed. That earned the Leafs' third baseman a trip to the showers. Jim Faulkner on the mound had his own issues with Crooke, and in the second game knocked the umpire over after a missed strike call.

"It is altogether likely that both players will be lost to the Leafs for some days just when their services are needed the most,"[12] said the *Star*'s Charlie Good. The two-man crew was standard throughout baseball in the 1920s, even in the big leagues; it didn't seem to occur to Major League owners, as their turnstiles were turning like never before in the Golden Age of Baseball, to have the best officiating for their sport. Violence against umpires, of course, was not new. "Kill the umpire" was first recorded in 1888 in Ernest L. Thayer's iconic "Casey at the Bat," but baseball didn't take the problem of attacks on umpires seriously until after World War II. But Crooke appeared to be able to dish it out as well as he could take it; this altercation was his third such incident in that week alone.

Reading police had to be called in to pull Faulkner off the prone Crooke. With temperatures rising in the dog days of August in the heat of a pennant race, it would have behooved League President Toole to crack down more on these incidents, but most of the punishments he handed out were minor. Team owners, not wanting to lose a star box-office attraction (and maybe pointing out Crooke's reputation), likely put considerable pressure on him to go lightly.

The big story from the weekend in the big leagues involved the defending World Series champs Pittsburgh. The Pirates had just dropped a weekend doubleheader to the next-to-last-place Boston Braves, a pair of losses that the first-place Bucs found embarrassing. Despite the Pirates' success, the team was slowly being torn apart from dissension involving former manager Fred Clarke. Clarke had been a legendary Pirates player and manager, leading the team to two World Series appearances (winning once), but had been away from the team for several years when owner Barney Dreyfuss invited him back for one last hurrah to sit in the Pittsburgh dugout and serve as an assistant to Bill McKechnie in 1925. Clarke frequently second-guessed McKechnie right in front of players in the dugout; the Bucs still managed to win the World Series, but things only deteriorated the following year.

Players later said they repeatedly heard Clarke giving orders to the batter going up to the plate that would conflict with McKechnie's signals from the coaching lines. Things came to a head between games of the Boston doubleheader, when Clarke told McKechnie that slumping star centre fielder Max Carey, a 15-year veteran and future Hall of Famer, should be replaced. Several players overheard the remark and approached Carey, who as captain of the team felt compelled to put Clarke's meddling to an end. Carey, along with the two players who told him of Clarke's words, immediately called a team meeting and put forward a resolution that Clarke be removed from the Pirates' dugout.[13]

Of course, there was no Players Association in those days; star players could speak out, but the conventional baseball wisdom was that how smart you were was determined by your batting average or win totals. Carey may have been a star, but at 35 and having suffered through a respiratory illness for much of the year, was on the downside of his career. Likely feeling the pressure of potential repercussions from management, the players—many of whom knew they were replaceable, World Series rings or not—voted against Carey's resolution, 18-6.

When Pirates' owner Dreyfuss (under pressure from Clarke, a team shareholder) got wind of what the press called "The Great Pirate Mutiny," he surprisingly released all three players. With a third of their lineup gone, Pittsburgh stumbled to a third-place finish.

The Leafs' sweep, combined with Newark's win and Baltimore's loss, meant that the three teams were now tied for first. Next stop: Jersey City.

CHAPTER 28
THE FIRST PLACE LEAFS

The Maple Leafs found themselves atop the International League standings after sweeping the three-game series over the weekend of August 15-16 at Jersey City. The Leafs had won seven in a row against the league's lesser lights, and 12 of 13 since Howley invited Jim Shaw to sit in the dugout at Maple Leaf Stadium. Toronto was on quite a roll, and big-league clubs were taking notice; scouts from several Major League teams had become a regular presence at Leaf games.

"Both Wally Stewart and Herman Layne will be with Toronto until the close of the season," Howley said in a special dispatch to the *Globe*. "Our chances of winning the pennant are entirely too good to even consider disposing of either Stewart or Layne…it would not be fair to our team or our city if we should sell any players now."[1] Big-league teams were gearing up for the stretch run, looking to bolster their lineups. Pittsburgh, whose pennant hopes were fading and desperately needing a replacement for the released Carey, had a scout following the team and filing reports on Layne, and legendary Yankees ivory hunter* Paul Krichell had been on hand to watch a

---

* A scout who searches for young, talented players; one who "seeks diamond phenoms" (*The Sporting News*, Oct. 13, 1913).

masterful start by Stewart. It was rumoured that as many as five MLB teams had put in an offer for the left-hander.

No doubt Howley was presented offers for both, but he knew that the team's chances of winning would take a hit if he sold the players. A pennant was the goal, not just for the team and city, but because it would no doubt increase the value of such players to be part of a championship team, and it certainly would look good on Howley's resumé, too. But in the end, Lol Solman had the last word in such matters, and he accepted an offer of $50,000 and two players for Layne. Under the terms of the agreement, Layne would finish the season in Toronto, and the two players would join the team the following year.

Toronto had six more games (two more at Jersey, then four games with Newark that were key for both teams) before returning home. Hewitt had noticed Howley's handling of his pitchers at home and on the road was markedly different in his *Star* column:

> For some reason or other, the Leaf leader showed much diffidence in the handling of his pitchers at the stadium. He refused to switch his original pitching nominee unless circumstances were such that he was compelled to make a change. On the road he stands for little loose work yanking his boxmen at the slightest sign of wavering, and as a consequence the Leafs have been winning the majority of close games.[2]

While the Leafs were in New Jersey over the weekend, back in Toronto a contest was held at Sunnyside Pavilion to name Miss Toronto. Over 35,000 spectators jammed the waterfront park to watch a "21 year old Scottish Canadian lass," as page one of the *Star* described Miss Jean Ford Tolmie. Tolmie was secretly entered in the contest by her brother under her mother's maiden name of Ford. Her father strenuously objected to beauty contests, but he was over-whelmed when a panel of five judges determined she was the most beautiful woman in the city. "I suppose I am a typical Scotchman," the

Edinburgh native told the *Star*. "but I don't take to that sort of thing or believe in it. It's not the way they do things in the old land."[3]

When asked if he was proud of his daughter, the elder Tolmie replied, "Well, I will say that girl can take care of herself. She is witty, and she is wise. She will hold her head all right." Young Miss Tomie, educated at a Toronto convent, said she loved swimming, ate mostly vegetables and not much meat, and had recently given up candies. Her prize for being named Miss Toronto was an all-expense-paid trip to Atlantic City; she hoped her mother would be allowed to chaperone her.

The Newark series would feature a matchup between the league's two hottest teams. Newark had the best record in the loop, but the Leafs came into town supremely confident, having won 14 of their last 16 games, and 12 of 16 against the Bears on the season. Packed houses were predicted for the series, but crowds fell short of expectations. The pennant pressure may have been too much for Newark pitcher Ed Tomlin in the Saturday game. After having given up five runs in the first inning—the last four on a grand slam by Mickey Heath—Newark manager Fred Burchell came out to replace Tomlin with a relief pitcher. Tomlin at first refused to leave the game, then attacked the manager. After being restrained and led to the dugout by his teammates, Tomlin drove his fist through a water cooler in the dugout. Newark fined Tomlin $500 and suspended him for the rest of the season.

The Leafs continued their torrid stretch, winning the first three games before rain forced a postponement of the final game. With Baltimore stumbling, not only would the Leafs come home in first place, they would do so with a bit of a lead. The second-place Orioles had fallen three games off the lead, Newark a half game behind that, and Buffalo in fourth was now seven games back, and fading fast. The *Buffalo Evening News* noted that, "it has been a long time since at this stage of the season the Orioles had been in such danger." Whoever opened up a lead on the O's would need a significant one, "according to the schedule Baltimore winds up the season with three successive double-headers against Reading."[4] The Leafs' chances of extending that lead were excellent, as Jersey City was first up on the homestand.

As the Leafs prepared to take on the Black Cats on Monday, August 23, Wilson in the *Globe* warned against counting chickens before they hatched, but went on to predict what would happen when —not if—Toronto won the pennant. The Leafs would face the champions of the American Association, currently led by Milwaukee, in a best-of-nine Junior World Series. From there, Wilson speculated that they might "trek across the continent to take on winners of the Pacific Coast League."[5] There was even a suggestion from Detroit, Wilson added, that the Leafs and Tigers play a best-of-three series at the conclusion of the American League season so that the big club could determine first-hand the progress of some of their prospects. With all but 10 of the Leafs remaining 35 games at home, coupled with Baltimore's August swoon, Wilson's optimism was understandable.

Jersey City continued to be easy fodder for the Leafs, losing four straight to the home side, increasing Toronto's lead over Baltimore to four games. Rescued from the scrap heap when Buffalo let him go, Clarence Fisher had been a revelation for Howley, who used him both in long relief and as a replacement for Hubbell in the second game of doubleheaders. Fisher picked up his eighth win, against no losses, in the nightcap of the Tuesday twin bill. With the series sweep, Toronto had won 18 of its last 20.

In the dugout, every move Howley made seemed to work. While Leaf pitchers were shutting down Jersey hitters, allowing only three runs in four games, the Leaf hitters were having their own struggles. Howley used what Rodden of the *Globe* called "inside ball," to squeeze in what proved to be the winning run in the fifth inning of the final game. As they had been for much of the season, pitching and defence were the keys for the Leafs. In the same article, Rodden singled out Gilhooley in centre field, and Miller at shortstop for outstanding plays.

*Poster for the Canadian National Exhibition, the grand dame of
Canadian fall fairs.*

It truly was an exciting time in Toronto. The Canadian National
Exhibition, the country's largest Fall Fair—The Ex, as locals call it—
was once known as the Toronto Industrial Exhibition, originally
designed to promote agriculture and technology in the Toronto area.
The small country fair morphed over its first century into one of the
top such events in North America. By the 1920s, The Ex included a

carnival, live music, a midway, parades, sporting events, art shows, and a building entirely devoted to food vendors. The Ex for many generations before and after was the place to be in late summer.

A highlight of the 1926 fair was the opening of the Ontario Government building, a reinforced concrete Beaux Arts building designed by the same firm that drew up the plans for Maple Leaf Stadium. It was to be a showcase "to display the products of Ontario," according to a government press release.

Maple Leaf Stadium sprung up about three solid line drives east of the grounds; many Exhibition goers planned to take in a Leafs game while down on the waterfront. With the Leafs at home throughout the length of the Exhibition, which ended on September 11, the *Globe*'s Wilson estimated the club might draw as many as 300,000 fans during that stretch. As The Ex was winding down by mid-September, the Toronto Argonauts of the Interprovincial Rugby Football Union would be opening their training camp. Several of their games would be played at Maple Leaf Stadium. With baseball, football, and national lacrosse playoffs going on, it was a busy time in Toronto sports, and the city's main daily newspapers reflected that in their multipage coverage.

Newark, sitting now in third, five-and-a-half games behind the Leafs, would be in town next for five games in three days.

CHAPTER 29
"PLAYING WONDERFUL BALL NOW"

TORONTO CONTINUED ITS WINNING WAYS WITH NEWARK IN TOWN, sweeping a doubleheader to open the series on Thursday, August 26. With Baltimore incredibly dropping their fifth straight game to Syracuse, the Leafs' lead over the Orioles was now at six games. "Yesterday was the biggest day in baseball Toronto has experienced in almost a decade,"[1] gushed Wilson in the *Globe*. Trailing 1-0 in the sixth inning of the second game (scheduled for seven), the game was halted because of showers drifting in off the lake. When play resumed, the Leafs played small ball to plate three runs to take the lead, shutting out Newark in the seventh to seal the win. Over at the *Star*, Charlie Good felt that President Solman should have received credit for at least one of the wins, as Cleo Carlyle ranged over several times to catch fly balls that would have been ruled doubles before Solman took out the left-field bleachers earlier in the month. His editor, Hewitt, who had been critical of the club more often than not, showed how a nine-game winning streak can cure a lot of ills when he wrote in the same edition, "They are playing wonderful ball now and deserve all their success."[2]

Newark was able to stop Toronto's win streak with a 6-3 victory on the last Friday of August. Owen Carroll was his usual wild self, although not so effectively this time, hitting a Newark hitter in the head with a pitch. Once again, he was ineffective after that, but gamely hung in until the eighth. He seemed on the verge of getting out of a jam when an easy fly ball was lofted into foul territory in left field. Carlyle was poised to make the catch when three fans, perhaps caught up in the pennant frenzy, jumped on the field to try to beat him to the ball. Carlyle, no doubt distracted by the sight, dropped the ball. On the next pitch, the Newark hitter laced a run-scoring double down the line.

The Leafs split a Saturday doubleheader with the Bears, Clarence Fisher winning his ninth straight in the second game. With an off day on Sunday, the Leafs were now comfortably in the lead, with Baltimore trailing by six-and-a-half games and departing Newark seven and a half. Close to 14,000 fans piled into Maple Leaf Stadium on Saturday, the biggest crowd of the year. With Reading, already at 104 losses on the season, scheduled to come into town next, Hewitt, in the *Star*, suggested Toronto fans were looking past that series and toward the weekend, when the Orioles came to town. "What the fans want to see more than anything else is for the Leafs to show real championship form when the Baltimore Birds come here," he wrote. "Those are the games the fans want most to see the Leafs win, so as to make up for the disappointment of past years."[3]

Reading came to town with the thinnest of rosters and was swept in five games by Toronto. The Reading starting pitcher in the first game of the series, Lefty Beard, was left in to absorb a 22-3 beating, because the Keys didn't bring a relief pitcher to town. Before they left Toronto, Reading sold their best player (shortstop Frank Sigaloos) to the Philadelphia Athletics. Reading went through three managers on the season, none of whom had much to work with. The syndicate owners feuded with each other all season, and the front-office internecine warfare spilled onto the field. Less than 100 fans typically attended a Keys' game early in the season, and when management began their midsummer fire sale of the team's best players, only a handful of diehards were in the stands. The team that Toronto had to rally to beat on the home opener was a shell of its former self, its players a ragtag group of players no one wanted. The Leafs finished the season 22-2 against one of the worst minor-league teams of all time; Reading would win only 31 of 160 games.

The standings at the end of August, per the *Globe*:

Baseball Record

INTERNATIONAL LEAGUE.

	Won.	Lost.	P.C.
Toronto	93	51	.646
Newark	84	59	.587
Buffalo	85	60	.586
Baltimore	83	59	.585
Rochester	72	73	.497
Jersey City	64	78	.451
Syracuse	58	82	.414
Reading	30	107	.219

Yesterday's Results.

Toronto	3	Reading	1
Newark	9	Syracuse	7
Buffalo	5	Baltimore	4
Jersey City	9	Rochester	2

Games today—Reading at Toronto (2); Baltimore at Buffalo; Jersey City at Rochester; Newark at Syracuse.

Baltimore was next, having beaten Buffalo on the weekend to climb back into third place. But time was not on the Orioles' side. Trailing Toronto by eight-and-a-half games, the O's would have to win 23 of their final 26 and the Leafs split their remaining 22 games to edge them out for the pennant. The six-time defending champs' pennant hopes were clinging by the thinnest of threads.

CHAPTER 30
THE ORIOLES
LIMP INTO TOWN

THE GROWTH OF RADIO IN THE FIRST HALF OF THE 1920S HAD BEEN modest, at best. Few homes had one, mainly because the setup, involving large batteries and an antenna array, was as unsightly as it was expensive. The batteries also tended to leak, needed frequent recharging, and produced a hum that was louder than the radio itself.

Edward Samuel Rogers was a Toronto born-and-raised son of a wealthy local businessman. Young Ted, as he was known, was obsessed with radio communications from an early age. At 13, he was recognized in the *Toronto Telegram* for receiving a telegraph report from Cape Cod on his home receiver about a shipwreck off the coast of Ireland. When he was 21, Rogers became the first Canadian amateur to send a radio signal across the Atlantic Ocean.

Rogers attended the University of Toronto from 1919 to 21 but left early to pursue a career as a radio engineer. One of his first jobs in the industry was to help the *Star* set up their radio station, CFCA ("Canada First Covers America"), and designing the *Toronto Star* Radio Car, a custom-built truck with its own wave coil antenna, receiving set, and large amplified speaker. The Radio Car, the only one of its kind in Canada, was driven by Rogers to parks and beaches in the city, where crowds would gather to listen to CFCA programming.

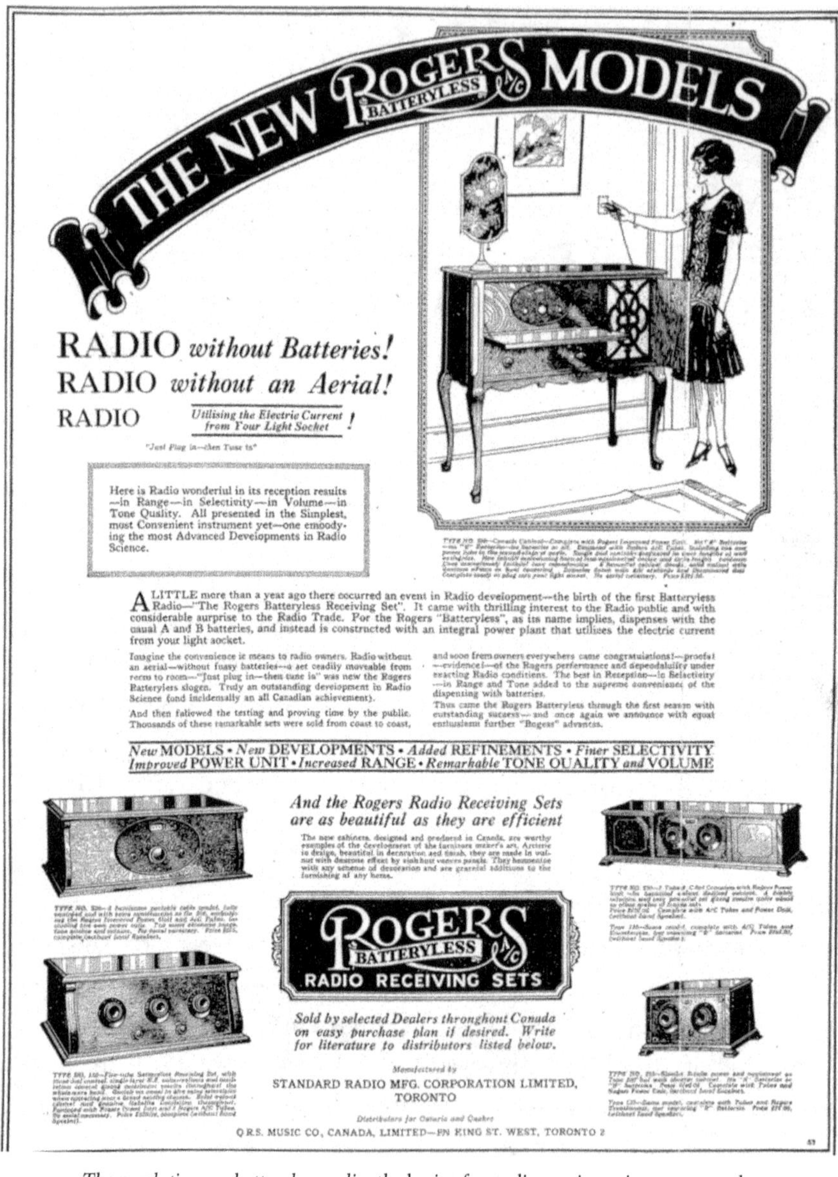

The revolutionary batteryless radio, the basis of a media empire so important to the Toronto baseball scene.

While on a visit to the labs of Westinghouse, then a major radio manufacturer based in Pittsburgh, Rogers saw the prototypes of a vacuum tube that would run on alternating current—the form of electricity now standard in all homes. He obtained the patent for some of these tubes and set to work on them when he returned home. Within a year, Rogers had produced his first batteryless radio; with the help of his father, he founded the Rogers Batteryless Radio, the first in the world that ran on regular household current.

Production of both the Rogers Batteryless and an adaptor for non-Rogers radios began in June, 1925, over a year before competitors' models in the United States. Rogers set up a display at the Exhibition the following year, attracting large crowds. Even though a Rogers set cost $260 (roughly three months' wages for the average Canadian worker), sales were brisk, and Ted Rogers' company—Standard Radio Manufacturing—gave birth to what would become a multimedia empire. And one day, a big-league Toronto ballclub would play in a stadium that bears his family's name two blocks to the east of where Maple Leaf Stadium once stood.

And as fans were getting ready for single Leafs-Orioles games on the Thursday and Friday heading into the Labour Day weekend, along with a Saturday doubleheader and maybe a trip to Sunnyside or The Ex, the Toronto papers carried a story of a 75-year-old woman who accidentally stepped off a train traveling 40 mph in Northern Ontario, and survived. A woman identified as Mrs. MacKenzie of Ottawa apparently walked off of the moving harvester train near Nakina, a railway community five hours northeast of Fort William, now part of modern-day Thunder Bay.

The conductor noticed her missing, and a frantic search aboard the train ensued. Fearing the worst, section men were sent out in either direction along the railway right-of-way to search for her. "They expected to find her dead," read the article on the front page of Friday's *Star*. Shortly after dawn, MacKenzie was found "lying in a muskeg," with a cut on her head, injured shoulder, and suffering from fatigue, but "still living." Nonetheless, she "greeted her rescuers cheerfully," as she was rushed onto a special train for treatment at the Nakina hospital.[1]

Perhaps a story about a woman who nearly tragically stepped off a moving train in the middle of the country would be an odd choice of front-page coverage on one of the nation's leading daily newspapers. Such a story showed the intense competition in the Toronto market. "If it bleeds, it ledes," was apparently standard for newspapers in the 1920s. All four city dailies featured similar sensationalistic stories on their front pages on almost a daily basis.

The Orioles limped into Toronto very much like a team that was out of contention, dropping the first two games of the series to fall into fourth place, 10 games back of the Leafs. The pair of victories gave Toronto an incredible 30 wins in its last 34 games. Baltimore's Dunn, who Toronto papers had few good things to say about and made for a good Snidely Whiplash-like villain, was quite charitable toward the Leafs.

"Toronto has a good ball club, and deserves a pennant," he told the *Star*. "I thought until last week that our team might come back to its old-time form (and we haven't been playing such bad ball, either), but we have no chance to win now." With his team's historic pennant streak coming to an end, Dunn was asked what happened to his team. "Well, I guess we've been winning too often and can't go on forever. I wish the Leafs the best of luck in the post-season series....I guess that will give some of the fans a laugh, but it's genuine, and I mean it."[2]

The crowd for Saturday's doubleheader was expected to be of the record variety, but rain washed out both ends—Leaf fans were hoping for a sweep, which would tie their season series with Baltimore. On Labour Day, over 9,000 fans watched the morning game of a scheduled doubleheader between the Leafs and Bisons, who moved in for a four-game series; 16,000 more attended the afternoon game, as the teams split the pair of games. It was indeed a heady time in Toronto. Both the *Star* and the *Globe* were devoting increased column space to accounts and analysis of Leaf games. More and more fans were tuning in to the broadcasts of the game on the *Star*'s CFCA; bags full of mail from appreciative listeners poured into the newsroom. L.W. Frood of Eden Mills, a hamlet west of the city, wrote, "That's what we call real entertainment, and in this small village we have as many as sixty listeners to every game, and they never leave until the last man is out."[3]

And in a city with big-league ambitions, talk of a third Major League fueled aspirations. "Thanks to Messrs. Solman, Dunn, and Dan Howley," penned Hewitt in his column the day after Labour Day, "the Queen City is once again back on the baseball map, and any plans in connection with the formation of a third major league would not be complete unless Toronto is given the highest consideration."[4] With the Yankees coming for an exhibition game at the end of the week, baseball interest and optimism was at an all-time high in the city.

Buffalo provided little opposition for the final two games of the series, appearing to save most of their combativeness for the umpires in a 16-0 drubbing in the final game—the Leafs' 100th victory. Slow Motion Doyle tossed a ten-inning complete-game gem in the series' third game, a 2-1 Leaf win. Doyle had become the club's most consistent starter during their torrid run, not having lost a start in six weeks. President Solman, with an eye toward the next season, reached an agreement with the Boston Red Sox for Cleo Carlyle, who would join the American League club the following year. On the downside, Otis Lawry, who had provided a great spark to the Leafs' attack, was struck by a line drive in pregame batting practice, and Howley was said to be concerned about the severity of the injury.

After a listless 5-0 loss to Rochester, Toronto hosted the mighty Yankees in an exhibition game on Friday, September 10. With both teams well out in front of their respective standings, the prospects for an entertaining game were slim. Both managers were content to let their regulars play only the first few innings before emptying their respective benches. Yankees' slugger Babe Ruth, whose last at bat in Toronto resulted in a home run when he played for Jack Dunn's Providence farm club, played first base and did not go deep in his return to the lakefront, managing only an infield hit in two trips to the plate. After the game, the Babe entertained a huge line of kids seeking his autograph. The next day was a Saturday doubleheader against Rochester, which the Leafs swept as both the Exhibition and their Maple Leaf Stadium schedule were winding down. No other ball games would be played at Maple Leaf Stadium that year, unless they were playoff contests, which seemed all but assured.

CHAPTER 31
TORONTO CLINCHES

The Maple Leafs clinched their first International League pennant with a Sunday, Sept. 12 doubleheader sweep of the Bisons in Buffalo. Former Bison Clarence Fisher shut down his old team over six shutout innings in the nightcap, securing at least a tie for the league title. The win was somewhat anticlimactic, as the outcome had not been in doubt for several weeks, and the twin-bill sweep extended Toronto's lead over second-place Newark to 11.5 games. From August 4 until September 3, the team had won an incredible 30 of 33 games, largely leaving the competition in the dust. A *Globe* editorial praised the Leafs:

"The series of triumphs by the Leafs has been a demonstration of marvellous skill and efficiency....The achievement of the Leafs reflects not just credit not only on themselves, but on Toronto and Canada generally, and the public of the Dominion acclaims their victory as good business and good ball."[1]

Voters went to the polls in the federal election the next day, September 14, and the electorate greeted the third such vote in the past five years with a collective yawn. Just under 67 percent of eligible voters exercised their franchise, a slight increase over the election a year earlier. The *Globe* threw their support behind the Liberals while the *Star*, clearly leaning toward the Conservatives, seemed resigned to the fact that the Liberals might win a majority (something perhaps causing modern readers to raise an eyebrow.) The *Star* did run a full-page story on page four, complete with photos, about four runaway freight cars that smashed into a streetcar in the city's east end. The car was full of passengers on their way home from The Exhibition. Two motor vehicles were severely damaged as well. Nine people were sent to hospital; luckily, there was no loss of life.

Baltimore and Newark Managers
—Dunn Lauds Howley and Toronto Hurlers—
Say Leafs Will Win Minor Series

(Special Despatch to The Globe.)

Baltimore, Md., Sept. 12.—Two managers of the International League praised Manager Dan Howley and his Toronto players late this afternoon when they heard that Toronto had made sure of the pennant by defeating Buffalo in two games. They were Jack Dunn, manager of the seven-time champion Orioles, and Fred Burchell, whose Newark team twice took a fall out of the Birds this afternoon.

Dunn declared that the Leafs were a team that any other would find hard to beat, and while dispirited at the recent poor showing of his hirelings, he was quick to give praise to the team which dimmed his vision of an eighth successive pennant. Discussing Toronto's victory, Dunn said:

"Let Dan Howley know that his team was too good to beat and that he handled his players in great fashion. His pitchers knew how to hurl, and the team had plenty of spirit as well as skill. We lost because we did not play well enough to win. The Leafs won because they were trying all the time, and that kind of baseball is the kind I like.

"No matter whether it is Louisville or Milwaukee that Toronto plays in the junior series, put Toronto down as the winner. Howley can send pitchers against them who will make their batters look cheap, and he has enough batting strength to score the runs he needs. The fielding should be O.K., too.

"While I would have liked to again win, I have nothing but congratulations for Toronto. The Orioles will be a different looking team next year, and I'll be in the pennant fight again."

Manager Burchell when informed that Toronto had made the pennant chase successfully, had nothing but good words for the team. He said:

"Toronto stuck to the pace and refused to slump. They will win by a big margin, and they deserve all the honors the fans can give them. I understand that Jack Dunn picks Toronto to win the Junior Series. Put me down as entertaining the same opinion. The Toronto pitching staff will turn the tide."

Toronto Globe, *Sept. 13, 1926.*

Mackenzie King had effectively campaigned against Lord Byng, the outgoing British-appointed Governor General, rather than his chief opponent, Conservative Arthur Meighen. King realized that he would not likely gain a majority of seats, so he enlisted the support of the Progressive and Liberal-Progressive parties to form another minority government. King's Liberals even agreed not to run candidates in some of their minority partners' ridings.

"Whether it is the closeness of the election to the preceding one a year ago, or the Exhibition, or the astounding pennant climb of the Leafs baseball team, is not readily apparent,"[2] said the *Globe* in trying to explain voter apathy a week prior to the election, as the turnout of 67 percent may have been more reflective of Canadians wearying of going to the polls for the third time in five years. Meighen's Conservatives defeated the Liberals in terms of ridings—232 to 208—but they did not have enough seats for a majority. Meighen lost his own riding, compounding matters for the Conservatives. Despite Toronto's growing multicultural demographics, a quarter of its citizens were born in the United Kingdom, and they voted overwhelmingly Tory— King's Liberals did not win a single Toronto seat.

Meighen's minority did not last a nonconfidence vote held shortly after the election, and King was returned to power. It was not a commanding electoral win, but King's strategy paid off. In his return to the Prime Minister's office, he continued Canada's push to loosen its British ties. Shortly after his return, King expanded Canada's Department of External Affairs and appointed the first Canadian-born ambassador, Vincent Massey. The scion of a wealthy farm equipment manufacturing family,[3] Massey took a turn at running the family business, but turned to politics when he found himself unsuited to corporate life. Massey was a lifelong friend of King's, later becoming the first Canadian-born Governor General of the country. The Massey family also built a concert hall in downtown Toronto in the 1890s that still stands today, known worldwide for its architecture and acoustics.

Howley would have a bit of challenge on his hands keeping his regulars sharp. The International League season would conclude on September 19. Louisville had already clinched the American Association crown, but their season would run a week longer. Certainly, Howley could use the final days of the regular season to give his core members some much-needed rest. Solman and Howley began to arrange some exhibition games to keep the Leafs sharp once the season ended. One such contest was scheduled for September 25 in Toronto, and one the following day in Montreal. Toronto's opposition would be an all-star team from the highly competitive amateur Ontario Intercounty League.

Maple Leaf Stadium after opening and development in the area. (City of Toronto Archives.)

CHAPTER 32

RUMOURS ABOUT HOWLEY'S FUTURE BEGIN

While the Leafs were in Buffalo, dates were being finalized for the Junior World Series, pitting the winners of the International League and American Association in a best-of-nine series. The series would begin on Tuesday, September 28, and the first five games would be played in Toronto. If games were necessary after that, the series would shift to Louisville. With the pennant salted away, Howley left the Leafs for Detroit to firm up deals for next year's team. This time around, with Steve O'Neill (who usually managed the club in Howley's absence) sent home to Cleveland to rest up for the playoffs, Howley left Flash Gilhooley in charge of the team. The veteran had managerial aspirations, and an International League rival had approached Lol Solman about acquiring him to run their team earlier in the season. Solman and Howley took the proposal to Gilhooley, who was not ready to give up playing and turned it down.

Toronto finished up the regular season with series in Syracuse and Rochester, sweeping the latter in a Sunday doubleheader on the final day. Howley used his bench in the final week of the season but was itching to get his regulars some action. In addition to the games against the Intercounty All Stars, Howley arranged an exhibition game at Maple Leaf Stadium against a team composed of players from Buffalo, Syracuse, and Rochester's rosters. The dates for the Little

World Series were changed slightly; now only the first four games would be played in Toronto. Louisville put forth a proposal to add three players to their postseason roster, a move Howley and Solman immediately protested. In the past, this was a regular practice—Baltimore added Toronto slugger Eddie Onslow just the year before to replace an injured player. In the *Star*, Charlie Good claimed, "Howley likes his team too well to make any changes in personnel at this stage."[1]

One change Howley did make was the reinsertion of a finally healthy Andy Harrington into the lineup. Otis Lawry's return date was still unknown, so Howley put Harrington at second, hoping his bat would give the batting order a boost. The day after the Leafs closed out their season with the Sunday doubleheader at Buffalo, they were back in Ontario in Brantford for their first tilt with the Buff/Syr/Roch Selects. The games would give Howley a chance to get Harrington some work to shake off the rust while giving some of his sparingly used pitchers some innings.

Army of Boxing Enthusiasts Takes Philadelphia by Storm

City of Brotherly Love Overrun With Fans—Crowd of 132,000 Expected—Dempsey Favored to Beat Tunney Tonight — Is He the Dempsey of Old?

Toronto Globe, September 23, 1926.

The biggest story of the week in the sports world, by far, was the World Heavyweight Championship bout between title holder Jack Dempsey and challenger Gene Tunney in Philadelphia. The 1920s were called the Golden Age of Sports, and there was no bigger star than Dempsey. He was bigger than Babe Ruth, football star Red Grange, tennis champion Bill Tilden, hockey star Howie Morenz, or golfer Bobby Jones. He was by far the largest drawing card and most popular athletic celebrity of his time.

Dempsey, the "Manassa Mauler," was a former bar fighter who first won the heavyweight title in 1919, knocking out defending champion Jess Willard despite giving up six inches in height and 80 pounds of weight to the titleholder. Dempsey was, according to famed *New York Times* sportswriter Red Smith, "187 pounds of unbridled violence."[2] Despite his smaller stature, Dempsey was a slugger, with the most feared right hand in all the sport. His victory over Willard and several subsequent successful title defences against much-heralded opponents vaulted Dempsey into icon status. The list of vaunted opponents did not include boxers of colour; Willard, on the other hand, won his first title over Black champion, Jack Johnson.

After retaining his belt against Argentinian contender Luis Angel Firpo in 1923, Dempsey spurned all challengers for three years. He found there was much money to be made in performing in exhibition matches, endorsing products, and starring in movies. It was said that Dempsey had gone Hollywood, although there may have been an understandable reason for his time away from the ring. His younger brother, desperate to make it as a movie star himself, was also a drug addict, and Dempsey likely moved to California to help look after him and his young family.

Tunney was definitely the underdog. The former World War I Marine had been steadily working his way up the boxing ranks. In 1921, he took a job as lumberjack in northern Ontario for lumber baron J.R. Booth's company.* He revealed his real name and identity to no one. According to the *Globe*, he wanted, "the solitude and the strenuous labors of the woods to help condition himself for the career that appeared before him."[3] Tunney was unusual for his day as a heavyweight boxer: rather than station himself in the middle of the

---

* Booth was a wealthy Ottawa timber and railroad tycoon. At one time, he was the largest lumber producer in the world and was said to control an area of timber rights larger than France.

ring and slug it out with his opponent, he relied on moving around the ring, using his footwork and jab to find weaknesses.

Over 120,000 tickets were sold, making the bout easily the largest sporting event in history. Big-league games were rescheduled to accommodate fans, and at least 1,000 Toronto fans, by Hewitt's estimate, made the trek to Pennsylvania either by automobile or one of the extra Pullman cars the railways added to their regular United States run.

The hype surrounding the event began to gather steam as early as mid-August, when over 2,000 fans attended a Tunney sparring session, while on the same day a thousand people paid one dollar each to watch Dempsey train. *The New York Times* published 75 articles on fight preparations in the weeks leading up to the fight.

Dignitaries such as the mayors of both New York City and Philadelphia, the Pennsylvania Governor (and those of several surrounding states), millionaires, and the U.S. Secretary of the Navy watched the fight in the pouring rain, and many more millions of people around the world followed the bout on radio or by telegraph.

Tunney danced around Dempsey for the whole match, getting numerous jabs to the champ's upper body and head. It was said that Dempsey landed only one hard punch. The bout lasted the full ten rounds, but there was no doubt about who had won. Tunney was the winner on all three judges' cards, a unanimous decision.

The defending champion came home bloody and blue, which so alarmed his wife that she asked what on earth had happened. "Honey," Dempsey replied, "I forgot to duck."[4]

With little to write about on the baseball front in the week between the end of the International League season and the Little World Series, both Wilson of the *Globe* and Good of the *Star* tackled the rumours of Howley's departure for greener managerial pastures. From various points across the United States, wrote Wilson, "reports are constantly emanating that Dan Howley of the Leafs will take over the leadership of the Detroit Tigers next season." Howley, Wilson said, "vehemently denies these rumours whenever he hears them." Furthermore, Wilson stated that Howley "...has not been approached by the

Detroit owners, has not made, and will not make, an effort to get the management of the Tigers or any other team, and will be manager of the Leafs next season if he wants the job."[5]

Meanwhile, Good wrote that rumours were circulating about another skipper coming in to take over in Toronto, as Howley's departure was viewed by many as imminent. "The latest product of the rumor factory comes from Jersey City, and Pat Donovan's name is attached to it." The rumour, according to Good, that Donovan—a long-time minor-league manager—"threw up his job as manager of the Black Cats in disgust," and he was being considered for the Toronto job. Good dismissed those reports as figments of some Jersey City sportswriter's imagination. "Howley," Good wrote, "with much vehemence asservates that he has no intention of cutting loose from the Leafs."[6]

With the baseball and lacrosse (the Mann Cup final for the senior championship of the nation, featuring Toronto's Weston Weston-men, was being contested) seasons winding down, rugby football was gearing up, and hockey training camps not far behind. Hewitt complained about this seasonal overlap. "If the schedule makers are wise," he suggested in his column, "they will curtail their seasons in future years so as to prevent conflicts with other more seasonal sports." The National Hockey League did not consult with Hewitt, doubling the length of their season from mid-November to April, as the league was growing by leaps and bounds. "The 'ironmen' of the game will be the star pro players this season," was his only response.[7]

In preparation for the series opener, the Leafs were to play a game against the Selects at Maple Leaf Stadium the Saturday prior, with the Toronto players getting the proceeds from ticket sales—but rain unfortunately canceled the contest. As late as the day before the first game, there was talk of the series winner heading west to take on the Pacific Coast League champs. Wilson had written earlier that if the Los Angeles Angels took the PCL title, the series would most defi-nitely take place. But Oakland took over top spot for a few weeks, and according to Wilson, interest from the IL waned, because "Oakland is not a good ball town," and "a series there would be an almost certain financial bust."[8]

For the series, both teams were limited to rosters of 20 players. Howley decided that Harrington was not quite ready, so his name was left off, as was Conacher's. Louisville had made this trip to the Junior World Series the season before, losing to Baltimore. Both the *Globe* and *Star* indicated the day before the first game that Howley was uncertain about his starting pitcher. Nineteen-game-winner Wally Stewart had been Toronto's best pitcher all season (Owen Carroll had won more games, but faded in the second half), but Jess Doyle had been the team's hottest starter since that Syracuse doubleheader sweep.

While baseball fans were getting ready for the series, businessmen in Toronto were more than concerned about auto manufacturer Henry Ford's decision to go from a six- to a five-day work week and doubling employee wages. Ford felt that his assembly line workers would be more productive with a shorter week, and with their increased leisure time, demand for his cars might increase. But several business owners the *Star* talked to were not convinced.

"LOCAL INDUSTRIAL CHIEFS DO NOT APPROVE FIVE-DAY WEEK," blared the front-page headline. E.C. Fox, president of a local pork-packing firm, said it would not work with perishable goods, like his business was engaged in. "Even under present conditions, a Sunday and holiday together seriously interfere with operations," Fox told the paper. "I don't believe the five-day week can be adopted by industry generally, certainly not the milling industry," said D.A. Campbell, general manager of Maple Leaf Milling. "We can't compete with the milling industry of other countries, unless these huge plants, involving a large capital investment, are kept running day and night, for six days a week." While Campbell said he was generally in favour of Ford's move and felt that workers should share in their company's prosperity, too much rest and relaxation time was not necessarily a good thing. "Man is born to work, and there is danger in excess leisure for any of us." C.L. Burton, first vice-president of retail giant Simpsons, was not keen on the idea either, saying that a five-day week would not apply well to the department-store industry. While he too expressed some support for Ford's efforts, he dismissed it as a "very interesting social experiment." Burton saw Canada's mission was "to people our country with the greatest number of the best settlers available." He too seemed to think idle hands are the devil's playground. "It was Mr. Burton's opinion," summarized the *Star*, "that the danger today is the tendency for people to use their leisure time more for amusement or physical or mental improvement." Burton felt "inclined to have doubts about workmen coming back from extended leisure time very much more keen for their work and able to produce in very noticeably large quantities."

The last word on the five-day work week subject belonged to T.A. Russell, president of automaker Willys-Overland. "I don't think the five day work week will spread to other automobile companies," he informed the *Star*.[9]

CHAPTER 33
THE SERIES OPENS

> ## SCANNING THE SPORT FIELD
> ### (By FREDERICK WILSON, Sports Editor of The Globe.)
>
> #### THE LEAFS' OPPONENTS.
>
> Statistics may be quoted to show the strength of the Louisville Colonels, who open the Junior World Series against the Leafs here today—they hit .309 as a team, and are strong defensively—but it is only necessary to point out that they established a remarkable record this season by beating every other team in the American Association in a majority of the games played against those teams throughout the league season. That does not happen often. The Colonels have been through the World Series mill too, which will be something in their favor, but it should be remembered that the champion Leafs are the strongest outfit the International League has boasted for years. Pitching is the thing in a short series, and the Howleys have nine fine flingers all ready for any kind of battle.

Toronto Globe, *September 28, 1926.*

"It is the Leafs' speed and power against our hitting power in this series," Louisville manager Bill Meyer told Mike Rodden of the *Globe.* And indeed it was the Colonels' bats that propelled them to the American Association pennant. The "quiet, earnest pilot," as the *Globe* described him, said that other than a few bumps and bruises, his team was in good shape and ready to go.[1] "The Colonels have been through the World Series mill, too," Wilson of the *Globe* observed, "but it should be remembered that the champion Leafs are the strongest outfit the International League has boasted for years."[2]

International League president J. Conway Toole drew comparisons to the Tunney-Dempsey fight of the week before in his series prediction in Hewitt's column:

"You know what the marine did to Jack; well, that's what I expect the Leafs to do to Louisville. What good is a punch when you can't get it over? The Toronto team is the best defensive aggregation I ever saw; the pitchers, in my opinion, are the best in the minors and I can't see anything but a victory for the International League representatives in this series."[3]

On paper, the Series appeared to be a close matchup. Under player-manager Meyer, the defending American Association champs Colonels finished with a 105-62 record, eight games ahead of second-place Indianapolis. Louisville had a potent attack, led by veteran catcher Al DeVormer (.368 batting average), outfielder Earl Webb (.333 average, 18 HRs), SS Clarke "Pinky" Pittenger (.312 average), 2B Bruno Betzel (.322 average), and 1B/OF Joe Guyon (.343 average). The Colonels' pitching rotation featured four starters with double-digit win totals, led by 39-year-old Nick Cullop (20-8 won-loss record), Ben Tincup (18-7), Joe Dawson (17-7), and Joe DeBerry (17-13). Meyer took over the club after future Hall of Famer Joe McCarthy was hired to manage the Chicago Cubs after the 1925 season.

Prior to the first game, the visiting Colonels arrived in town too late to get a workout in, but were still able to tour Maple Leaf Stadium, and "expressed themselves as being delighted with the park."[4] Louisville manager Meyer felt his team was the favourite because they had captured the American Association crown, "which according to his view, (was) a much stronger organization than the International."[5]

There was considerable speculation as to whom Howley would give the ball to start the Series. Owen Carroll had led the team with 21 wins, but his 120 bases on balls was far and away the highest total on the team. Under such an intense spotlight, Howley was probably concerned that a case of the jitters might be felt by the young starter. Lefty Stewart went 18-9 and was a candidate as well. Jess Doyle went 15-7 after his demotion to Toronto and was easily the Leafs' best starter over the final week of the season. Louisville had some pop from the right side, so Howley was likely leaning toward Doyle.

Louisville would counter with either Nick Cullop or Ben Tincup. Cullop had won 57 games for four big-league teams in the 1910s, but last pitched in the bigs in 1917. He won 42 games for the Colonels between 1925 and 1926. Tincup was a member of the Oklahoma Cherokee nation and was one of two indigenous Colonels; the other, Joe Guyon, hailed from the White Earth Reservation in Minnesota.* Tincup pitched briefly in the bigs with the Phillies, but like Cullop had been a minor leaguer for most of his career. Howley's batting order probably didn't strike a lot of fear into Louisville manager Meyer, but the betting was that if he went with southpaw Cullop, Howley would replace Cleo Carlyle in the lineup with Tillie Walker.

The series would attract a considerable radio audience on both sides of the border. The *Star's* CFCA would jointly broadcast the games with competitor CKCL (later to become CKEY, owned by future Leafs owner Jack Kent Cooke, who would go on to much greater fame and fortune in the United States). Louisville had set up a unique experience for fans in the Kentucky city. The games would be carried on local station WHAS; for those who wanted a more real-life view of the game, the Colonels' ballpark and two semi-pro teams were enlisted. "The 'radiogame,'" explained the *Louisville Courier-Journal*, "is a means whereby two teams at Parkway Field, each equipped with ear-phones will reproduce every play of the games at Toronto, so that the fans will see each inning enacted before their eyes, practically simultaneously with the Toronto contests."[6] No detail was too small to be overlooked in this re-creation. "Umpires and even bat boys will be supplied," added the *Courier-Journal* after a "rehearsal" the day before the first game. Newspapers in big-league cities had

---

* Guyon had played in Toronto before as a football player for Jim Thorpe's famous Carlisle Indians.

gone to great lengths to re-create World Series games over the past few decades. Fans would gather outside the newspaper offices to hear updates given regularly by an employee with a megaphone, who would relay results from a telegraph operator. Later, major papers erected large sign boards with a baseball diamond on them, and results would be posted with operators manipulating "runners" circling the bases. The Louisville re-creation was certainly among the most creative.

With Lawry's status still uncertain, there was talk that the Leafs—despite earlier objections—would ask permission to use Anderson of Buffalo in his place at second. "Nothing doing," Howley told reporters. "If we can't win with the players we have, I don't want to win at all."[7] Lawry's improved health likely had much to do with Howley's stance.

Meanwhile, plans for a series with the Pacific Coast champs were beginning to unravel. Howley indicated that his team would not make the trip unless his players agreed to it, and there was some doubt as to whether that would happen or not.

On the Louisville side, the team was healthy apart from catcher Al DeVormer. The former Yankees backup backstop had developed a serious staph infection on the back of his neck, and the team reluctantly stopped in Detroit to drop DeVormer off for surgery on the offending carbuncle. The Colonels' train continued across the border minus their catcher; manager Meyer told the press he was hopeful DeVormer would be available later in the series. His loss would be potentially a huge one.

It was a glorious time to be a Toronto sports pages reader. In addition to the Leafs and Colonels, the Yankees and Cardinals had both clinched their respective pennants, and the *Star* was full of analysis. Babe Ruth would be playing in his seventh World Series, more than any other player at the time. Amateur baseball playoffs were winding up in Ontario, and there was plenty of coverage. Football season in Canada was well underway, and the amateur lacrosse championships were wrapping up. Also, the NHL had just wrapped up their meetings, and with the dissolution of the Western Hockey League and the addition of several U.S.-based franchises, there was plenty of hockey news even though training camps were a month away from opening.

"Not always is the best baseball played in the postseason, majors or minors," Wilson led off the *Globe*'s coverage. "Yesterday's opening contest between the Leafs and Louisville was as fine a sample of baseball as a fan could ask for."[8] Jess Doyle kept Louisville hitters constantly off balance with his repertoire of curveballs and change-ups, and the Leafs rode their two strengths—pitching and defence—to a 2-0 victory in the opening game. With the sun shining brightly on Toronto harbour beyond the outfield wall, Louisville hitters claimed they had trouble tracking Doyle's pitches. "Any old excuse, etc etc," replied Good in the *Star*.[9]

Catcher DeVormer was a surprise starter for the visitors. Physicians in Detroit, where he was treated, said on Monday that the backstop would be out until the second game on Thursday at the earliest, but he managed to make his way to Toronto for the opener.

Louisville loaded the bases in the first inning, but Doyle got out of the jam. Ten of his outs came on flyballs, likely providing evidence of Maple Leaf Stadium's pitcher-friendly dimensions. Toronto scored a run in the fourth when Frank Gilhooley and Bill Mullen singled and were moved over by Otis Lawry's sacrifice bunt. Cleo Carlyle then plated Gilhooley with a sacrifice fly. Doyle helped his own cause with an RBI single the next inning. Otis Miller was singled out for a pair of outstanding defensive plays at shortstop. The reporter calling the games for local radio was stationed on top of the grandstand to deliver play-by-play for fans across southern Ontario and western New York. The unnamed announcer (likely Hewitt's son, Foster, who would go on to fame as the voice of Hockey Night In Canada*) described his view to his audience. "In front of me," he told his listeners, according to the *Star*'s daily radio column, "is the western gap, to my left the bay, and to the right the lake. All this water is as calm as a

---

* Hewitt had started calling hockey games for the *Star*'s CFCA three years earlier. In 1925, he and his father made what was believed to be the first ever radio broadcast of a horse race. With Edward Rogers' new radio innovation, the *Star* broadcast all manner of sporting events, with the younger Hewitt often at the microphone.

millpond."[10] Attendance was expected to reach 10,000 but was barely half that.

Leaf fans were able to get home in plenty of time for dinner, as the game was "played in an hour and sixteen minutes, snappily, without an error by either side," penned Wilson in the *Globe*.[11] His colleague Rodden wrote, "'Jess' Doyle was at his best. Nothing more be said." Rodden also was disappointed with the small turnout of fans, noting, "It was very disappointing to the owners and the players not to see a golden harvest at the turn-stiles." [12]

The *Courier-Journal* reporter covering the series in Toronto was not impressed after a breeze coming in off the lake dropped the game time temperature of 16°C (60°F) to 5°C (41°F) by game's end. "Whipped to refrigeration by one of Lake Ontario's choicest nor'westers," he wrote, "the Colonels of Louisville, champions of the American Association, were humiliated by the Maple Leafs of Toronto, International League gonfalon winners."[13] Adding to the disappointment for Louisville fans, a torrential Kentucky downpour cancelled the re-creation at Parkway Field.

CHAPTER 34
GAME TWO: AN EXTRA-INNING RALLY

Cullop vs. Carroll In Second Game of Series at Stadium

If Manager Meyer of the Colonels sends Cullop, his star lefthander into the box this afternoon, Tilly Walker will replace Carlyle in right field.

President J. Conway Toole of the International League was greatly elated over the Leafs' win but much disappointed over the smallness of the crowd.

When the Colonels filled the bases in the first inning it looked bad for Doyle, but he refused to lose his composure and easily disposed of Cotter.

Toronto Star, *September 29, 1926.*

HOWLEY SURPRISED FANS AND EXPERTS ALIKE WHEN HE DECIDED TO GO with Owen Carroll in the second game. Lefty Stewart had arguably been Toronto's best starter over the second half. Perhaps after a day of flailing at Doyle's soft offerings, Howley felt that Carroll's fastball would continue to throw off the timing of the Louisville hitters. No doubt he would have the hook ready if Carroll faltered early; Howley's nine-man staff, except for Jess Doyle, was well-rested.

Game Two was another classic, perhaps the most exciting game of the series. Carroll's fastball was blazing; he struck out four Colonels through three innings, then fanned the first two in the fourth. With two strikes on the next hitter, Carroll was one pitch away from getting out of the inning. Behind the plate, Steve O'Neill put down the sign for a curve on the outer half of the plate, but Carroll crossed him up, his fastball sailing inside. The Louisville hitter swung and missed, but so did O'Neill, who missed the pitch as it bounced to the back-stop, allowing the runner to reach first. Carroll next gave up a double, scoring the runner from first, and then an RBI single to stake the visitors to a 2-0 lead.

On the other side, Nick Cullop, the Louisville pitcher, was shutting down the Leafs. Carroll, according to Good of the *Star*, did not break down despite his shaky inning. "He kept his feet on the ground, and his head in the air," wrote Good, "and although in several tough spots after that managed to escape unscathed."[1] Good was likely referring to the ninth, when the Colonels, still up 2-0, had runners on second and third with no outs. But Carroll got out of the jam as the Leafs came up to bat in the home half of the ninth.

Many of the Leafs' victories during the season were of the come-from-behind variety, and the ninth set the stage for that. With one out, Lena Styles (who had replaced Mickey Heath at first base earlier as a pinch runner) singled, and Toronto had life. The next hitter, O'Neill, hit a line drive to second. The Louisville second baseman snagged the ball and tried to double off Styles, who had strayed too far from first, but hit Styles in the back with his throw. Carroll was up next, normally a situation for a pinch hitter. But Carroll was one of the Leafs' better hitting pitchers, and Howley showed faith in his hurler; Carroll rewarded Howley's belief in him by beating out a slow roller to third. The home side was down to its final out, but the top of the order was coming up. Frank Gilhooley, the leadoff hitter, hit a dribbler to the right side of the infield. Both the Louisville first and second basemen tried to field the ball; the latter scooped it up, but the former was too far from the bag, and the speedy Gilhooley raced across the bag safely. Toronto now had Bill Mullen—hitless on the day—up to bat. He singled to left, scoring both Styles and Carroll to tie the game. Lawry was unable to keep the inning going, and the two teams headed to extra innings.

Carroll gave up a one-out double but otherwise shut down the Colonels in the tenth. The Leafs loaded the bases with two out in the bottom half of the inning, but Carroll fanned to end the threat. Howley, not content to turn things over to the bullpen, sent Carroll back out for the eleventh, and he set Louisville down in order. In the Leafs' turn at bat, Lawry singled with two out, and Carlyle reached on an error by the Colonels second baseman. The mistake would prove fatal a few pitches later when Herman Layne laced a single to right, scoring Otis Lawry from second. Toronto had a 3-2 walk-off win, and a 2-0 lead in the series. It was a classic Howley triumph, led by pitching, defence, and small ball. Carroll fanned 13 hitters, and Good of the *Star* wrote, "If ever a twirler deserved to win any game, the twirler from Holy Cross University was entitled to capture this one."[2]

Once again, the *Courier-Journal* "Special Correspondent" was not impressed. "For eight innings the Colonels played superb ball behind the spectacular pitching of Norman A. Cullop," he observed. "After that they played like nine old maids. Poor fielding by Shanks and Betzel led to the heart-sickening defeat."[3] Good, in his account in the *Star*, said that the Colonels lost because "they didn't play smart baseball."[4]

Despite the beautiful weather and exciting baseball, attendance was once again underwhelming, with a crowd of about 5,000 on hand. A diehard fan wrote to Hewitt about the small crowds, and Hewitt ran it in his column:

What is the matter with the so-called sporting fraternity? Baseball fans have squawked for years for a park on the city side. They have it—one

of the finest plants in operation. They've wanted a pennant winner...
they have it now, and incidentally one of the best teams seen in the
minor leagues in some time...and now, after lukewarm support all
season, they turn it down cold....The odd thing is, when the team was
down, there were about fifty thousand knockers. Now that is on top,
where are all the boosters?[5]

After all the high expectations raised by the new ballpark, the
Maple Leafs finished third in International League attendance with
221,846 total fans, behind Newark (274,099) and Buffalo (241,013).
Still, Toronto more than doubled 1925's total of 115,592 fans.[6]

CHAPTER 35
GAME THREE: SORRELL SOARS

Frank Gilhooley Sending in the Tying Run

RIGHT MAN IN THE RIGHT PLACE

With the Colonels leading 1 to 0 in the fifth inning of yesterday's game Frank Gilhooley came to bat with Heath on third base and one out. It was decidedly up to him and the veteran did the needful in fine style, shooting a liner to right centre on the first pitch, which Guyon was fortunate to capture. Heath scored easily after the out.

Toronto Star, *October 1, 1926.*

THE LAST DAY OF SEPTEMBER—THE LATEST PROFESSIONAL BASEBALL HAD ever been played in the city, to anyone's recollection—saw another surprise Howley starter. Young Vic Sorrell had quietly won eight games against no losses since joining the team part way through the season, pitching very well in spot starts and relief roles in the Leafs' run to the pennant. With Louisville—whose team average of .309 led the American Association—heavy with right-handed bats, Howley decided to start right-handed Sorrell instead of the southpaw Lefty Stewart, who again may have been the logical choice to Leaf fans.

Once more, Howley made the right decision in electing to go with Sorrell. The young righty retired the first nine men in order before giving up a single run in the fourth, which the Leafs answered the following inning. The drought of runs for the visitors continued, as Sorrell retired the side in seven of the first nine innings he pitched. "Sorrell flashed a quick breaky curve," Good wrote in his postgame summary, "and a smoky one that had the opposition guessing."[1]

But runs were hard to come by for the home side as well. With one run already in thanks to a Gilhooley base hit, Sorrell himself had a chance to score the go-ahead run from second. An Otis Lawry two-out single to right field should have scored Sorrell in the fifth, but his inexperience on the bases forced him to stop at third, where he was stranded. The game headed into the ninth inning still knotted at one. Neither team could force a run across, and for the second day in a row, the game was headed to extra innings. Sorrell blanked Louisville in their half of the tenth, and when Bill Mullen led off the bottom of the frame with a base hit, Leaf fans were on their feet with the heart of the order coming up. But both Lawry and Cleo Carlyle popped out, and the game seemed destined to head to 11 innings once again. Then Herman Layne smashed a single through the left side of the Colonels' infield, and now the winning run—which would put a Leafs' stranglehold on the series—was on second. Miller drove a ball down the line that Louisville first baseman Hooks Cotter couldn't handle, and Mullen (on the move at the crack of the bat with two out) raced all the way around third and into home with the winning run.

Toronto now led the series 3-0, and even with four games coming up in Kentucky after the fourth and final contest at Maple Leaf Stadium, it would take something of a miracle for the Colonels to come back. Having scored only three runs in as many games, Louisville was clearly a frustrated lot, as Good noted in the *Star*. "Signs of dissension were in evidence yesterday," Good noted, "and they not only questioned every decision of the umpires, but yapped at one another with considerable gusto."[2] The *Courier-Journal* reporter covering the series was obviously tiring of Louisville's' lack of sharpness, noting, "The first Leaf run was another one of those little presents the Colonels have been distributing throughout the series."[3]

The Colonels had apparently planned to do some sightseeing prior to the crucial third game, but their bench boss put an end to that. "Manager Meyer had his charges out at the crack of dawn and put them through a morning workout that lasted almost until noon," reported the *Courier-Journal*. "All side trips to Niagara Falls and to other scenic spots planned by the team were called off."[4] After the workout, several players from both teams took to local golf courses; the two Colonels players of indigenous background—pitcher Ben Tincup and outfielder Joe Guyon—visited patients at the Indian Veterans Military Hospital. One has to wonder if the Colonels were really into this Series if sightseeing and getting in a round or two of golf before games were priorities.

Once again, attendance fell short of expectations—as it had all season long—and it's worth attempting to consider why. One has to wonder if the late 4 p.m. start time of the first three games persuaded many fans to either listen to the game at home, watch the updated scoreboards at various points in the downtown, or even listen on radio. With Daylight Saving Time having ended on September 19, fans from outlying parts of the city perhaps were not enamoured of the idea of returning home to a late supper in the dark. Since the streetcar line would not extend past the Maple Leaf Stadium for another year, that absence may have been a factor, as it likely had all year. The thought of walking, then standing in line waiting for the Bathurst car may have brought back memories of waiting for the island ferry home for some.

Wilson, in his column, pointed out that, "it is no easier to get to Leaf stadium, except by motor, than it was to get to the Island." With all the industrial activity along the waterfront, he suggested that "the air was better on the Island."[5] Wilson also suggested that increased ticket prices for the Series might also have forced some fans away. With a full slate of other sports running in the city at the time, there certainly were cheaper alternatives to Leaf playoff games. And while neither Wilson nor Hewitt addressed it, the Blue Laws making Sunday games an impossibility had to be a factor in the season's final attendance totals. Even though the team set a new single-season attendance record in the new stadium, the Leafs probably would have drawn more than the average crowd of 2,670 had there been games on the waterfront on the only day of the week most people had off. It would be another quarter century before Sunday baseball was allowed in Toronto (with a 6 p.m. curfew at that), in a province where Sunday shopping would not be legal until near the end of the 20th century. Finally, there was still a large contingent of fans who missed the island stadium at Hanlan's Point. Many made a day of going to a Leafs game there, partaking in the amusement park, strolling along its quiet streets, and picnicking on the shoreline, where the noise of the city was drowned out by the breaking Lake Ontario waves.

The weather does not appear to have been a factor for the Toronto portion of the series; game-time temperatures for Games Two and Three were around 14C (57F), perhaps not ideal for baseball, but still well within a northern sports fan's tolerance. No precipitation was recorded for the first three dates. Whatever the case, sportswriters were dismayed that the third game attracted only 2,900 fans; the story of the disappointing attendance was overshadowing the three exciting games that had been played.

The following day was a built-in off day in the event of rain, and the fourth and final game of the series at Maple Leaf Stadium was scheduled for 2 p.m. the day after. This gave both teams the chance to catch a special train bound for Louisville after the game. In any case, the hope was a sizable crowd would come out to watch the last Leafs' home game of the year.

CHAPTER 36
GAME FOUR: ANOTHER ONE-RUN VICTORY

A. A. Champs Must Win All of Remaining Five Tilts to Take Series

By STAFF CORRESPONDENT.

Maple Leaf Stadium, Toronto, Ontario, Oct. 2.—The Colonels of Louisville lost the fourth straight game of the series for the junior baseball championship of the world to

(Continued on Page 8.)

Louisville Courier-Journal, *October 3, 1926.*

ON THE SCHEDULED OFF-DAY ON OCTOBER 1, THE PROVINCIAL HIGH-school track and field championships (for boys only, even though women would be competing at the Olympics for the first time just two years later) were held at the stadium. The star of the meet was Harry Shanacy from the high school in Midland, a short drive from Jim Shaw's home of Port McNicoll, two hours north of the city. Shanacy defeated the Canadian high-school high-jump record holder and added a first in the javelin and another in the standing broad jump. Teammate W. Finlayson won the 100-yard dash, finishing second in the 220—quite an accomplishment for the small school.

Howley told reporters that Jess Doyle would be his Game Four starter. Doyle had won 12 decisions in a row and had thoroughly flummoxed Louisville hitters in the first game. Depending on the outcome of the games in Kentucky, this outing might be his last in a Leafs uniform. Doyle had been with the Tigers in spring training the year before, but Ty Cobb thought so little of his pitching that he was primarily used as an umpire during exhibition games. But what a difference a year made—Cobb was on his way out as manager, and the Tigers admitted his mistake by selecting Doyle in a special draft held on the day of Game Four.*

While the Leafs and Colonels were playing their fourth game, the Yankees hosted the Cardinals in front of 61,000 fans in the first game of the World Series, as veteran Grover Cleveland Alexander "unfurled the ancient power in his mighty right arm to pitch the Cardinals to victory," in the words of a wire service report.

On the field in Toronto, the biggest crowd of the series (just over 7,000) watched the Leafs take another one-run victory, 4-3. Doyle faltered in the fifth inning, giving up three runs and the only hits the visitors would muster all day. Howley didn't hesitate to summon a well-rested Clarence Fisher from the bullpen, and he shut the door the rest of the way. Down a run after the three-run outburst by the Colonels, the Leafs tied the game in the fifth on Mickey Heath's home run (the only longball of the Series) and scored the eventual winning run in the sixth. The two teams scrambled to make their five o'clock train, but it had to be a dispirited Louisville group that boarded their Pullman car for the trip home. "The only thing that can be said about the Colonels in this fourth game of the series is that they played a much brainier game than they played in the other three games," the *Courier-Journal* said. "Their chances of becoming champions are very, yea verily, very remote."[1]

---

* The drafting of minor-league players by major-league teams began in 1892 and has taken many forms over the years. The Rule 5 draft is the most well-known version and has been in place since 1920. When minor-league teams were independent, they fought the premise of a draft because it placed a defined monetary value on players. Minor-league owners like Jack Dunn, understandably, wanted to obtain a higher price for their talent.

CHAPTER 37

GAME FIVE: A DASH TO VICTORY

SCANNING THE SPORT FIELD

(By FREDERICK WILSON, Sports Editor of The Globe.)

CHAMPIONS "AS ARE" CHAMPIONS.

Not only did the Leafs beat Baltimore and at least two other contenders in the International League, but they administered a most decisive beating to the Louisville champions of the American Association in five consecutive victories, four here and the fifth and final game of the set by 7-0 in the Kentucky metropolis yesterday. It is too much to say that the Howleys outclassed the Colonels, even though they beat them five times in a row. The Kentuckians were far from outclassed. In the Junior World Series two teams of almost exactly the same stripe were the rivals. Brilliant defensive organizations supported by sparkling pitching, they were both light in hitting. Louisville's team batting average of .309 for the season was not reflected in their work in the series, which is a tribute to the pitching strength of the Leafs. On the other hand, there were several teams in the International with better team batting averages than the Leafs, but the Howleys were able to negotiate the Louisville pitching. Howley's strategy against a team of approximately the same strength and style of play as that of the Leafs was an important factor in the victory of the International Leaguers. He directed the play with excellent judgment in every game. The Toronto manager, after winning four straight with right-handers, did the sporting thing by putting in Stewart, a southpaw, yesterday, although there were plenty of capable right-handers available. At that, Stewart has been just as effective as any pitcher in the league this season, and undoubtedly will lead the circuit again, as in 1925. There is very little likelihood of the Leafs going to the Coast for a series with Los Angeles, winners of the Pacific Coast League title. Howley will not take a composite team, and many of his regulars refuse to make the trip to California. The Leafs have done well enough without crossing the Rockies. The World Series has been won in four games, but the junior set has never before been taken in five straight.

* * * * *

Toronto Globe, *October 4, 1926.*

HOWLEY FINALLY GAVE LEFTY STEWART A START IN THE JUNIOR WORLD
Series on a hot and sweltering Sunday afternoon in Kentucky, just 24

hours later. The Colonels, who had much of the steam taken out of them in Toronto, put up little opposition in losing 7-0 to the Leafs. Louisville had promising innings in both the first and second, but scoring opportunities were wiped out by Leafs' double plays, and the home side seemed to be interested only in getting the whole series over and done with.

The Howleyites won, as they had all season, on the strength of their starting pitching; Clarence Fisher was the only reliever he turned to the whole series. The Leafs won by scratching out runs with walks, sacrifice bunts, speed on the bases, and defense, letting the pitching do the rest. Winning on the road certainly helped as well. Howley rode his core players hard, but the results spoke for themselves. Toronto's five-game sweep was the first of its kind at any level.

The home crowd of over 8,000 wasn't really into the game either, according to the *Courier-Journal*. "They did not seem to have the confidence which a charging team instills in its supporters. The cheering was half-hearted, and the call for a rally had lost its ominous boom."[1] The heat did not appear to bother the Leafs, wrote Charlie Good, "who played with much more snap and dash than in any other game of the series."[2] Tensions boiled over as the Colonels, who lost to Baltimore in eight games the previous year, were about to fail to capture the Series once again. When Frank Gilhooley was called safe on a very close play at the plate, the Louisville public address announcer, "went so far as to come onto the field and threaten the arbiter."[3]

Four Colonels regulars had been sold to big-league teams for the following year, and one has to wonder if traveling to a foreign country for four games after winning the pennant of what they probably believed to be a superior league had them as motivated as they could have been.

In addition to Toronto's pitching, the Louisville press thought the team's speed, both on the bases and in the field, as the key to victory. "Several games were lost to the Canadian team by slight margins. A little more speed may have turned the tables," was one reporter's observation.[4] Total attendance for the five games was just over

26,000, almost a third of that coming in the final game at Louisville. Gate receipts totaled $31,642. After expenses, the Leafs would get 60 percent of the remaining total, the Colonels 40 percent.

During the Series, Howley canvassed his players to gauge their interest in a series with the Pacific Coast League champs. The Los Angeles Angels, the PCL titlists, had offered to pay the Leafs' expenses to make the trip. Interest was lukewarm, to say the least, and the proposed games were quickly abandoned. Toronto had just played (including regular season, exhibition, and playoffs) 174 games in just 172 days, and the team must have been a worn-out bunch. Toronto played an astounding 27 doubleheaders (often with no day off afterward), and on a half dozen occasions, the team had to catch a train for Sunday games immediately after a Saturday contest, then either return home or continue on the road. The Coast League played a longer (200 games) schedule than the International League and the American Association, thanks to the milder West Coast weather. Even though the Angels had clinched the league title, there were still two weeks left to play in the regular season, and another series would have potentially extended the season into November. Understandably, the Leafs were not willing to extend their season that much longer. Several Leafs players who hailed from the southern United States boarded trains for home from Kentucky right after the final game.

There was also some grumbling among the Toronto players over the city's lack of celebration of the team's victory—a proposal at City Council to hold a dinner for the team and award medals to the players was voted down. "St. Louis gave Rogers Hornsby a $5,000 sedan," W.A. Hewitt remarked in his column, "Toronto gave Dan Howley an engrossed resolution of thanks."[5] Or maybe there just wasn't a lot to prove by going west. "The Leafs have done well enough without having to cross the Rockies,"[6] Wilson commented. The smaller-than-anticipated players' share of the gate receipts from the Junior World Series may have been front of mind for many on the team. Hewitt wrote that President Solman "is convinced he has a club strong enough to meet any team, major or minor, in the country, and he is willing to match the Leafs in a series with the Yankees on a sixty-forty basis and pay all expenses."[7] The Yankees, who would lose the seventh game of the World Series a week later when Babe Ruth was caught trying to steal second, ending the game, apparently were not interested in Solman's offer.

The Leafs had captured the attention of America's sporting press with their torrid run to the pennant. No less an authority than *The Sporting News* called the team the best in all minor-league baseball, Toronto's pitching staff singled out. "Dan Howley provided an innovation for the minors in winning his flag with a pitching staff as big as a major league team might boast," observed *TSN*'s Charles J. Foreman, who added, "there is no doubt that it was superior to some of those in the majors." Howley's strength, in the eyes of Foreman, was his ability to shore up his club's weaknesses as the season went on:

"Dan opened the season with weak hitting recruits at first and second base, a lame third baseman, and a good but ill outfield. But he found a life-saver as a catcher, in old Steve O'Neill. The old boy cost nothing…however, he was good enough to catch 136 games for a pennant winner and assist considerably in starring the pitching staff."

As for the Leafs' attendance issues, Foreman blamed the team's early struggles for a poor showing at the gate: "Toronto didn't break any records at its new and expensive stadium. The citizenry didn't have a great deal of faith in the team until most of the year was spent."[8]

The baseball season may have been over, but Maple Leaf Stadium was going to continue to be busy for the next two months, as the Interprovincial Rugby Football Union, "the Big Four," was about to commence play.* The Ottawa Senators, Hamilton Tigers, Montreal AAA Winged Wheelers, and Toronto Argonauts (coached by *Globe* columnist Mike Rodden†) would compete for the right to play in the Grey Cup. The Argos would play their home games in the IRFU's six-game schedule at the Stadium. Rodden's club finished third, but a

---

* The IRFU was the precursor of the Canadian Football League's Eastern Division.

† Rodden, who later became sports editor of the *Globe*, was also a respected hockey referee. He became the first person elected to both the Hockey Hall of Fame (1962) and the Canadian Football Hall of Fame (1964).

Toronto team did make it to the Grey Cup final. The University of Toronto Blues of the Intercollegiate Rugby Football Union replaced Regina in the traditional east-west final, losing to Ottawa in a snowy early December game played at U of T's Varsity Stadium.* Maple Leaf Stadium also hosted games for the Ontario Rugby Football Union, a lesser but still popular provincial league.† Football star Red Grange brought his American Football League New York Yankees to the Stadium for a Thanksgiving Day‡ exhibition game against the Pacific Coast Wildcatters. Writing in the *Star*, Hewitt commented that, "The consensus of opinion was that the American game is a sort of glorified basket-ball game."[9]

Maple Leaf Stadium hosted ball games, track meets, police games, a traveling horse show, boxing matches, and rugby football in its first eight months. The following year promised to have even more dates. The stadium had firmly established itself as the center of the Toronto sports scene (at least during non-winter months) for decades to come.

---

* Regina won the West, but as their season ended in early November, they bowed out of further competition. Varsity Stadium hosted 30 Grey Cups, the last in 1957.

† The Canadian version of football was very popular across the country. In addition to leagues like the ORFU, Intercollegiate RFU, and professional IRFU, there were junior and senior leagues across the province. Most towns and cities had entries in one of the many grassroots leagues.

‡ Canadian Thanksgiving was not moved to its October date until an act of Parliament was passed in 1957.

CHAPTER 38
"A BIG FROG IN A SMALL PUDDLE"

LEAVING for States, subletting my choice apartment at 400 Avenue road, five rooms, balcony, elevator service, $100 per month. Dan Howley, Apartment 409.

B

AFTER A DECADE OF COACHING AND MANAGING IN BOTH THE MINORS and the bigs, the job Howley did with his 1926 team firmly cemented his reputation as a master of player development and game management.

Sportswriters of the day no doubt talked to the ballplayers on a regular basis. They were at the park every day, travelled with the team (sharing the same railway cars, hotels, and drinking establishments), and generally knew the minutest of details about the everyday functioning of the club. But the texts of their conversations were generally private; reporters didn't seek them out for postgame quotes. From the few snippets available, it's easy to understand how Howley's players felt about him. He no doubt was something of a demanding boss—witness the number of impromptu workouts he ordered on off days or when a scheduled game was postponed by rain.

But it's likely no accident that many players had the best years of their careers under Howling Dan. He had an eye for detail, an ability to find the slightest mechanical flaw that often kept a player from reaching his potential. Pitcher Myles Thomas was one of the many reclamation projects Howley took on when he came to Toronto.

Thomas was a much-heralded collegian at Penn State, was signed by the Yankees, and threw a no-hitter in his first professional start in 1921. But he struggled to get hitters out, and 20 months later after his sizzling debut, he was on the scrap heap; Toronto purchased his contract from Reading. Through spring training and the first few weeks of the season, Thomas continued to get hit hard. In late April, it was suggested that Thomas's "stay in Toronto was doubtful."[1]

But Howley saw something in Thomas. It only took one or two looks at Thomas for Howley to pick up that the pitcher was "short-arming" the ball. Thomas had an issue with walks, and somewhere in his first two pro seasons he altered his delivery (possibly without realizing it) to keep his throwing elbow close to his body to try to maximize his control. The alternation in his mechanics caused him to lose velocity and probably was hard on the elbow as well. Howley worked patiently with Thomas to lengthen his delivery, and while it obviously took some time for Thomas to get back to his old motion, his manager was willing to stick with him while Thomas figured things out. In much the same fashion as he used Carl Hubbell in 1926, Howley eased Thomas into action in 1923, pitching him in the second game as doubleheaders began to pile up in June. Thomas responded by winning 13 games, boosting Howley's confidence in him with every start. By the next season, Thomas was a fixture in the Leafs rotation, and when he won 28 games for Howley in 1925, the Yankees came calling once again, obtaining him for the following season. Two years later, Thomas won seven games in a swingman role for the 1927 World Champions.[2]

Similarly, Mickey Heath enjoyed the best season of his career in 1926. Howley stuck with him after a subpar season at the plate the year before, and Heath responded with a batting average 110 points higher than the prior year, banging out 52 extra-base hits. Challenged in spring training by the young slugger Dale Alexander, Howley must have taken Heath aside and said, "you're my first baseman, no matter what." He certainly was—Heath appeared in all 164 of Toronto's regular-season games, although Alexander's contract was sold to Toronto as the season wound down, and he would be the Leafs' first baseman in 1927.

Howley expected hard work and excellent fundamental play from his teams. He would go to battle for them in the face of unfavourable umpire's calls. He would work with them to correct flaws but never call a player out publicly for a mistake. Later Howley told a reporter that while he ran a tight ship, "You have to treat every man differently...but I have laid down a few rules for myself. I have never called a man down on the field. I never like to be humiliated, and I have never humiliated a player by calling him down for a mistake on the field."[3] Howley was honest with his players, showed patience with them, and let them know their roles on the team. In return, they would all but go through a wall for him.

After returning to Toronto, Howley took off on a two-week hunting and fishing trip in northern Ontario with his good friend Cobb. While he was gone, the rumour mill was going full tilt. Reports had him under consideration for managing jobs in St. Louis, Boston, and Pittsburgh. One thing was for certain: Howley had established a reputation as a master acquirer and developer of top-flight talent. His work with the 1926 Leafs likely made him the leading candidate for a number of openings as the offseason began. While Howley made all the right noises about staying in Toronto, it had been no secret for some time that he was on to bigger and better things. Howley may have helped Solman christen a new ballpark with a championship, but the club president wouldn't stand in his manager's way if a big-league job was offered to him.

Legendary Boston Globe *illustrator Gene Mack weighs in on Howley's suitability for the Boston Red Sox managerial post.*

Charlie Good, in an October 19 article in the *Star*, suggested that the job in Boston, given that Howley was from the area, was the opening that made the most sense. But Good said Howley was content and would remain in Toronto. "Dan muchly prefers being a big frog in a small puddle," he told his readers, "to being a small frog in a big pool."[4] While Howley did not take the Red Sox job, the man who Boston fired after the 1926 season, Lee Fohl, would take over in Toronto the following year.

Howley had long since ruled out replacing his good friend Cobb in Detroit, and when the Georgia Peach announced his resignation at the end of the 1926 season, there were no rumours connecting Howley with the job. Former player-turned-umpire George Moriarity, considered the front-runner for the Red Sox job, was hired to replace Cobb.

The *Detroit Free Press* said Howley was in line to take over the Pirates after Bill McKechnie resigned after a tumultuous season. "They say Howley can handle ball players of all types, and that he would make a good leader for any big team,"[5] the paper reported. Howley reportedly met with Pittsburgh owner Barney Dreyfuss, but it was uncertain as to whether he was offered the job or not. Given the controversy surrounding the team in the aftermath of a disappointing and dissension-racked season, Howley would have been well advised to steer clear of that situation, anyway.

As October gave way to November, the Toronto papers were reporting that Howley had indicated to Solman that he would be returning to the fold. But it was well known that Solman would not stand in the way of a big-league job offer, and it was not exactly a secret that Howley had crisscrossed much of America east of the Mississippi interviewing for a Major League posting; Good called it a "case of keepitunderyourhat-itis."[6]

On November 3, the *St. Louis Post-Dispatch* reported that Howley had agreed to manage the St. Louis Browns and was given a three-year contract. Howley was to replace player-manager George Sisler, a future Hall of Famer, who decided to give up the managing duties. Browns owner and president Phil Ball, an ice-manufacturing mogul whose clients included the Anheuser-Busch brewery, was a cantankerous, meddling type, who Howley had likely been warned about. "Howley and I have been dickering for about two weeks," he told reporters at a press conference announcing his signing, "but reached an agreement, subject to approval of the Toronto owners, last Saturday."[7]

As for matters regarding player personnel, Ball said, "I told Howley that he would have an absolute charge of the club, subject only to veto by the president. No other official with the club will have authority over Howley." Ball told reporters that after the Browns stumbled to a 92-loss, seven-place finish, he had some convincing to do to get Howley to agree to take on the job. "He called attention to the (next-to-last) standing, and to the supposition that we had bad actors on the club," Ball continued. "However, Howley said he would take responsibility if he had absolute authority. He has it. Howley is known as a disciplinarian, and he said that he would gain control of the club, or quit if he could not." Ball claimed that of the 20 applicants he had considered for the job, Howley was easily the most impressive. Financial terms of Howley's three-year deal were not disclosed, but a few days later Hewitt wrote that the contract called for a salary of $20,000 per year.

A few days later, Hewitt relayed a conversation he'd had with a visiting *Post-Dispatch* reporter, who was sent north of the border to research a profile on Howley. Howley's hiring, the reporter said, "created a mild surprise in St. Louis, as his name was not mentioned in connection with the position."[8] Hewitt was also told Howley "has a big job on his hands," with the Browns. A *Star* reader wrote to Hewitt that he was certain Howley would keep a soft spot for his former home, and that "there will be plenty of times next summer, that his memory will turn to the south end of Bathurst St, and he will wish that he was back there where the air and water—even if highly flavored—were always cool."[9]

Howley took the visiting St. Louis reporter on an extensive tour of Toronto, showing him the "fine new ballpark, and the ice rink where two professional teams were practising." The writer put together a profile of Howley in the Sunday, November 7 edition of the *Post-Dispatch*, with the headline on the jump, "ONLY HUSTLERS CAN PLAY BALL FOR ME - DAN P. HOWLEY." In the interview that followed, Howley pledged that he would add a scout to the Browns' staff, "a man I know and whose ability I recognize." As was the case in Toronto, Howley knew the name of the game was pitching. "You can't place too much importance on pitching, I learned that from Matty," Howley advised, invoking the name of future Hall of Famer Christy Mathewson. Howley also promised, as the headline inferred, that "The Browns, under my management, will hustle….the entire Browns team will be in condition next spring—I can say that right now."[10]

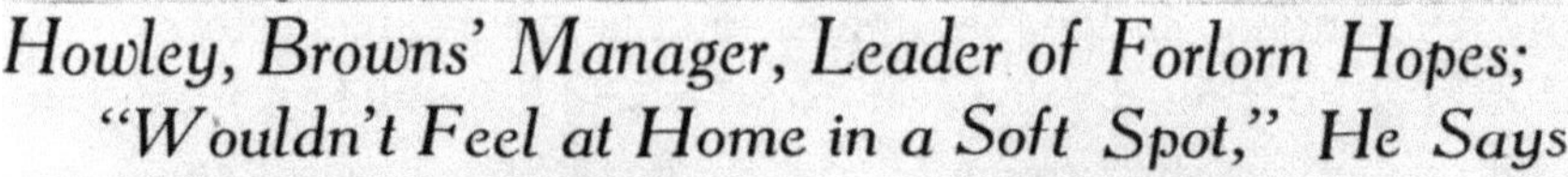

Howley, Browns' Manager, Leader of Forlorn Hopes;
"Wouldn't Feel at Home in a Soft Spot," He Says

DANIEL P. HOWLEY.
In baseball uniform and at his desk.

Man Who Led Toronto to Pennant Tells Roy Stockton His Plans for Handling the St. Louis Situation.

By J. Roy Stockton,
Of the Post-Dispatch Sport Staff.

TORONTO, Ont., Nov. 6.—If you have a forlorn hope and it is sufficiently forlorn, call on Daniel Philip Howley. If the prospects are bright, or the future promising, if you see so much as one ray of light, don't bother Mr. Howley. But if your forlorn hope is like unto Mrs. Luella Nonesuch Schmalz of Macon, Ga., before she started taking pink pills, and all your friends have given it up, then call Mr. Howley. Forlorn hopes are his specialty. He dotes on them.

Howley has no time for bright futures or promising prospects. He is too busy rescuing floundering ships in the baseball seas and steering them safely into pennant port, with all flags flying, all seams caulked and all the paint restored on the former drifting hulk.

No Places Open For Rum Hounds On Howley's Club

TORONTO, Nov. 6.—Daniel Philip Howley

St. Louis Post-Dispatch, *Nov. 7, 1926.*

Howley had a huge rebuilding job on his hands, which is likely why Ball granted him a three-year contract. "They tell me I've got a tough job in St. Louis," he told the *Post-Dispatch* reporter. "I love tough jobs. I've had tough sledding all my life—I wouldn't be at home in a soft spot." The *Buffalo News* was more blunt in the challenge that lay ahead for the Bisons' former rival manager. "Dan Howley, drum major of the pennant-winning Toronto Maple Leafs, moves 'up' to the Saint Louis Browns as manager, though there are some who will call it a demotion."[11]

After returning to Toronto to wrap up some business (Hewitt in the *Star* speculated that Howley approached Solman about taking St. Louis native Otis Miller with him to the Midwest), Howley made his second—but not final—departure from the city all but official with a classified ad in Hewitt's paper to lease his mid-town apartment in a building that still stands today. Howling Dan was leaving Toronto again, but he would one day return.

POSTSCRIPT

Players formed a cross to honor the late Lol Solman on the 1931 Opening Day at Maple Leaf Stadium, as the Maple Leafs hosted the Jersey City Skeeters. (City of Toronto Archives, Globe and Mail fonds, Fonds 1266, Item 23783.)

After the 1926 season ended the Leafs scattered across the continent. Many of Howley's players followed him to the big leagues, and just over half of the roster returned to Toronto. Here, in no particular order, is where the players went:

Owen Carroll returned to the big leagues with the Tigers in 1927, winning 26 games over the next two seasons. He hurt his arm part way through the 1929 season, and while he hung on for a few years (he reconnected with Howley in Cincinnati in 1931), he was never the same pitcher again. After his playing career ended, Carroll coached at Seton Hall from 1948 to 1972. The playing field there is named in his honour.[1]

Wally "Lefty" Stewart nearly died after his appendix ruptured while he was on a hunting trip following the 1926 season; doctors felt he might not pitch again. But Stewart recovered quickly, and Howley acquired him for the '27 Browns. He pitched in the bigs for ten years, winning 20 games for the last-place Browns in 1930.[2]

Jess "Slow Motion" Doyle returned to Toronto in 1927, winning 14 games. But one has to wonder if the toll of pitching a career-high 280 innings for Howley in 1926 had exacted a heavy toll. After being drafted from Toronto by the Tigers late in the 1926 season, Doyle made the club the following year, but by 1928 was a .500 pitcher, and he was sent back to Toronto and released by the Leafs in 1929 after losing his first seven decisions.[3]

Jim Faulkner won 15 games and led the Leafs in innings pitched in 1926. He returned to Toronto and was sold to the Giants late in the 1927 season. One day the following season, he gave up a walk-off home run to the Cubs; fiery Giants' manager John McGraw tore a strip off Faulkner in front of the team in the clubhouse after the game. "You *never* throw a curveball in that situation!" he screamed, even though the pitch was a fastball. When asked why he withstood McGraw's tirade in silence, Faulkner said to respond would have provoked McGraw even further. Faulkner retired after the 1931 season and ran a flight school in Florida for many years after that.[4]

Herman Layne seemed poised to earn a big-league job in 1927 after hitting .350 and leading the International League in triples with the '26 Leafs. But he was beaten out in spring training by future Hall of Famer Lloyd Waner. Layne was used sparingly by the Pirates, appearing in only 11 games (eight as a pinch runner) and going hitless in six plate appearances before being sent back to the minors, never to return.[5]

Carl Hubbell's story is well known. Despite showing promise in those exhibition games against big-league clubs and in the second games of doubleheaders, Howley must have received word from the Tigers to limit the use of Hubbell and his screwball, and he appeared sparingly after the Dominion Day weekend. Detroit pitched for two more nondescript minor-league seasons for the Tigers before the New York Giants signed him and sent him to Beaumont of the Texas League, where his manager, Claude Robertson—a former catcher—said to go ahead and use the pitch, and Hubbell had a dozen wins by midseason. Legendary Giants scout "Sinister" Dick Kinsella was in Houston in July for the 1928 Democratic National Convention and was convinced to go and watch Hubbell compete against the local team. Hubbell dominated that day—as he had all season—and was in the big leagues two weeks later. His biggest achievement may have been striking out five consecutive future Hall of Famers at the 1934 All Star game. Ty Cobb didn't want Hubbell using the screwball because it might hurt his arm, and it did—twelve years, 253 wins, two MVP awards, and nine All-Star Games later.[6]

Frank "Flash" Gilhooley gave the Leafs' offence quite a boost at the top of their batting order, leading the International League in singles. But at 35, the former big leaguer was—in the eyes of Solman and new manager Lee Fohl—getting on in years. To that end, they signed outfielder Vern Spencer to give him some competition. Gilhooley balked at the signing and even made a February trip from his home in Toledo to talk things over with Solman.[7] Gilhooley wanted to secure his future by asking for a two-year contract, but Solman refused. Gilhooley held out and missed all of spring training, displeasing his new skipper, who traded him to Rochester a week into the season. Gilhooley finished his career as player-manager of Jersey

City. His son, Frank Jr, was a long-time radio broadcaster for the Toledo Mud Hens.

Andy Harrington had shown considerable promise by reaching the bigs—albeit only for a cup of coffee—at the age of 22 in 1925. Injuries limited his contributions to the Leafs championship season, although he was a productive player in Toronto the following season. Harrington would play another 13 years in the minors after that, peaking in the Pacific Coast League before finishing his career in Class C ball.[8]

Mickey Heath is one of many players who benefitted from Howley's tutelage. His sale to Hollywood of the PCL two months into the 1927 season was a major surprise to Leafs followers, and was one of the reasons Lee Fohl was asked to resign as manager six weeks later. Heath starred for Hollywood before reconnecting with Howley in Cincinnati for two seasons. He returned to the minors for good in 1932 but still had a number of good offensive years before retiring in 1939. Heath married a Toronto woman and kept his connections with the city for many years.[9]

Otis Lawry gave the Leafs' offence a boost when he joined the team halfway through the 1926 season. Like Heath, he was surprisingly let go by Toronto in the first half of the following season. It was said that when he played the outfield, Lawry liked to loudly call balls and strikes, much to the consternation of the home plate ump. Lawry finished his career with Jersey City in 1928.[10]

Joe Maley was used mostly in long relief and mop-up roles in 1926. He was given a starting role the following season, struggled, and was sold to Albany of the Eastern League in 1928. Maley's career ended in 1931.[11]

Otis Miller had a career year under Howley in 1926, following him to St. Louis for the 1927 campaign. He was sold to Milwaukee of the American Association in 1928 and was back in the minors for a couple of years before the Red Sox picked him up in 1930. After his career ended in 1932, Miller returned to his hometown of Belleville, Illinois, for which he served in the Illinois state legislature for 16 years.[12]

Billy Mullen also had the best year of his career under Howley, set to become his starting third baseman in St. Louis before tearing up his knee in training camp. The Browns' trainer "immediately went to work on Mullen," reported the *Post-Dispatch*, "using psychology and other forms of salve, including a knee baking process to hasten the restoration of the injured member."[13] But the treatment was to no avail, and Mullen missed the entire 1927 season and much of the next. Mullen appears to have retired after playing for Galveston of the Texas League in 1931, but he came back to hit .327 in 61 games for Jacksonville in 1939 in the Class C East Texas League at the age of 43.[14]

Steve O'Neill deservedly received much of the credit for his handling of Toronto's pitching staff. He resurrected his big-league career, too, as a result of his time with the Leafs, and was another player who joined Howley in St. Louis. O'Neill was involved in a serious motor vehicle accident in New York City in 1928. A cab he was riding in was hit by a truck, and O'Neill's injuries were so critical that a priest was called to administer the last rites. O'Neill recovered, but his full-time playing days were over. He returned to Toronto to serve as the Leafs player-coach from 1929-31, then limited his onfield duties to pinch-hitting for two more seasons while he was Toronto's bench boss. O'Neill went on to manage Cleveland, the Philadelphia Phillies, and Boston Red Sox in a career that spanned 44 years. As a manager, he never had a losing season.[15]

Claude Satterfield was nominally a relief pitcher, but Howley used him more as a pinch-hitter and late-inning defensive replacement as much as he used him on the mound in 1926. Satterfield played for three more seasons with the Leafs after their championship season. Unlike many of his teammates, Satterfield lived in Toronto year-round, coaching and refereeing basketball in his spare time. When he was sold by the Leafs in 1929 to a Texas League team, Satterfield was so attached to Toronto that he refused to report, instead pitching for the semi-pro Oslers in town.[16] He spent the next several years bouncing around the low minors before retiring after the 1932 season.

Carl Schmehl won a lot of fans over with his defensive play, but he played mostly in a reserve role after Toronto acquired Otis Lawry from Baltimore. A ruptured appendix caused him to miss most of spring training the year after the Leafs' championship run, and he was traded to Rochester part way through the 1927 season. Schmehl retired the following year.[17]

Vic Sorrell pitched mostly in relief after joining the Leafs part way through the '26 season. He won 14 games as a starter the following year, earning him a promotion to Detroit. The Tigers were just entering a very lean period, yet he managed to win 57 games between 1929 and 1933. Just as the Tigers returned to contention, Sorrell's arm gave out. After retiring in 1940, Sorrell coached the North Carolina State ball team for 21 years.[18]

Cleo Carlyle was sold to the Red Sox after the championship season. As a rookie, Carlyle was broken in slowly, but by midseason was playing on a regular basis in the Red Sox outfield. He was bothered by appendicitis from mid-August on and would have his appendix removed after the season. The illness cost Carlyle his spot on the roster, and he was sold to Hollywood of the Pacific Coast League after the 1927 season. Carlyle played for 10 seasons in the PCL before retiring.[19]

Clarence Fisher was perhaps the most important midseason acquisition the Leafs made, and it was odd that Buffalo—for whom he had been a rotation stalwart for half a decade—let him go, to a rival no less. But the submarining Fisher, who pitched mostly in the second half of doubleheaders, helped the Leafs immensely in that department, winning ten straight decisions. Because his delivery did not cause much wear and tear on his pitching arm, Howley could also call upon him out of the bullpen—he was the only reliever Howley trusted enough to use in the postseason. Late in the season, Fisher was involved in an automobile accident in downtown Toronto. At the intersection of Yonge and College streets, he hit a man emerging from a vehicle. Fisher, the driver, had teammate Jess Doyle as a passenger, and when police officers came on the scene, a bottle of beer was discovered. Doyle was later released, but Fisher spent the night in jail.

The next morning, he was charged with reckless use of an automobile, while charges related to the alcohol were dropped.[20] Fisher pitched for the Leafs for three more seasons before being sold to Montreal, who had reentered the International League. He retired after the 1935 season.[21]

Tillie Walker's bat gave the Leafs' offence a considerable boost when he was acquired in midseason. Approaching 40 years of age, the 13-year big-league veteran was a defensive liability in the outfield, and he was sold to Mobile of the Southern Association the following year. After his playing career, he umpired and managed in Class D ball before becoming a highway patrolman in his native Tennessee.[22]

Lionel Conacher had high hopes of becoming one of the Leafs' first home-grown stars, but the multisport athlete was glued to the Leafs' bench, appearing in only three games as a late-inning defensive replacement. Dan Howley had a pennant to win, and there was no place in his lineup for a player who had not taken even one at bat in a lower-level league before signing with the Leafs. A case of tonsillitis he suffered during the season did not help his cause.

Conacher went back to hockey after 1926, winning Stanley Cups with Chicago and Montreal Maroons. During his athletic career, he won boxing titles, played on national championship lacrosse teams, and won a Grey Cup with the Toronto Argonauts—he is one of only three men to have his name engraved on both the Grey and Stanley Cups.

After retiring from sports in 1937, Conacher became involved with provincial and federal politics, many of his political associations involving sports. In 1949, while playing in a charity softball game on Parliament Hill in Ottawa, he suffered a heart attack while trying to stretch a double into a triple; he died 20 minutes later.

Conacher was awarded numerous honours after his death. He was named Canada's Athlete of the Half-Century in 1950, and was later inducted into the Canadian Sports, Football, and Lacrosse Halls of Fame, as well as the Hockey Hall of Fame. The Canadian Press award for Canada's Male Athlete of the Year is named after him.[23]

Conacher conquered many sports in his career, but professional baseball was not one of them. One wonders, given his prodigious talent, if he had been signed not to sell tickets, but to start in the low minors and work his way up, learning the game and honing his skills in the process, how far he would have gone in the diamond game.

Lol Solman Maple Leaf Stadium was perhaps Solman's crowning achievement in a career as an entertainment entrepreneur.

The increased costs for the new ballpark, Solman's willingness to spare no expense when it came to obtaining players to end the Orioles' run, and lower than planned attendance meant that the Leafs reported an undisclosed financial loss on the season.[24]

When the Depression hit, his team's fortunes both on and off the field took a turn for the worse. Attendance dropped off as the Leafs were mired in the middle of the International League standings. The team was already floating in a sea of red ink when Solman died of pneumonia in 1931. His funeral was one of the largest Toronto had ever seen: "Lol always loved a good crowd," eulogized Lou Marsh of the *Star*.[25]

The Leafs hit rock bottom the season after Solman passed, losing 113 games and finishing dead last. Just under 600 fans on average came out to watch the moribund team. To compound matters, the Harbour Commission, which had never received a lease payment from Solman for the land the stadium was built on, stepped in and took over the ballpark. Had the Commission not done so, the city may have put the stadium up for auction (which might have seen the team leave Toronto) to recoup back taxes Solman had not paid. Solman's original deal with the city was not as sweet as it first seemed. Attendance for the first several years of Maple Leaf Stadium fell below expectations, the Great Depression took leisure money out of the pockets of many, and Solman failed to plan for rainy days (and not of the diamond variety). Late in the 1932 season, the International League had to take over ownership of the club to ensure the players were paid. A new ownership group was formed in 1933 to take over the Leafs; they managed to lure Howley back to Toronto again to manage it.

Dan Howley took the St. Louis Browns from a seventh-place, 59-

94 season in 1927, to an 82-72, third-place finish the following year, a feat earning him "Miracle Man of 1928" honours from *The Sporting News*.[26] But he couldn't move the Browns up from that finish; they dropped to fourth, 79-73, in 1929. Howley feuded with owner Phil Ball for much of the season over personnel matters, and his three-year contract was not renewed at the end of the season. But Howley's sterling reputation as a player's manager and developer of talent, if anything, was enhanced by his time with the Browns, and he was quickly signed to another three-year deal by Cincinnati in 1929. But the Reds' owner, Sidney Weil, lost much of his personal fortune in the stock-market crash that took place three weeks after Howley was hired.

As a result of Weil's financial losses, the team was run on a shoestring for much of Howley's tenure, and he resigned at the end of his contract after the 1932 campaign. Howley returned to manage the Leafs for the 1933 season, but he sat out the following year when his bid to become a part owner of the team failed. Howley returned in 1935 in a general manager's role, but after two seasons was back in the dugout. He stepped away from the team in 1940, returning to his native Massachusetts to work with the Red Sox as an amateur scout.

Prime Minister William Lyon Mackenzie King left a complicated legacy far beyond the powers of this book to document. Suffice to say that he served his country through the Roaring Twenties, Great Depression, and World War II, although the country saw fit to vote him out of office more than once. King forged greater economic and military ties with America and led the charge for full Canadian independence from Britain. He oversaw the implementation of social programs like unemployment insurance and a national pension plan. At the same time, according to historian Mark Bourrie, "Smart men, even those who worked closest to him, despised him. They knew he was vindictive, superstitious, bigoted, and grasping."[27] During King's time in power, the Chinese Immigration Act, intended to limit Chinese immigration, was passed, he refused to expand immigration opportunities for Jewish refugees escaping Nazi oppression, and his handling of the Conscription Crisis in WWII greatly divided the country.[28]

Maple Leaf Stadium ushered in a new era of civic pride when it was completed. Unfortunately, it did not age well, becoming something of a White Elephant at a relatively young age.

The combined municipal budget belt-tightening of the Great Depression and World War II meant that upkeep for the ballpark was done on a shoestring budget, if at all. The Harbour Commission took on a debt of $30,000 just before Solman passed and was reluctant to put any money into the team or the stadium before selling the club, but retaining ownership of the facility.[29]

Jack Kent Cooke with players in the ballpark dugout. (City of Toronto Archives, Fonds 1257, Series 1057, Item 2609.)

When broadcasting entrepreneur Jack Kent Cooke purchased the team in 1951, he immediately lobbied the Commission and City Council for funding of much-needed repairs. Cooke had turned the team around on the field and at the box office, making Maple Leaf Stadium the place to be, but the neglect of the park continued. When the St. Louis Browns were up for sale after the 1952 season, Cooke all but had a deal in place to purchase the team, but the Commission balked at paying for the installation of centre field bleachers, which would have brought the park's seating capacity up to MLB standards. The Browns moved to Baltimore instead.

Cooke even offered to buy the stadium from the Harbour Commission, but was turned down by the board, citing the need to study the impact of added traffic congestion (if Cooke was successful in landing an MLB team) along Lakeshore Boulevard. Toronto then missed out on bringing the Boston Braves and the Philadelphia Athletics because of the limitations of Maple Leaf Stadium. Under Cooke's ownership, the Leafs won four International League pennants in the 1950s, but he tired of his battles with city officials over the need to upgrade the ballpark, sold the team in 1961, and moved south of the border to find considerable fortune in the cable-TV business. and fame as the owner of the Los Angeles Kings and Lakers, and the Washington Redskins.[30]

As a result of the lack of maintenance, Maple Leaf Stadium—which was labelled state-of-the-art when it opened—became known as one of the worst in all Minor League Baseball. Opposing players and IL beat writers called the park's infield, lighting, and clubhouse facilities the worst in the league as early as the late 1950s. While Cooke put the team up for sale, the decay continued. An International League beat reporter called Maple Leaf Stadium "an ugly step daughter of the Harbour Commission that is fundamentally sound, could use some face-lifting, and will probably end up on the scrap heap if the commission has its way."[31]

Truth be told, a combination of factors likely convinced city officials that the stadium was beyond salvaging by the early '60s. Television beamed Major League teams into fans' living rooms, and the minor-league product—at least in the eyes of Torontonians—was just that. Cooke's pursuit of a big-league team certainly sent the message to local baseball fans that the International League was second-best.

The city had plans to redevelop both the Exhibition grounds and the area around it, and an aged ballpark, a relic of the 1920s, did not fit. Maple Leaf Stadium soon became the place to be only for marauding flocks of starlings; the city had to bring in a wildlife biologist to bring the avian population, which had taken up much of the underside of the grandstand roof, under control. Damage from several fires over the ballpark's final decade only contributed to its growingly decrepit state.

At the start of what would be the Leafs' last season in Toronto in 1967, local ownership did not have the funds to operate the team in place until mid-April. Predictably, the team struggled on the field, and fewer than 90,000 fans came through the turnstiles. For the last two weeks of the season, the team was kept afloat only by the parent Boston Red Sox taking over the club's payroll. Heading into the season's final month, the Leafs were in third place and in a playoff spot, but with the uncertainty over the team likely a factor, they stumbled to an 8-23 finish, falling to sixth place. On September 4, only 800 fans bothered to show up for what would be the final game in team history. Over 23,000 soccer fans had shown up to watch a game featuring a Greek club team the week before, and close to 5,000 would be drawn to a pro wrestling card the week after. Toronto fans had clearly moved on from minor league baseball.[32]

Some local ownership groups had expressed interest in the team. Harold Ballard, then the executive vice-president of the Maple Leafs hockey club, made a proposition to buy his baseball cousins. But Ballard's plans were for a big-league team, and the $250,000 ($2.1 million in today's dollars) estimated cost of patching up Maple Leaf Stadium until a new one could be built likely proved prohibitive.

A month after that final game, ownership (which had lost over $400,000 in a half dozen years) sold the team to a Louisville businessman for $60,000. The Leafs would be headed to the site of their greatest triumph 41 years earlier. An auction was held in December to disperse the team's few remaining assets, in "perfect funeral weather," according to one report.[33] The Toronto Old-Timers Baseball Association bought 100 bats for $1.15 each and 40 batting practice balls for

30 cents apiece, which were to be distributed to playground teams in the city. The team's whirlpool tub sold for $85, and an auction participant picked up two dirt-encrusted home plates for $5 each. The proceeds of the event netted about $5,000. Everything that wasn't nailed down—including home plate—was sold.[34]

After Christmas, the stadium was condemned by the city by officials who feared children would be injured playing in it. When the snow lifted in April, 70-plus years of baseball history bit the dust when Maple Leaf Stadium met the wrecker's ball. The Harbour Commission said they had no immediate plans for the site, but the city did rezone the area for commercial and residential use later. The former Maple Leaf Stadium grounds today host a small ballpark, playground, and a townhouse development. A commemorative plaque, placed in 2019 just steps from where home plate once sat, celebrates the stadium and Toronto's baseball history.[35]

The 1926 Toronto Maple Leafs were the only team that brought a Junior World Series title to Toronto in the Modern Era (the Series ended in 1971). During the centennial celebration of the the National Association of Baseball Leagues, the Howleyites were ranked as #39 on a listing of the Top 100 Minor League teams of all time.[36]

Nineteen-twenty-six was a year of tremendous growth of the game in Toronto. The team and the stadium, in the eyes of Toronto fans at the time, were big league, matching the aspirations of many Torontontians for the city to start to take its place as the country's leader in business, sports, and the arts. Banting and Best, the Group of Seven, Mackenzie King appointing the first ever Canadian-born diplomat, and the Leafs catching the attention of the baseball world gave Canadians in general, and Toronto residents in particular, reason to feel proud of their young nation. Even though all but one of the players on the Leafs' end of season roster was born south of the border, the team gave its home fans reason to be proud to be Canadians.

APPENDIX: TORONTO MAPLE LEAFS 1926 GAME-BY GAME RESULTS (REGULAR SEASON)

Home games **in bold**. x=10-inning game. y=11-inning game. z=12-inning game. +=7-inning game (second half of doubleheader). a=clinched pennant.

April 14: Toronto 8, Reading 2 (1-0)

April 15: Toronto 6, Reading 1 (2-0)

April 16: Toronto 4, Reading 3 (3-0)

April 17: Toronto 14, Reading 5 (4-0)

April 18: Baltimore 6, Toronto 4 (4-1)

April 18: Baltimore 8, Toronto 6 (4-2)

April 19: Baltimore, postponed

April 20: Baltimore, postponed

April 21: Toronto 7, Newark 6 x (5-2)

April 22: Toronto 13, Newark 4 (6-2)

April 23: Toronto 17, Newark 13 (7-2)

April 24: Newark 11, Toronto 5 (7-3)

April 25: Jersey City 3, Toronto 2 (7-4)

April 25: Toronto 8, Jersey City 2 (8-4)

April 26: Toronto 6, Jersey City 1 (9-4)

April 28: Reading, postponed

April 29: Toronto 6, Reading 5 (10-4)

April 30: Reading, postponed
May 1: Reading 4, Toronto 3 (10-5)
May 1: Toronto 2, Reading 1 y (11-5)
May 3: Newark 10, Toronto 8 x (11-6)
May 4: Toronto 2, Newark 1 x (12-6)
May 5: Toronto 3, Newark 1 (13-6)
May 5: Newark 5, Toronto 3 y (13-7)
May 6: Toronto 4, Baltimore 3 x (14-7)
May 7: Baltimore 6, Toronto 1 (14-8)
May 8: Baltimore 1, Toronto 10 (14-9)
May 10: Baltimore, postponed
May 11: Toronto 2, Jersey City 1 (15-9)
May 12: Toronto 5, Jersey City 3 (16-9)
May 12: Toronto 1, Jersey City 0 z (17-9)
May 13: Jersey City 6, Toronto 0 (17-10)
May 14: Toronto 10, Jersey City 1 (18-10)
May 15: Buffalo 8, Toronto 2 (18-11)
May 15: Buffalo 8, Toronto 0 y (18-12)
May 16: Buffalo 15, Toronto 7 (18-13)
May 17: Toronto 8, Buffalo 3 (19-13)
May 19: Syracuse, postponed
May 20: Toronto 4, Syracuse 0 (20-13)
May 21: Syracuse, postponed
May 22: Toronto 7, Syracuse 6 x (21-13)
May 23: Toronto 7, Rochester 6 x (22-13)
May 24: Toronto 8, Rochester 1 (23-13)
May 24: Toronto 13, Rochester 6 y (24-13)
May 25: Rochester 6, Toronto 3 (24-14)
May 26: Toronto 6, Rochester 3 (25-14)
May 27: Toronto 4, Syracuse 3 (26-14)
May 28: Toronto 3, Syracuse 2 (27-14)
May 29: Toronto 8, Syracuse 6 (28-14)
May 30: Toronto 3, Syracuse 0 (29-14)
May 31: Rochester 4, Toronto 2 (29-15)
May 31: Toronto 9, Rochester 6 y (30-15)

June 2: Rochester 11, Toronto 5 (30-16)
June 4: Toronto 10, Buffalo 3 (31-16)
June 5: Toronto 9, Buffalo 0 (32-16)
June 5: Toronto 3, Buffalo 2 y (33-16)
June 6: Buffalo 4, Toronto 3 (33-17)
June 7: Newark, postponed
June 8: Toronto 10, Newark 7 (34-17)
June 8: Toronto 6, Newark 3 (35-17)
June 9: Toronto 8, Newark 0 (36-17)
June 10: Toronto 8, Newark 2 (37-17)
June 11: Jersey City 5, Toronto 1 (37-18)
June 12: Jersey City, postponed
June 13: Jersey City 3, Toronto 0 (37-19)
June 13: Toronto 8, Jersey City 1 (38-19)
June 14: Toronto 8, Jersey City 5 (39-19)
June 15: Toronto 6, Reading 1 (40-19)
June 16: Toronto 10, Reading 2 (41-19)
June 17: Reading 6, Toronto 2 (41-20)
June 18: Toronto 3, Reading 1 (42-20)
June 19: Toronto 4, Baltimore 3 (43-20)
June 19: Toronto 10, Baltimore 2 (44-20)
June 20: Baltimore 7, Toronto 4 (44-21)
June 20: Baltimore 11, Toronto 1 (44-22)
June 21: Baltimore 7, Toronto 3 (44-23)
June 22: Baltimore 4, Toronto 3 (44-24)
June 23: Rochester, postponed
June 24: Rochester 5, Toronto 2 (44-25)
June 25: Toronto 6, Rochester 1 (45-25)
June 26: Rochester 12, Toronto 5 (45-26)
June 26: Rochester 4, Toronto 3 (45-27)
June 27: Buffalo 7, Toronto 4 (45-28)
June 28: Buffalo 8, Toronto 4 (45-29)
June 29: Buffalo 4, Toronto 3 (45-30)
June 20: Buffalo 6, Toronto 4 (45-31)
July 1: Toronto 6, Syracuse 3 (46-31)

July 1: Toronto 11, Syracuse 7 (47-31)
July 2: Toronto 9, Syracuse 4 (48-31)
July 3: Toronto 2, Syracuse 0 (49-31)
July 3: Syracuse 1, Toronto 0 (49-32)
July 4: Rochester 6, Toronto 5 (49-33)
July 4: Toronto 11, Rochester 2 (50-33)
July 5: Rochester 4, Toronto 2 (50-34)
July 5: Toronto 7, Rochester 6 x (51-34)
July 6: Toronto 5, Rochester 4 (52-34)
July 8: Toronto 9, Reading 2 (53-34)
July 9: Toronto 19, Reading 2 (54-34)
July 10: Toronto 12, Reading 7 (55-34)
July 10: Toronto 5, Reading 4 (56-34)
July 12: Baltimore 6, Toronto 5 x (56-35)
July 12: Baltimore 4, Toronto 0 (56-36)
July 13: Toronto 18, Baltimore 9 (57-36)
July 14: Baltimore 11, Toronto 1 (57-37)
July 15: Toronto 4, Baltimore 3 (58-37)
July 16: Toronto 4, Newark 3 (59-37)
July 17: Newark 7, Toronto 6 x (59-38)
July 17: Newark, postponed
July 19: Toronto 4, Newark 3 (60-38)
July 19: Toronto 3, Newark 1 y (61-38)
July 20: Toronto 4, Jersey City 1 (62-38)
July 21: Jersey City 9, Toronto 7 (62-39)
July 22: Jersey City, postponed
July 23: Jersey City 6, Toronto 4 (62-40)
July 23: Toronto 5, Jersey City 4 (63-40)
July 24: Syracuse 2, Toronto 1 (63-41)
July 25: Syracuse 8, Toronto 1 (63-42)
July 25: Syracuse 3, Toronto 1 (63-43)
July 27: Toronto 8, Syracuse 3 (64-43)
July 28: Buffalo, postponed
July 29: Toronto 10, Buffalo 5 (65-43)
July 29: Buffalo 7, Toronto 5 (65-44)

July 31: Toronto 5, Buffalo 4 (66-44)
July 31: Toronto 7, Buffalo 5 y (67-44)
August 1: Rochester 1, Toronto 0 (67-45)
August 2: Syracuse 12, Toronto 7 (67-46)
August 2: Toronto 7, Syracuse 6 z (68-46)
August 3: Syracuse 6, Toronto 4 (68-47)
August 4: Toronto 5, Syracuse 3 (69-47)
August 4: Toronto 7, Syracuse 2 (70-47)
August 6: Toronto 7, Baltimore 6 z (71-47)
August 7: Toronto 8, Baltimore 5 z (72-47)
August 8: Toronto 6, Baltimore 5 x (73-47)
August 8: Baltimore 10, Toronto 8 x (73-48)
August 10: Toronto 5, Reading 3 (74-48)
August 11: Toronto 8, Reading 6 + (75-48)
August 12: Reading, postponed
August 13: Toronto 8, Reading 6 x (76-48)
August 13: Toronto 5, Reading 3 x (77-48)
August 14: Toronto 6, Jersey City 0 (78-48)
August 14: Toronto 4, Jersey City 1 (79-48)
August 15: Toronto 4, Jersey City 1 (80-48)
August 17: Jersey City 5, Toronto 3 (80-49)
August 18: Jersey City, postponed
August 19: Toronto 5, Newark 1 (81-49)
August 20: Toronto 11, Newark 2 (82-49)
August 21: Toronto 10, Newark 1 (83-49)
August 22: Newark, postponed
August 23: Toronto 3, Jersey City 0 (84-49)
August 24: Toronto 4, Jersey City 2 (85-49)
August 24: Toronto 3, Jersey City 0 (86-49)
August 24: Toronto 5, Jersey City 0 (87-49)
August 26: Toronto 3, Newark 2 (88-49)
August 26: Toronto 3, Newark 1 (89-49)
August 27: Newark 6, Toronto 3 (89-50)
August 28: Newark 3, Toronto 1 x (89-51)
August 28: Toronto 3, Newark 1 y (90-51)

August 30: Toronto 22, Reading 3 (91-51)
August 30: Toronto 8, Reading 7 (92-51)
August 31: Toronto 3, Reading 1 (93-51)
September 1: Toronto 2, Reading 1 (94-51)
September 1: Toronto 8, Reading 0 y (95-51)
September 2: Toronto 7, Baltimore 4 (96-51)
September 3: Toronto 7, Baltimore 2 (96-51)
September 4: Baltimore, postponed
September 4: Baltimore, postponed
September 6: Toronto 3, Buffalo 2 (98-51)
September 6: Buffalo 6, Toronto 5 (98-52)
September 7: Toronto 2, Buffalo 1 x (99-52)
September 8: Toronto 16, Buffalo 0 (100-52)
September 9: Rochester 5, Toronto 3 (100-53)
September 11: Toronto 3, Rochester 2 (101-53)
September 11: Toronto 2, Rochester 0 (102-53)
September 12: Toronto 9, Buffalo 8 (103-53)
September 12: Toronto 4, Buffalo 0 a (104-53)
September 13: Toronto 10, Buffalo 4 (105-53)
September 14: Toronto 8, Buffalo 3 (106-53)
September 15: Syracuse 10, Toronto 9 (106-54)
September 15: Syracuse 4, Toronto 3 (106-55)
September 17: Toronto 4, Syracuse 3 (107-55)
September 17: Syracuse 6, Toronto 1 (107-56)
September 18: Rochester 12, Toronto 5 (107-57)
September 19: Toronto 8, Rochester 4 (108-57)
September 19: Toronto 3, Rochester 0 x (109-57)

GONE, BUT NOT FORGOTTEN...

There are two individuals I would like to recognize as being important motivators behind this book's creation.

My father Douglas Sr. came to Toronto fresh off the eastern Ontario family farm in the early 1950s to work as a courier for Canadian Pacific telegraph services in the city's downtown. He lived in a rooming house in Parkdale, not far from Maple Leaf Stadium. Dad spent many Saturday afternoons down at the ballpark watching Leaf doubleheaders. This was his ballpark.

Dad passed away months before I finished this manuscript. I still miss his Friday night phone calls wondering where the Jays game (carried on Apple TV, rather than his usual Sportsnet), was broadcast.

My late mother-in-law Kay (Donnelley) Taylor was born and raised in the city's west end six months after the Leafs won the Junior World Series. This was her city.

While I never saw a game at Maple Leaf Stadium, I have long been fascinated with the Leafs' history. It was a thrill to be able to include the Canadian National Exhibition in this story. In 1974, my baseball team advanced to the semifinals of the *Toronto Star* PeeWee baseball tournament. Prior to what was to be our final game in the tourney, our coach had arranged for us to sit in the old grandstand at The Ex while we watched Canadian supergroup Lighthouse open for Evel

Knievel, who thrilled our little group of 12-year-olds by jumping 13 Mack trucks.

Former big leaguer Clyde Engle, Shaw, and Howley at a Leafs' open tryout camp in Owen Sound, Ontario. Courtesy Barb Benson.

Finally, being able to include Jim Shaw in this book closes a circle in my research and writing efforts of this era. I first came across Shaw while researching my first book, *On Account of Darkness: The Summer Ontario Baseball Broke the Colour Barrier.* In 1934, Shaw was brought in to manage a local promising but raw young pitching phenom from nearby Penetanguishene named Phil Marchildon, who would win 19 games for the 1947 Athletics. Shaw and Howley had been fishing and baseball buddies for several years. Shaw's granddaughter, Barb Benson, now lives in her grandparents' home in Port McNicoll, and she loaned me a scrapbook of her grandpa's clippings, correspondence, and photos that was an absolute treasure trove. As I wrote in this book, Howley sent his ailing slugger Chick Hafey to stay with the Shaws in the middle of the 1932 season—just imagine the Blue Jays doing something similar with Bo Bichette when he injured his knee during the 2025 pennant run. I returned the album to Barb several months ago; she wasn't home, so she said to leave it in the door. Before I left, I sat on the porch overlooking Hogg's Bay, imagining Jim and Chick sipping lemonade and talking baseball one July night in 1932, just days before my Dad was born.

One final personal link: when I was growing up in Midland, Ontario, our town team was dominant in Ontario Intermediate (small town) circles, having won multiple provincial titles in the 1960s. The team was led by a big righthanded pitcher named Gordie Dyment, who pitched briefly in the Phillies organization before accepting a job as a Canadian Pacific Railway policeman in Port McNicoll. Gordie pitched well into his 40s and would often pitch batting practice to Midland minor league ball teams, including my own. The guy sure could spin a curveball.

Gordie tried pro ball again with the New York Giants organization in the early 50s. His pitching coach in Class C ball in 1954 was Carl Hubbell.

BIBLIOGRAPHY

As noted throughout the book, Toronto newspapers of 1926—the *Star* and *Globe*—are the primary sources I used. Both are available through the Toronto Public Library via ProQuest, as well as newspapers.com. Several out of print books were available on the Internet Archive site: archive.org.

- Blaisdell, Lloyd L. *Carl Hubbell: a Biography of the Screwball King*. McFarland & Company Inc., Publishers, 2011.
- Bourrie, Mark. *Big Men Fear Me*. Biblioasis, 2022.
- Cauz, Louis. *Baseball's Back in Town: From the Don to the Blue Jays a History of Baseball in Toronto*. Controlled Media Publications, 1977.
- Grey, Zane. *The Redheaded Outfield: And Other Baseball Stories*. The Floating Press, 2011.
- Humber, William. *Diamonds of the North: A Concise History of Baseball in Canada*. Oxford University Press eBooks, 1995.
- Havill, Adrian. *The Last Mogul: An Unauthorized Biography of Jack Kent Cooke*. St. Martin's Press, 1992.
- Innis, Harold Adams. *The Fur Trade in Canada: An Introduction to Canadian Economic History*. University of Toronto Press, 1999.
- James, Bill. *Bill James Historical Baseball Abstract*, Villard Books, 1985.
- Murray, Joan. *Masterpieces: Tom Thomson and the Group of Seven*. Key Porter Books Limited, 1994.
- Papalas, Anthony. "L'il Rastus Was Ty Cobb's Good Luck Charm." *Baseball Research Journal*, 1984.
- Seymour, Harold, and Dorothy Seymour. *Baseball: The Golden Age*. Oxford University Press, 1971.
- Sowers, Mike. *The Pitch That Killed: The Story of Carl Mays, Ray Chapman, and the Pennant Race of 1920*. Ivan R. Dee Publishing, 1989.
- White, Randall. *Too Good to Be True: Toronto in the 1920s*. Dundurn Press, Toronto & Oxford, 1993.
- Young Scott. *He Shoots, He Scores! The Life and Times of Foster Hewitt*. Harper-Collins, 1985.

ACKNOWLEDGMENTS

One of the biggest challenges I have found in the course of writing a book is to recall all the people who have helped along the way.

My wife Sherry Taylor-Fox, while not a baseball fan,* is my faithful copy editor. Her ability to harness my run-on sentences, round up my inconsistencies, and generally lend a sharpness to my prose that it sometimes lacks is All-Star game worthy. Her eye for detail is uncanny.

Bill Humber, who wrote the introduction to this book, has been very supportive of my writing efforts, going back to my first book. We met at the Canadian Baseball History Conference several years ago; meeting the dean of baseball historians on this side of the border was a thrill. It was an honour to have him provide his memories of Maple Leaf Stadium.

Jamie Bradburn and Adam Bunch are Toronto historians and big-league storytellers in their own rights. Jamie was extremely helpful in painting a picture of the Toronto newspaper landscape in the 1920s, which was truly a Golden Era of print media in the city. Adam helped me understand the underground liquor economy of the Roaring Twenties thanks to Prohibition.

My son Liam Fox, a Ph.D. student at the University of Toronto, helped me with the herculean task of organizing my citations. One of the greatest days of my baseball life was when Liam flew in from Vancouver and joined me and his brother Taylor at Game Six of the

---

* My wife became a huge fan in 2025 with the Blue Jays' World Series run. Let's hope this is a long-term development.

Dodgers-Blue Jays World Series. Both of our sons have been tremendously supportive of my writing.

Drew Hayes is a pitching coach in the Toronto Blue Jays minor league system. He has patiently answered my many questions about pitching over the years, which helped me understand what Dan Howley was thinking when he assembled one of the best pitching rotations in Minor League Baseball history in 1926. Prior to my conversations with Drew, about the only thing I knew about good pitching was that I couldn't hit it.

John Thorn is the official historian for Major League Baseball, and a legendary baseball writer in his own right. He helped me track down statistics, rules, and information about the 1926 season that was not easy to find by putting me in touch with baseball researcher John Cronin.

Thomas Paradis is a baseball and hockey writer and researcher from Midland, Ontario, who was a good childhood friend. It was Tom who mentioned the story of Dan Howley sending Chick Hafey to the little town next door, Port McNicoll, in the summer of 1932. Tom also put me in touch with Barb Benson, whose grandparents Hafey stayed with. It was from Barb that I learned the story of her grandfather sitting in the Leafs dugout for that August doubleheader which was the turning point of the season.

Cassidy Lent, Manager of Reference Services at the Baseball Hall of Fame, provided me with copies of the Hall's Dan Howley files, which I have made extensive use of over the past few years.

Blake Murphy of Sportsnet The FAN 590 in Toronto took a chance several years ago when he invited a blogger (that is, me) on to his excellent show, Jays Talk Plus. My appearances on his show have both helped grow the audience for my writing and encouraged me to keep at it.

Last but certainly not least is my editor, Kevin Reichard, who took a chance on a writing prospect to further develop his skills.

D.M. Fox
Nottawa, Ontario, January 2026

BIOGRAPHY

For most Canadian kids, baseball was something to play between hockey seasons.

For D.M. Fox, it was quite the other way around.

Fox's love of baseball literature and lore dates back to when his parents forbade him to read Jim Bouton's iconic *Ball Four* as an adolescent. Far from corrupting him, it made him want to read everything and anything he could get his hands on about the game. He couldn't wait for allowance day, when he raced to Parker's Variety in downtown Midland, Ontario, to walk on the store's ancient creaky wooden floors back to the magazine section, where he picked up the latest issue of *The Sporting News*.

D.M. Fox began writing about the Toronto Blue Jays farm system in 2013, amassing a list full of contacts in the organization from CEO Mark Shapiro to Niall O'Donohoe, the PA announcer for the team's Vancouver Canadians affiliate. His work has been featured in numerous online publications, and he's a regular guest on Sportsnet The FAN 590 in Toronto with updates about Blue Jays prospects.

Fox has written two books of historical baseball fiction. *On Account of Darkness: the Summer Ontario Baseball Broke the Colour Barrier*, re-creates the historic and dramatic 1934 season, when Ontario integrated the game over a decade before MLB did. *Severn*

Sound: A Big Leaguer Comes to Port McNicoll is a story (based on real events) about a future Hall of Famer, friendship, and an Edwardian-era Great Lakes steamship.

D.M. Fox, his wife Sherry Taylor-Fox, and their American cocker spaniel Mabel live in Nottawa, Ontario.

NOTES

1. THE TOAST OF THE MINORS

1. "Miller Gets Down Off His High Horse," *Toronto Star*, March 18, 1926.
2. "W.A. Hewitt, "Sporting Views and Reviews," *Toronto Star*, October 2, 1926.
3. Foreman, Charles, J., "Remarkable Pitching Carries Toronto to Championship," *The Sporting News*, October 25, 1926.

2. THE CITY GAME

1. North, Andrew. "The Beachville Game," March 20, 2023. *https://sabr.org/journal/article/the-beachville-game/*.
2. "Base Ball," *Toronto Globe*, August 8, 1859.
3. Cauz, Louis, *Baseball's Back in Town: From the Don to the Blue Jays—A History of Baseball in Toronto*, Controlled Media Corp., 1977, p. 11.

3. HOWLING DAN

1. *Elmira (NY) Star-Gazette*, March 24, 1913.
2. "Lichtenhein Out of Hockey and Baseball," *Toronto Globe*, January 8, 1918.
3. Sowell, Mike, *The Pitch That Killed: The Story of Carl Mays, Ray Chapman, and the Pennant Race of 1920*, Lyons Press, 2016, p. 31.
4. Ibid.
5. Sowell, p. 32-33.
6. *Toronto Globe*, April 3, 1918.
7. *Toronto Globe*, December 14, 1918.
8. Kieran, John, "Howling Dan of Tampa Bay," *The New York Times*, March 13, 1932.

4. THE KING OF WEEKENDS

1. *Buffalo News*, February 13, 1923

5. THE MIGHTY ORIOLES

1. James, Bill, *Bill James Historical Baseball Abstract*, Villard Books, New York (1988), p. 140.
2. James, p. 141.
3. James, p. 142.
4. Keenan, Jimmy. "Jack Dunn," January 4, 2012. *https://sabr.org/bioproj/person/jack-dunn/*.

5. Hewitt, W.A., "Sporting News and Reviews," *Toronto Star*, Monday, September 14, 1924.

6. THE CHANGING
PERSPECTIVE OF THE CITY

1. Ernest Hemingway, *Complete Poems*, ed. Nicholas Gerogiannis, rev. edn. (Lincoln and London: University of Nebraska Press, 1992): 66-67.
2. Ibid.
3. Bourrie, Mark, *Big Men Fear Me: The Fast Life and Quick Death of Canada's Most Famous Media Mogul*, E-book edition, 27.
4. Murray, Joan. *Masterpieces: Tom Thomson and the Group of Seven*, Key Porter Books, 1995, p. 12.

7. HOWLING DAN RETURNS

1. James, Bill, *The Bill James Historical Baseball Abstract*, p. 88.
2. James, 81.

8. TORONTO ON THE MOVE

1. White, Randall, *Too Good to Be True: Toronto in the 1920s*, Dundurn Press, 1993, p. 117.

9. THE LEAFS TAKE SHAPE

1. Hausman, John, "Toledo's Flash," *Toledo Magazine*, June 18-24, 1989.

10. THE STADIUM DEBATE

1. *Toronto Star*, July 26, 1924.
2. *Toronto Globe*, December 8, 1922.
3. *Toronto Star*, January 31, 1925.
4. Ibid.

11. SILENT CHARLIE AND
MORE PIECES OF THE PUZZLE

1. "Charlie Gehringer," October 25, 2024. *https://sabr.org/bioproj/person/charlie-gehringer*.
2. Forsey, E. A. (2015, March 4). "King-Byng affair," The Canadian Encyclopedia. *https://thecanadianencyclopedia.ca/en/article/king-byng-affair*.

12. MAPLE LEAF STADIUM
RISES ON THE WATERFRONT

1. "Rivalry of Unions Blamed for Strike at Toronto Stadium," *Hamilton Spectator*, January 7, 1926.
2. "Karpe's Comment," *Buffalo News*, January 13, 1926.
3. Good, Charlie, "Choice Dates For the Toronto Club," *Toronto Star*, February 18, 1926.

13. THE HOWLEYITES
TAKE THEIR FINAL SHAPE

1. Good, Charlie, "Faulkner's Request Denied by Farrell," *Toronto Star*, November 19, 1925.

14. SPRING TRAINING APPROACHES

1. Wilson, Frederick, "Scanning the Sport Field," *Toronto Globe*, January 27, 1926.
2. Baseball-Reference.com. "Carl Hubbell Minor Leagues Statistics | Baseball-Reference.Com," n.d. *https://www.baseball-reference.com/register/player.fcgi?id= hubbel001car*.
3. "With the Leafs in the Land of Cotton and Red Clay Diamonds," *Toronto Star*, March 29, 1926.
4. Blaisdell, Lowell L., *Carl Hubbell: A Biography of the Screwball King*, 2011, McFarland & Co. Publishers, p. 11.
5. Chester, Carl W., "Wiltse Loses Out When Bisons Fail," *The Sporting News*, August 21, 1924.

15. THE LEAFS HEAD NORTH

1. "Leafs Win Another, but Lose Alexander," *Toronto Star*, April 8, 1926.
2. "Howley Hopeful That Leafs Will Be Team To Beat," *Toronto Star Weekly*, April 3, 1926.
3. Ibid.
4. Ibid.
5. Ibid.
6. "Leafs Lose Services of Dale Alexander, Refuse to Include Heath in Deal," *Toronto Globe*, April 8, 1926.
7. "It's Opening Day in International," *Toronto Globe*, April 14,1926.
8. "Another Flag is Predicted for the Birds," *Toronto Star Weekly*, April 17, 1926.
9. "Howley Changes Toronto Line-Up," *Toronto Globe*, April 14, 1926.

16. MAPLE LEAF STADIUM
NEARS COMPLETION

1. Wilson, Frederick, "Scanning the Field," *Toronto Globe*, April 14, 1926.
2. Hewitt, W.A., "Sporting Views and Reviews," *Toronto Star*, April 27, 1926.
3. Cox, Kevin, "Nova Scotia's Marathon Man," *Toronto Globe*, June 18, 2003.
4. Goldstein, Richard, "Johnny Miles - Boston Marathon Winner in 1926," *The New York Times*, June 22, 2003.
5. "The Result Was No Surprise to Johnny Miles," *Brooklyn Eagle*, April 28, 1926.
6. Marsh, Lou, "With Pick and Shovel," *Toronto Star*, April 28, 1926.
7. Hewitt, W.A., "Sporting Views and Reviews," *Toronto Star*, April 28, 1926.

17. SEASON OPENER

1. Wilson, Frederick, "Scanning the Sport Field," *Toronto Globe*, April 15, 1926.
2. Hewitt, W.A., "Sporting Views and Reviews," *Toronto Star*, April 24, 1926.
3. Good, Charlie, "Opening Ball Game Played To-Morrow," *Toronto Star*, April 24, 1926.
4. "Newark's Winning Streak Stopped by 'Lefty' Faulkner," *Toronto Globe*, April 22, 1926.
5. "Leafs Take Count Lose to 'Sally' Boys," *Toronto Star*, April 6, 1926.
6. "Temperamental," *Toronto Globe*, April 26, 1926.
7. "Wilson, Frederick, "Shaughnessy Through in Reading," *Toronto Globe*, April 26, 1926.

18. BASEBALL ON THE MAINLAND

1. *Toronto Globe*, special insert, April 28, 1926.
2. "Sporting Gossip," *Toronto Mail and Empire*, April 27, 1926.
3. Good, Charlie, "Opening Ball Game Played To-Morrow," *Toronto Star*, April 28, 1926.
4. "Big Mogul of Baseball Here," *Toronto Mail and Empire*, April 28, 1926.
5. "Sporting Gossip," *Toronto Mail and Empire*, April 29, 1926.
6. Wilson, Frederick, "Scanning the Sport Field," *Toronto Globe*, April 29, 1926.
7. "Opening of Maple Leaf Stadium Featured by Sensational Victory," *Toronto Mail and Empire*, April 30, 1926.
8. Good, Charlie, "Leafs Come Through With a Great Finish," *Toronto Star*, April 30, 1926.
9. "Sporting Gossip," *Toronto Mail and Empire*, April 30, 1926.

19. OFF TO A COLD START

1. Hewitt, W.A., "Slaney's Southpaw Slants Too Good for Leafs," *Toronto Star*, May 1, 1926.
2. Linthicum, Jesse A., "Comment on Sports," *Baltimore Evening Sun*, May 6, 2005.

20. TORONTO'S STUMBLES CONTINUE

1. *Toronto Star*, May 3, 1926.
2. Hewitt, W.A., "Sporting Views and Reviews," *Toronto Star*, May 13, 1926.
3. Gray, Zane, *The Redheaded Outfield and Other Stories* (McClure Syndicate, 1915).
4. "Karpe's Comment," *Buffalo Evening News*, May 18, 1926.
5. "Leafs Come From Behind to Take Lead in Sixth," *Toronto Star Weekly*, May 22, 1926.
6. Neyer, Rob, *Rob Neyer's Big Book of Baseball Legends* (Touchstone, 2008), pp. 247-48.

21. SIGNS OF A TURNAROUND

1. Wilson, Frederick, "Hayworth, Not O'Neill to Detroit," *Toronto Globe*, May 29, 1926.
2. Good, Charlie, "Baseball," *Toronto Star Weekly*, May 29, 1926.
3. Good, Charlie, "Hubbell Too Good for the Harrismen," *Toronto Star*, June 4, 1926.
4. Good, Charlie, "Carroll Stops Bisons for His Ninth Victory," *Toronto Star*, June 5, 1926.
5. Good, Charlie, "Leafs Lose at Buffalo and Bisons Lead Again," *Toronto Star*, June 7, 1926.

22. DOES BASEBALL MAKE GIRLS MASCULINE?

1. "Does Baseball Make Girls More Masculine?" *Toronto Star Weekly*, May 29, 1926.
2. "Howleyites Defeat Bears Twice And Creep Up Close to Leaders," *Toronto Globe*, June 9, 1926.
3. *Toronto Globe*, June 10.
4. "Vic Sorrell, From Bluefields, Another Brilliant Hurling Find," *Toronto Globe*, June 11, 1926.

23. SHINBONE

1. Seymour, Harold, *Baseball: The Golden Age.* (Oxford University Press, New York, 1971), p.128.
2. Livicari, Gary, "Baseball Mascots and Clowns," *https://www.baseballhistorycomesalive.com/baseball-mascots-and-clowns/*, April 20, 2016.
3. Morris, Peter, "Eddie Bennett," *https://sabr.org/bioproj/person/eddie-bennett/*.
4. Anthony Papalas, "L'il Rastus Was Ty Cobb's Good Luck Charm," *https://sabr.org/journal/article/lil-rastus-cobbs-good-luck-charm/*, 1984.
5. "Shinbone Does It," *Toronto Globe*, June 11, 1926.
6. Good, Charlie, "Leafs Move Up When Bisons Take Tumble," *Toronto Star*, June 10, 1926.
7. Hewitt, W.A., "Sporting Views and Reviews," *Toronto Star*, June 17, 1926.
8. "Toronto Loses Golden Opportunity to Share First Place With Orioles, *Toronto Globe*, June 18, 1926.

24. ORIOLES FANS ARE "PENNANT SORE"

1. Linthicum, Jesse A., "Comment on Sports," *Baltimore Evening Sun*, June 16, 1926.
2. Ibid.
3. Wilson, Frederick, "Scanning the Sport Field," *Toronto Globe*, June 16, 1926.
4. Wilson, Frederick, "Leafs Hold Lead One Day and then Lose Twice to Orioles," *Toronto Globe*, June 21, 1926.
5. Ibid.
6. Ibid.
7. "Circuit Blows Help Dunnmen," *Baltimore Evening Sun*, June 21, 1926.
8. "Howleyites Return Full of Confidence," *Toronto Globe*, June 24, 1926.
9. Wilson, Frederick, "Scanning the Sport Field," *Toronto Globe*, June 24, 1926.
10. "Thormahlen, Horne Hurl Good Games to Provide Locals Edge For Series," *Rochester Democrat and Chronicle*, June 27, 1926.

25. NOT A "SEMBLANCE OF A SMILE" ON JACK DUNN'S "CAREWORN FACE"

1. Reed, Don B., "Kelly's Bat Brings Home Hard Hit Game," *Buffalo News*, July 1, 1926.
2. Ibid.
3. White, p. 152.
4. Rodden, M.J., "Leafs Take Two From Stars and Gain on Orioles and Bisons," *Toronto Globe*, July 2nd, 1926.
5. Hewitt, W.A., "Sporting Views and Reviews," Toronto *Star*, July 6, 1926.
6. Rodden, M.J., "Double Victory Over Howleyites Gives Champions Commanding Lead," *Toronto Globe*, July 13, 1926.
7. "Random Notes on Current Sport," *Toronto Star*, July 13, 1926.
8. Ibid.
9. Rodden, M.J., "Double Victory Over Howleyites Gives Champions Commanding Lead," *Toronto Globe*, July 13, 1926.
10. "Boosters' Day and Baltimore Birds At the Ball Park," *Toronto Star*, July 14, 1926.
11. Rodden, M.J., "Five Pitchers Shelled Off Mound While Leafs Pile Up 18 Runs," *Toronto Globe*, July 14, 1926.
12. Rodden, M.J., "Orioles Batsmen in Their Glory When Leafs Lose, Eleven to One," *Toronto Globe*, July 15, 1926.
13. Hewitt, W.A., "Sporting Views and Reviews," *Toronto Star*, July 15, 1926.
14. Hewitt, W.A., "Sporting Views and Reviews," *Toronto Star*, July 16, 1926.
15. Rodden, M.J., "Faulkner 'Hero' in Rescue Role," *Toronto Globe*, July 17, 1926.
16. Marsh, Lou, "With Pick and Shovel," *Toronto Star*, July 21, 1926.

26. LEAFS "HANGING ONTO SECOND PLACE BY AN EYELASH"

1. Bunch, Adam, "The King of the Bootleggers," *The Toronto Time Traveller*, *https:// torontohistory.substack.com/p/the-king-of-the-bootleggers*.
2. Hewitt, W.A., "Sporting Views and Reviews," *Toronto Star*, July 26, 1926.

3. Hewitt, W.A., "Sporting Views and Reviews," *Toronto Star*, July 27, 1926.
4. Hewitt, W.A., "Sporting Views and Reviews," *Toronto Star*, August 3, 1926.

27. A VISITOR GIVES THE LEAFS A LIFT

1. Rodden, M.J., "Good Luck Accompanies Visitor to Leafs Bench," *Toronto Globe*, August 5, 1926.
2. Rodden, M.J., "On the Highways of Sport," *Toronto Globe*, May 18, 1937.
3. Ibid.
4. Ibid.
5. Ibid.
6. "Owen Carroll Hurls in Dunnville Today," *Toronto Globe*, August 6, 1926.
7. Hewitt, W.A., "Sporting News and Reviews," *Toronto Star*, August 4, 1926.
8. Hewitt, W.A., "Sporting News and Reviews," *Toronto Star*, August 7, 1926.
9. Reed, Don B., "International Has Red Hot Flag Race," *Buffalo News*, August 9, 1926.
10. "Bisons Pay $4200 for Whitman of Reading," *Buffalo News*, August 13, 1926.
11. Hewitt, W.A., "Sporting News and Reviews," *Toronto Star*, August 13, 1926.
12. Good, Charlie, "Leafs Clean Up at Expense of Keys," *Toronto Star*, August 14, 1926.
13. Corbett, Warren, "Bill McKechnie," Society for American Baseball Research, *https://sabr.org/bioproj/person/bill-mckechnie/*.

28. THE FIRST PLACE LEAFS

1. "Stewart and Layne Sought by Majors," *Toronto Globe*, August 16, 1926.
2. Hewitt, W.A., "Sporting Views and Reviews," *Toronto Star*, August 16, 1926.
3. "Miss Toronto's Father Objects to Beauty Contests, So Mother's Name Used," *Toronto Star*, August 17, 1926.
4. "Karpe's Comment," *Buffalo Evening News*, August 16, 1926.
5. Wilson, Frederick, "Scanning the Sport Field," *Toronto* Globe, August 24, 1926.

29. "PLAYING WONDERFUL BALL NOW"

1. Wilson, Frederick, "Scanning the Sport Field," *Toronto Globe*, Friday, August 27, 1926.
2. Hewitt, W.A., "Sporting Views and Reviews," *Toronto Star*, Friday, August 27, 1926.
3. Hewitt, W.A.,. "Sporting Views and Reviews," *Toronto Star*, Monday August 30, 1926.

30. THE ORIOLES LIMP INTO TOWN

1. "Woman, 75, Steps Off Train Going 40 Miles Per Hour is Found Alive Next Day," *Toronto Star*, September 3, 1926.
2. Hewitt, W.A., "Sporting Views and Reviews," *Toronto Star*, September 3, 1926.
3. "Sixty Persons in One Village Listen to Baseball," *Star Weekly*, September 4, 1926.
4. Hewitt, W.A., "Sporting Views and Reviews," *Toronto Star*, September 7, 1926.

31. TORONTO CLINCHES

1. "The Victory of the Leafs," *Toronto Globe*, September 14, 1926.
2. "The Political Plot," *Toronto Globe*, September 6, 1926.
3. Massey-Harris Co., later emerging as Massey-Ferguson after a 1954 merger.

32. RUMOURS ABOUT
HOWLEY'S FUTURE BEGIN

1. Good, Charlie, "Leafs All Set for Junior Ball Series," *Toronto Star*, September 20, 1926.
2. Smith, Red, "Jack Dempsey Was a Soft Touch Outside of Ring," *Toronto Globe and Mail*, June 1, 1983.
3. "Tunney Was Lumberjack for an Ottawa Company," *Toronto Globe*, September 28, 1926.
4. "Dempsey Insisting on Return Contest," *Toronto Globe*, September 25, 1926.
5. Wilson, Frederick, "Scanning the Sport Field," *Toronto Globe*, September 23, 1926.
6. Good, Charlie, "Dan Howley Says He'll Stick With Leafs," *Toronto Star*, September 23, 1926.
7. Hewitt, W.A., "Sporting Views and Reviews," *Toronto Star*, September 25, 1926.
8. Wilson, Frederick, "Scanning the Sport Field," September 27, 1926.
9. "Local Industrial Chiefs Do Not Approve Five-Day Week," *Toronto Star*, September 27, 1926.

33. THE SERIES OPENS

1. Rodden, M.J., "Doyle on Mound for Leafs Today," *Toronto Globe*, September 28, 1926.
2. Wilson, Frederick, "Scanning the Sport Field," *Toronto Globe*, September 28, 1926.
3. Hewitt, W.A., "Sporting Views and Reviews," *Toronto Star*, September 28, 1926.
4. Good, Charlie, "Pres. Toole Fancies the Leafs' Chances," *Toronto Star*, September 28, 1926.
5. Ibid.
6. "C.-J. 'Radiogame' Teams to Rehearse This Afternoon at Parkway Field," *Louisville Courier-Journal*, September 27, 1926.
7. Hewitt, W.A., "Sporting Views and Reviews," *Toronto Star*, September 28, 1926.
8. Wilson, Frederick, "Scanning the Sport Field," *Toronto Globe*, September 29, 1926.
9. Good, Charlie, "Leafs Get Off to a Running Start in Minor World Series," *Toronto Star*, September 29, 1926.
10. "Facing Millpond in Baseball Broadcast," *Toronto Star*, September 29, 1926.
11. Wilson, Frederick, "Scanning the Sport Field," *Toronto Globe*, September 29, 1926.
12. Rodden, M.J., "Heard at Leaf Stadium," *Toronto Globe*, September 29, 1926.
13. "Sacrifice Fly Scores First Run and Second Comes on Infield Out," *Louisville Courier-Journal*, September 29, 1926.

34. GAME TWO: AN EXTRA-INNING RALLY

1. Good, Charlie, "Battling Leafs Win From Colonels in Extra Innings," *Toronto Star*, September 30, 1926.
2. Ibid.
3. "Cullop Blanks Leafs Until Defense Cracks With Two Outs in Ninth," *Louisville Courier-Journal*, September 30, 1926.
4. Good.
5. Hewitt, W.A., "Sporting News and Reviews," *Toronto Star*, September 30, 1926.
6. Johnson, Lloyd and Wolff, Miles, *The Encyclopedia of Minor League Baseball*, 2nd edition (Baseball America, 1997), p. 243.

35. GAME THREE: SORRELL SOARS

1. Good, Charlie, "Sorrell Too Good for Colonels in Third Game," *Toronto Star*, October 1, 1926.
2. Ibid.
3. "Colonels Lose to Leafs, 2-1," *Louisville Courier-Journal*, October 1, 1926.
4. "Colonels Fail to Hold High Standard on Field," *Louisville Courier-Journal*, October 2, 1926.
5. Wilson, Frederick, "Scanning the Sport Field," *Toronto Globe*, October 1, 1926.

36. GAME FOUR: ANOTHER ONE-RUN VICTORY

1. "Colonels Lose to Leafs, 4-3," *Louisville Courier-Journal*, October 3, 1926.

37. GAME FIVE: A DASH TO VICTORY

1. "Colonels Drop Last Game Here," *Louisville Courier-Journal*, October 4, 1926.
2. Good, Charlie, "Leafs Make a Clean Sweep in Louisville," *Toronto Star*, October 4, 1926.
3. "Highlights on Leafs Victory in Louisville," *Toronto Star*, October 4, 1926.
4. "Leafs Superior Speed Cost Louisville Title in Junior World Series," *Louisville Courier-Dispatch*, October 5, 1926.
5. Hewitt, W.A., "Sporting News and Reviews," *Toronto Star*, October 5, 1926.
6. Wilson, Frederick, "Scanning the Sport Field," *Toronto Globe*, October 4, 1926.
7. Hewitt, W.A., "Sporting Views and Reviews," *Toronto Star*, October 4, 1926.
8. Foreman, Charles J., "Remarkable Pitching Carries Toronto to Championship," *The Sporting News*, October 28, 1926.
9. Hewitt, W.A., "Sporting News and Reviews," *Toronto Star*, November 9, 1926.

38. "A BIG FROG IN A SMALL PUDDLE"

1. *Toronto Star Weekly*, April 21, 1923.
2. "The Appearance of Control," *The Diary of Myles Thomas*, https://medium.com/the-diary-of-myles-thomas/the-appearance-of-control-f576a56849e.
3. Holmes, Thomas, "Dan Howley, Never Star Player, Has Chance to Emulate Joe McCarthy," *Brooklyn Eagle*, November 10, 1926.
4. Good, Charlie, "Dan Howley Likely to Go to Big Loop," *Toronto Star*, October 19, 1926.
5. "Bancroft Sought to Pilot Pirates," *Detroit Free Press*, October 21, 1926.
6. Good, Charlie, "Howley Slated to Take Major Berth," *Toronto Star*, November 3, 1926.
7. "Leader of Champion Toronto Leafs Gets Three-Year Contract," *St. Louis Post-Dispatch*, November 3, 1926.
8. "Man Who Led to Pennant Tells Stockton His Plan for Handling the St. Louis Situation," *St. Louis Post-Dispatch*, November 7, 1926.
9. "Six-Bit Critic," *Toronto Star*, November 6, 1926.
10. "Only Hustlers Can Play Ball for Me - Dan P. Howley," *St. Louis Post-Dispatch*, November 7, 1926.
11. "Sport Comment," *Buffalo News*, November 4, 1926.

POSTSCRIPT

1. "Ownie Carroll - BR Bullpen," n.d. *https://www.baseball-reference.com/bullpen/Ownie_Carroll.*
2. "Lefty Stewart - BR Bullpen," n.d. *https://www.baseball-reference.com/bullpen/Lefty_Stewart.*
3. Doyle's Baseball Reference page: *https://www.baseball-reference.com/players/d/doyleje01.shtml*
4. "Reminiscence: An Era Most Have Forgotten," November 23, 2020. *https://sabr.org/journal/article/reminiscence-an-era-most-have-forgotten/.*
5. "Herman Layne - BR Bullpen," n.d. *https://www.baseball-reference.com/bullpen/Herman_Layne.*
6. "Carl Hubbell," February 8, 2025. *https://sabr.org/bioproj/person/carl-hubbell/.*
7. "Champion Leafs Leave Shortly for Southland," *Star Weekly*, February 26, 1927.
8. "Andy Harrington (Harrian02) - BR Bullpen," n.d. *https://www.baseball-reference.com/bullpen/Andy_Harrington_(harrian02).*
9. "Mickey Heath," January 4, 2012. *https://sabr.org/bioproj/person/mickey-heath/.*
10. "Otis Lawry - BR Bullpen," n.d. *https://www.baseball-reference.com/bullpen/Otis_Lawry.*
11. Baseball-Reference.com. "Joe Maley Minor Leagues Statistics | Baseball-Reference.Com," n.d. *https://www.baseball-reference.com/register/player.fcgi?id=maley-001jos.*
12. "Otis Miller," June 6, 2012. *https://sabr.org/bioproj/person/Otis-Miller/.*
13. Wray, John E., "Absence Leaves Fight For Far Corner Job Wide Open," *St. Louis Post-Dispatch*, March 14, 1927.
14. *https://www.baseball-reference.com/register/player.fcgi?id=mullen002wil*

15. "Steve O'Neill," December 22, 2021. *https://sabr.org/bioproj/person/steve-oneill/*.

16. Rodden, Mike, "On the Highways of Sport," *Toronto Globe*, June 22, 1929.

17. Baseball-Reference.com. "Carl Schmehl Minor Leagues Statistics | Baseball-Reference.Com," n.d. *https://www.baseball-reference.com/register/player.fcgi?id=schmeh001car*.

18. "Vic Sorrell," October 9, 2020. *https://sabr.org/bioproj/person/vic-sorrell/*.

19. "Cleo Carlyle," March 18, 2014. *https://sabr.org/bioproj/person/cleo-carlyle/*.

20. "Fine Clarence Fisher Toronto Ball Player," *Toronto Star*, September 17, 1926.

21. Baseball-Reference.com. "Clarence Fisher Minor Leagues Statistics | Baseball-Reference.Com," n.d. *https://www.baseball-reference.com/register/player.fcgi?id=fisher001cla*.

22. Baseball-Reference.com. "Tillie Walker Minor Leagues Statistics | Baseball-Reference.Com," n.d. *https://www.baseball-reference.com/register/player.fcgi?id=walker001cla*.

23. The Canadian Encyclopedia. "Lionel Conacher," n.d. *https://thecanadianencyclopedia.ca/en/article/lionel-conacher*.

24. "Karpe's Comment," *Buffalo Evening News*, October 27, 1926.

25. Marsh, Lou "'Lol' Solman Dead After Long Illness," *Toronto Star*, March 24, 1931.

26. "The Miracle Man of 1928," *The Sporting News*, November 1, 1928.

27. Bourrie, Mark, p. 442.

28. Dictionary of Canadian Biography. "KING, WILLIAM LYON MACKENZIE – Dictionary of Canadian Biography," n.d. *https://www.biographi.ca/en/bio/king_william_lyon_mackenzie_17E.html*.

29. Cauz, Louis, "*Baseball's Back in Town, From the Don to the Blue Jays, A History of Baseball in Toronto*," Controlled Media Corporation (1977), p. 77.

30. Havill, Adrian, "*The Last Mogul: An Unauthorized Biography of Jack Kent Cooke*," St Martin's Press (1992) is an excellent resource not only for this tycoon's life, but for the early days of Toronto radio, and the 1950s Leafs.

31. Vanderschmidt, Bill, "Wings Split with Leafs On Leonhard 4-hitter," *Rochester Democrat and Chronicle*, May 23, 1967.

32. Dechman, Phillip, "Powerless Leafs bow 7-2 in final game of the season," *Toronto Globe and Mail*, September 5, 1967.

33. Dechman, Phillip, "The last Leafs of summer fall," *Toronto Globe and Mail*, December 19, 1967.

34. McCarl, Neill, "The remains are auctioned off at last rites for Leafs," *Toronto Star*, December 19, 1967.

35. "The Way We Were: City plaques tell a story," *Toronto Sun*, May 12, 2019.

36. *https://www.baseball-reference.com/bullpen/100_Best_Minor_League_Baseball_Teams*

INDEX

The pages referenced in this index refer to the page numbers in the print edition. If you are accessing this index on an eBook reader, please use your device's search function.

ALSO FROM AUGUST PUBLICATIONS

Before They Wore Dodger Blue: Tommy Lasorda and the Greatest Draft
    Class in Baseball History
Jim Gilliam: The Forgotten Dodger
The Complete Guide to Spring Training 2027 / Florida
The Complete Guide to Spring Training 2027 / Arizona
The Right Thing to Do: The True Pioneers of College Football Integration
Raye of Light: Jimmy Raye, Duffy Daugherty, The Integration of College
    Football, and the 1965-1966 Michigan State Spartans
My 1961
Goodfellows: The Champions of St. Ambrose
Baseball Like It Ought To Be: How a Shoe Salesman's Madison Mallards and
    His Renegade Staff Ignited a Summer Collegiate Baseball Revolution
Home Runs: Tales of Tonks, Taters, Contests and Derbies
The Baseball Thesaurus, 3e
The Football Thesaurus, 2e
Cradle of the Game: North Carolina Baseball Past and Present

Available from Amazon, Ingram, and *augustpublications.com.*